Foreword

The name of George Frederick Cooke is often coupled with that of Edmund Kean in popular memory as examples of great actors ruined by drink: a simplistic view at best. And if without quite the overwhelming genius of Kean, Cooke was arguably the more complex, and, whatever his failings, the more sympathetic personality. It is the duality of Cooke as actor and as man which Arnold Hare explores in his study.

Professionally Cooke was the product of the Georgian provincial theatre – in an acting life of at least 38 years he spent only twelve as a London (and American) star. This biography therefore sets out also to fill in much of the detail of those all-important years which made Cooke not only the man but the actor he was.

The Society wishes gratefully to acknowledge assistance from the University of Bristol towards the publication of this book.

KATHLEEN BARKER
Editor for the
Society for Theatre Research

Acknowledgements

By no means the least of the enjoyments of research is the kindness and help with which one so often meets, and it is a pleasure to acknowledge it here. Bernard Miles (as he then was), with his generous loan of Cooke's Memorandum Book, started me off on the trail many years ago. Since then the librarians and staffs of many libraries have helped me on my way – the national collections of the British Library in Bloomsbury and Colindale, the Victoria and Albert Museum, the National Library of Ireland in Dublin; the University Libraries of Bristol, Trinity College Dublin, Glasgow, and the Harvard Theatre Collection; the City Libraries of Bath, Berwick, Birmingham, Boston, Canterbury, Chester, Derby, Edinburgh, Glasgow, Grantham, Lancaster, Leicester, Lincoln, Liverpool, Loughborough, Manchester, Newcastle-upon-Tyne, Norwich, Nottingham, Preston, Sheffield, and York; the County Libraries of Westmoreland and Wiltshire; the Record Offices of Greater London and Lancaster; the offices of the *Chester Chronicle* and the *Stamford Mercury*. I am particularly grateful to Norma Armstrong of Edinburgh for opening her own researches to me, to Bernard Barr of the Minster Library in York for introducing me to the Hailstone Collection, and the later gift of photocopies, to Elizabeth Leach for giving me the freedom of the Manchester stack rooms, and to Charles Parrish of the Library of the Literary and Philosophical Society of Newcastle for lending me a photocopy of Cooke's *Hamlet* prompt book, and for giving up time to show me the changes in a library I once knew so well; to George Nash of the Gabrielle Enthoven Collection, and especially to A. S. Latham for, among other things, producing Cooke's *Man of the World* prompt book like a magician out of a hat; to George Hauger for introducing me to "A Veteran Stager", to David Rostron for his loan of a copy of the sale catalogue of Kemble's library, to Don B. Wilmeth for a copy of his Index to Dunlap, to Peter Husbands for his helpful reconnaissance in Dublin that saved me much time when I went there myself, to Christopher Hare for extracting information from Sheffield and

GEORGE FREDERICK COOKE

The Actor and the Man

by

ARNOLD HARE

THE SOCIETY FOR THEATRE RESEARCH

To

CHRISTOPHER, JOHN,
JUDY, and SIMON

who cheerfully shared me with G.F.C.
for more years than I dare to recall

ISBN 0 85430 0317

Text set in 10/12 pt Photon Baskerville, printed and
bound in Great Britain at The Pitman Press, Bath

Cheltenham for me, to Mary and John Tully for their hospitality in Durham, and to Norman Marshall for a glorious afternoon among the portraits of the Garrick Club. Three old friends have given special help – Kathleen Barker, out of her unique store of knowledge of the Bristol Theatre Royal, passed on to me far more information about Cooke in Bristol than in the end I was able to use and later, as my editor, not only enlivened with wit and wisdom the agonising process of cutting and revision, but with her great sense of consistency improved the text, and especially the notes; George Rowell encouraged and stimulated me, and read the typescript with his acute but sympathetic eye, and Geoffrey Cunliffe saw to it that I was able to make many of the journeys without which the vast bulk of material could not have been collected. Ruth Greaves and Janet Parker made the first typescript, Linda Lambshead the second; Simon Hare took some of the photographs. To all of them, my thanks. As always, my most fundamental debt is to my wife, who comforted me with apples and stayed me with flagons throughout the whole undertaking. To her, my love.

A few words need to be said about my use of Dunlap's *Life of George Frederick Cooke*. Dunlap knew Cooke in the United States of America during the last eighteen months of the actor's life. To him Cooke left such records and papers as he had with him, and they seem to have had some conversations on the understanding that Dunlap would write his life. On these, together with such current theatrical publications as were available across the Atlantic, and Dunlap's own reminiscences, the work was based; and it still remains a primary source. But Dunlap's perspective is not a well-balanced one. Over a quarter of his book is devoted to the events of the last eighteen months of Cooke's life, over five-sixths to the last twelve years; and since his book was first published in America within a year of the actor's death, Dunlap was in no position to check Cooke's recollections and notes by reference to English sources. This I have tried to do. Obviously I have quoted much from Dunlap whenever he reprints Cooke's own words or had first-hand information, but where he quotes other sources I have gone back to the originals wherever possible; I have made no attempt to include all of Dunlap's material for the later years, but have given much more attention to the pre-1800 period, and to post-1800 information not available to him. To that extent the hope is that the two biographies may be found to be complementary.

Some of the conclusions and a few actual paragraphs from this study were incorporated in a paper read to a Symposium on the *18th Century English Stage* at the University of Manchester in 1971, and subsequently published in its Proceedings, in 1972, by Methuen & Co.

Arnold Hare
University of Bristol. August 1979

Contents

CONTENTS

Chapter I

"In my end is my beginning"

I

On the evening of Wednesday the 21st of November, 1810, in and around the twelve-year-old Park Theatre in New York, the excitement was intense. There had never been such crowds trying to get into the theatre, and they jostled and pushed and fought for priority. The normal box-office arrangements were overwhelmed, and in the confusion people were pushed through the doors without payment. Many of those, especially ladies, who had already taken places for the performance, found no way through the confusion to the normal entrance to the boxes. In the end they had to be taken round to the back door of the playhouse in Theatre-alley, and there conducted over the stage and into the boxes from behind the curtain. There were one thousand three hundred and fifty eight of them in the three tiers of boxes, and in a house normally expected to hold about two thousand it was estimated that at least another two hundred were crammed in. The managers took in one thousand eight hundred and twenty dollars, and if all had paid would have received much more. Nothing like it had ever been known before.[1]

The cause of all this excitement was an English actor now in his middle fifties, about to appear for the first time in the American continent, and in one of his most famous roles – Richard III. Many rumours had preceded his arrival, not only about his extraordinary power as an actor, but of the wildness and irregularity of his private life; but when William Dunlap met him for the first time on the evening of November 16th, he had seen no indication of the latter.

He looked older than men I had been used to seeing of his age, but vigorous and healthful. The neatness of his dress, his sober suit of grey, his powdered grey hairs, and suavity of address, gave no indication of the eccentric being, whose weaknesses had been the theme of the English fugitive publications.[2]

1

Now, five days later, in the tension before curtain rise, the strain was noticeable. Ten years before, there had been an occasion something like this. After twenty five years as an actor up and down the provincial playhouses of England and Ireland, he was making his first appearance at London's Theatre Royal in Covent Garden, in the same play, and before an equally packed house. It was a moment that would decide his reputation as a great actor, and he trembled like a young player about to expose himself to an audience for the first time. Now he was a decade older, he was appearing in a new continent before audiences whose taste and judgment he had no opportunity of assessing. He had great successes behind him, and embarrassing failures.

But the moment George Frederick Cooke stepped on to the boards and the roar of welcome burst from the packed assembly, any trace of hesitation vanished.

He entered on the right hand of the audience, and with a dignified erect deportment, walked to the centre of the stage, amidst their plaudits. His appearance was picturesque and proudly noble: his head elevated, his step firm, his eye beaming fire. I saw no vestige of the venerable grey-haired old gentleman I had been introduced to at the coffee house; and the utmost effort of imagination could not have reconciled the figure I now saw, with that of imbecility and intemperance. He returned the salutes of the audience, not as a player to the public on whom he depended, but as a victorious prince, acknowledging the acclamations of the populace on his return from a successful campaign – as Richard Duke of Gloster, the most valiant branch of the triumphant House of York. When he spoke:
"Now is the winter of our discontent
Made glorious summer by the sun of York,
And all the clouds that lower'd upon our house
In the deep bosom of the ocean buried!
Now are our brows bound with victorious wreaths,
Our stern alarums, etc."
the high key in which he pitched his voice, and its sharp and rather grating tones, caused a sensation of disappointment in some, and a fear in others, that such tones could not be modulated to the various cadences of nature, or such a voice have compass for the varied expressions of harmonious diction and distracting passion, which the characters of Shakespeare require; but disappointment and fear vanished, and conviction and admiration succeeded, and increased to the dropping of the curtain; then reiterated plaudits expressed the

fulness with which expectation had been realised, and taste and feeling gratified.[3]

This first engagement lasted just over a month. In that time he gave seventeen performances, including most of his most famous roles – Richard III (three times), Sir Pertinax MacSycophant (three), Shylock (three), Sir Archy MacSarcasm (three), Sir Giles Overreach (twice), Falstaff (twice), Macbeth, and others – and the management took in a total of $21,578 – an average of $1,296 a night. There could be no doubt about George Frederick Cooke's initial theatrical success in New York.

II

Three months later, at about ten o'clock in the morning of 19 February 1811, the same observer, who by this time had seen most of Cooke's public performances and some of his private ones, received a brief note in the theatre. It read simply – but almost illegibly –

Dear Dunlap, send me one hundred dollars.

G. F. Cooke.

It had been one of the worst nights of a bitter cold winter, and the streets were choked with ice and snow. Questioned, the little girl who brought the note told how in the early hours of the morning she was sitting up with her sick mother at their house in Reed-street, when a negro and a watchman known to them brought a strange gentleman to the house and asked if he could sit by the fire. At first reluctant to enter, the strange man then said "Let me lay down here and die"; later, having sent out for two quarts of brandy, he settled down with the bottle, brooding and talking in a rambling way in which, by Dunlap's account, his own situation and that of Lear in the storm became in his mind inextricably mixed.

Inquiries revealed that on the previous evening Price the manager, with whom Cooke was staying, had insisted on his going to bed to avoid a noisy drunken evening developing; but after the family had all retired, Cooke let himself out of the house and in to the arctic west wind, presumably in search of the conviviality he felt he was being denied. The rest had followed.

Dunlap took the money requested and was guided to a small wooden building behind the hospital. The scene he found there was almost Hogarthian. The room was dark, and seemed full of people.

I soon found that they were the neighbours, brought in to gaze at the strange crazy gentleman, and sheriff's officers distraining for the rent on

3

the furniture of the sick widow who occupied the house. The bed of the sick woman filled one corner of the room, surrounded by cur-tains – sheriff's officers, a table, with pen, ink and inventory, occupied another portion – a motley group, of whom Cooke was one, hid the fire-place from view, and the remainder of the apartment was filled by cartmen, watchmen, women and children.

When I recognised Cooke, he had turned from the fire, and his eye was on me, with an expression of shame and chagrin at being found in such a situation. His skin and eyes were red, his linen dirty, his hair wildly point-ing in every direction from his "distracted globe", and over his knee was spread an infant's bib, or something else, with which, having lost his pocket-handkerchief, he wiped his incessantly moistened visage. After a wild stare at me, he changed from the first expression of his countenance, and welcomed me. He asked me why I had come? I replied that I had received his note and brought him the money. I sat down by him, and replied to his repeated intreaties of "don't leave me" by promises of remaining with him, but told him we must leave that place. He agreed, but added with vehemence, "Not back to his house – no – never! never!!" which apparent resolution he confirmed with vehe-ment and reiterated oaths. The officer let me know, that the gentleman had stopped the levying on the goods, and agreed to pay the quarter's rent. I was proceeding to make some inquiries, but Cooke in the most peremptory tone, required that the money should be paid, as if fearing that his ability to fulfil his promise should be doubted by the bystanders. I paid the money and demanded a receipt. The officer, who was nearly drunk, asked for the gentleman's christian name, when with all the dignity of the buskin, the drooping hero raised his head, and roared out most discordantly, "George Frederick! George Frederick Cooke!" The peculiar sharpness of the higher tones of his voice, joined to the un-melodious, broken and croaking notes of debauchery, with his assumed dignity and squalid appearance, were truly comic, though pitiable.

Dunlap paid the widow's rent arrears in full, took the Marshal's receipt, and eventually persuaded Cooke to leave.

He rose from his chair, his step was not steady, and some of the crowd offered to assist him, but he put them by with his hand in a style of court-ly contempt. He accepted my arm, but before we reached the door stopped to wipe his face, and having left the piece of dirty linen he had before used, he made enquiry for his handkerchief. It was not to be found, and I, fearing a change, and somewhat impatient of my own situation, offered him a white handkerchief which I had put in my pocket

4

but a few minutes before receiving his note, and which, after seeing the filthy rag he had been using and displaying on his knee before the fire, I did not hesitate to present to him; but he put it aside with a most princely motion, saying "a gentleman cannot accept a handkerchief that has been used."

With considerable difficulty Dunlap cajoled the reluctant Cooke back to Price's house, and by the early afternoon into bed, having undertaken to apologise to his landlord for him. With that, this particular incident ended; but the experience had been a traumatic one. Never again was Dunlap to be able to regard Cooke as a normal human being.[4]

III

Within a month of this incident the triumphs of that first appearance in New York were being repeated at the Chestnut-street playhouse in Philadelphia. "Why, this beats Sarah," said Cooke cheerfully, as the hordes around the theatre prevented him from even reaching the Stage Door; and again, when the performance was at last given, his success was complete.[5]

Two days later, at six o'clock in the morning, Dunlap found him "nearly the same disgusting object which I found in the house of the poor widow in Reed street", fulminating alcoholically against comparisons of himself with the American actor Cooper, and swearing that he would never play in New York again. Yet after a few hours, sober once more and in good spirits, he ate a combined breakfast and dinner, drank a pint of wine, and went cheerfully to the theatre to play Richard III.[6]

This was a pattern that had now become established in Cooke's way of life and within two years would lead to a lonely death in exile. It had in it hours of glory and days of wretchedness and squalor; gestures of generosity and kindness, and incidents of reckless profligacy; something of comedy, much of tragedy. What was it that had brought him to this Jekyll-and-Hyde existence, this strange amalgam of good and evil, this epitome of the human dilemma at its most extreme?

Chapter II

Early Years – 1756-1773

I

The Cooke problems begin even with his birth and parentage. Several different accounts have survived, and in none of them can one feel complete confidence. The account which Dunlap accepts, and which he had from Cooke himself, was that he was born on Saturday 17 April 1756, in Westminster, his father a "high Irish Officer, and Captain in the 4th Dragoons", his mother a Benton, daughter of the Laird of Benton, near Lamberton.[1] Nevertheless, Dunlap feels bound to put on record that many accounts of his life speak of him as an Irishman, and some make Berwick or Dublin his birthplace. On the face of it, Cooke's own statement should be preferable; but by the time it was made, in the last year of his life, Dunlap had noted in other contexts "his habit of romancing, and imagining himself other than he was",[2] and recorded elsewhere a conversation in which, asked if he were born in October 1755, Cooke stated firmly that he was born in October, "but not 55".[3] No record of such a birth in Westminster has so far come to light.

Of contemporary accounts, the *Thespian Dictionary* of 1802 confirms the date of 17th April 1756, but places the birth in Dublin, where his father was a subaltern in one of the regiments of the garrison,[4] as does the biographical footnote by "A Veteran Stager", who also knew Cooke and quotes the account given in Cooke's presence in 1806, by an Irish sergeant and his wife, who claimed to remember his birth "in the barracks of Dublin". The essence of their account is that his father was a non-commissioned officer in the 70th Regiment ("the Black Cuffs") and a native of Kelso, who had married the daughter of an innkeeper in Drogheda. He had gone to America with his regiment, she remaining behind as one of the barrack nurses. Thirteen months after his birth she too went to America, where she died before he was four, leaving his father to bring him back and deposit him with his brother, a printer at Berwick, who brought him up

6

and later took him on as an apprentice.[5]

Dunlap's account continues that, after the death of her husband, Mrs Cooke went to live at Berwick-on-Tweed, and later, after her death, her son stayed on there or in the neighbourhood with two aunts, her sisters, who sent him to school.[6]

Two accounts of 1800 (presumably inspired by his appearance and success at Covent Garden) provide further variations on the theme. According to the *Monthly Mirror* he was born in 1756 in the barracks of Dublin where his father was an officer in the army, at that time quartered there, and he was barely three when his father removed him to England, where he received his early education in London, afterwards finished in the north of England.[7] At about the same time, the *Albion* was recording that Cooke was "the son of an eminent schoolmaster, who lived about thirty or forty years since in Mount Street, Grosvenor Square."[8]

To sort out fact from gossip, or perhaps deliberate obfuscation, is not easy, but one or two matters can be clarified, and if they in turn suggest a further conjecture, it should be emphasised that in the present state of our knowledge it can be no more than that.

Apart from the *Albion*, which may have been quoting newspaper gossip and Cooke's late statement to Dunlap, which, as we have suggested, may well be suspect, along with other statements at that time, there seems most agreement about the birth in Dublin (and if A Veteran Stager can be relied upon, he seems to imply that Cooke himself confirmed this). It seems fairly common ground, too, that his father was in the army, and (with the exception of A Veteran Stager) that his mother was a girl from near Berwick-on-Tweed.

A Veteran Stager's account is interesting in that it follows two others in all the essential pattern of the story, but differs in detail, e.g. it gives his birth as 1758, makes his mother an *Irish* girl, and has him apprenticed in Berwick to his *father's brother*. These discrepancies may well reflect a conversation with two old people carried out over more than one "glass of Peter Kearney's Inashone whiskey punch"[9], and recorded later when memory of detail was hazy and unreliable. But it may suggest that, differences of detail notwithstanding, the account should not be dismissed where it fits in with others.

The Registers of Trinity Church, Berwick-on-Tweed have no record of Cooke's baptism there during the years 1754–64[10]; but they do record, on the 3rd of January 1754, the marriage of "Jas Moore, Soldr. & Eliza Renton".[11] Dunlap records that Cooke's account of his mother was that she was a "Benton, daughter of the laird of Benton", near Lamberton. Lamberton is a border village near Berwick which, like Gretna Green, on the other side of the country, profited from a legal loop-hole in the eighteenth and nineteenth centuries and became a recognised place for the carrying out of runaway marriages. There is no Benton near it; but there is a *Renton*, an easy transliteration. The conjunction of the names is suggestive. At this time, less than a decade after the rebellion of 1745, Berwick was an important military, naval and garrison town. A Veteran Stager describes Cooke's mother as

> the daughter of a very respectable inn-keeper ... in whose house George's father chanced to be quartered. There a mutual attachment took place, and notwithstanding the opposition of her father, the indissoluble knot was tied by the chaplain of the regiment. "She packed up her tatters, and followed the drum." She was a woman of strong mind, with acquirements and education superior to her station in life.[12]

A plausible pattern is beginning to emerge. A garrison town, a lively and intelligent girl, whether daughter of a small land-owner or prosperous inn-keeper hardly matters, falling in love with a soldier and strong-willed enough to marry him despite family opposition; following him with his regiment eventually to Dublin, by which time he has perhaps become an N.C.O., and there, in the barracks, giving birth to a child. The husband leaving her, perhaps because of a posting to the American colonies; and not returning, either because of death or desertion, so that in the end she has to return with the child to her border family, where, after her death or departure in his early years, he is left parentless to be brought up by her sisters.

A story of this kind may well, in broad outline, lie behind Cooke's origins. What of the "high ranking Irish Officer" and, if there should be any connection between the marriage of Eliza Renton and James Moore, of the name George Frederick Cooke? The simplest explanations may be the best – the former the embroidering of a man given to such embroideries and in the heyday of his success wanting his origins to be thought more genteel than they actually were; the latter the simple adoption of the married surname of one of his guardians, a practice common enough in those days and not requiring the same legal sanction as nowadays. But there could be another, and perhaps more significant explanation.

Dunlap has remarked, and we shall have cause to remind ourselves of the fact on a number of later occasions, that Cooke

> not only in his writing, but also in conversation, sedulously avoided the mention of such transactions of his life, as were either dishonourable, or which, in his opinion, detracted from his dignity as a gentleman.[13]

8

And in his paragraphs on Cooke, in his account of the history of the theatre in Glasgow, Walter Baynham makes the statement about him that

> Like Kean, too, he was an illegitimate child, and like Kean he had served as a sailor.[14]

Unfortunately Baynham does not give his authority for the statement, and since the book was not published until 1892, one's immediate reaction is to dismiss the notion as theatrical gossip or hearsay. But Baynham had met and had long talks with Charles Mayne Young, in his later years, and Young was a direct link with Cooke. He had acted with him many times, both in the provinces and at Covent Garden, and Young had also been one of Cooke's managers in Manchester. Was this something about Cooke that was known to some of his intimates in the theatre, but that he himself did not wish to be widely known? By the time of his conversations with Dunlap Cooke had already suggested to him that he might become his biographer, and had promised to leave him his papers. One of Dunlap's major sources is Cooke's own Ms. Chronicle of his life, which, as we shall later see, is sometimes significantly selective. Was the assertion of his birth in Westminster an attempt to forestall inquiries in Dublin that might in the end have revealed more than he wished to be known? Could his mother, deserted by her husband, have become the common-law wife of another – perhaps in this case even an officer of the name of Cooke? And was the knowledge of this, and the parentless years that followed, one of the basic causes of that fundamental insecurity which may have helped to condition him into the kind of man he became?

Again, it must be emphasised that in the present state of our knowledge this can be no more than speculation. It is an attempt to take into account the greatest amount of matter common to the various stories that have come down to us, without any positive collateral documentary evidence to enable us to evaluate them. It may be suggestive. But it is not established fact.

II

What does seem established is that Cooke grew up under the guardianship of his two aunts and was educated and apprenticed to a trade in the little border town of Berwick-on-Tweed. "My old school-town" he called it when he went from Edinburgh to play there in 1807.[15]

Although it has grown in size since then, it is comparatively easy still to visualise the little town as it must have been in the seventeen sixties, when Cooke first knew it, since the fortified walls which then surrounded it still remain. They enclose a squat, solid little town, of no great area – a walk round the complete walls takes less than half an hour – and the Governor's House, the Customs House, the great Barracks and the Gaol remain still to remind the visitor of its importance as a border garrison and trading post in the troubled years after the Act of Union. But it had a little culture, too. The Town Hall had been rebuilt in the baroque style in 1754, and with its pillared portico and its clock and lantern tower surmounted by an elegant spire still dominates the High Street or Marygate. Six years later the Butter-market was rebuilt at the rear, and the little complex of buildings must have been the social and commercial centre of the town. The church is peripheral and insignificant by contrast. To the Town Hall came the local gentry and the Officers of the Regiments quartered there for their Balls and Assemblies and – now and again – the theatre, when a strolling company from Edinburgh or summer visitors from London came for a short season.[16]

Educationally Berwick seems to have been well served. There was a Grammar School and four or five educational charities; whatever Border dominie taught the young boy was successful in one matter – he left him with a love of reading that remained with him throughout his adult life. And in Berwick, too, Cooke acquired his passion for the theatre.

While still at school he had seen some prints of actors in character – he particularly remembered one of Henry Woodward as Mercutio – and he had seen a puppet show which had given him his first incoherent idea of a stage performance. But in 1767 some of the Edinburgh company came to the Town Hall on one of their visits, and for the first time he saw the real thing, a performance of Colley Cibber's *The Provok'd Husband, or a Journey to London*, followed by Garrick's farce of *The Lying Valet*.[17]

The company was not without talent. It was led by James Aickin, an Irishman who had for some time been a favourite leading player of the Edinburgh Company, and was soon to establish himself at Drury Lane: and Mr. and Mrs. Didier, later to become stalwarts of the Bath and Bristol Company, for whom Mrs. Didier was playing well into the first decade of the nineteenth century. Aickin played Lord Townly and Mrs. Didier Miss Jenny; Didier played Count Basset, and Sharp in the farce. Aickin was playing at Drury Lane by November 1767,[18] and he had gone to London after the Edinburgh Playhouse had been broken up by a riot staged by young members of the audience in support of an actor called Stayley who had been discharged from the company. Aickin, as Leading Man, had been called on to apologise publicly and get down on his knees to do it. This with some spirit he had refused to do, whereupon the young bloods erupted on to the stage with swords drawn. Aickin escaped through a back window, but the rioters destroyed most of the scenery and tried to set fire to the Green Room. As a result the theatre had to be closed prematurely, and the company dispersed, and it may well have been in consequence that a group of them made the particular foray into Berwick which had such a seminal effect on Cooke.[19] If so, though he might well not have known it at the time, he would have doubtless been told years later; for he records that in his periodic visits to Bath and Bristol as a guest star in the early nineteenth century he talked with Mrs. Didier again about that performance. One can well understand this; for however good or indifferent it may have been it sparked off the imagination of the young boy. In his own account, from that time on, plays and playing were rarely absent from his thoughts.[20]

From one source or another, plays were borrowed and read avidly; he recalled later that the first he ever read was Otway's *Venice Preserv'd*, no easy assignment for a young boy. But more than that, with a group of his contemporaries he began to prepare a performance of Rowe's pathetic tragedy, *The Fair Penitent*. It was doubtless little more than children's imaginative play, and the performance was never given, but he learnt his first lines as an actor, in the part of Horatio, lines that years later he was to speak many times in his professional life. But that professional life may not yet have been dreamed of. Of his contemporaries who took part in the game, none was to follow him into the theatre. Altamont died young; Lothario became surgeon of a regiment of light dragoons in the East Indies, Rossano became a respectable tradesman in Berwick, and Sciolto kept a chemist's shop in London.[21]

In April 1769, the fires were rekindled when another detachment of the Edinburgh Company visited Berwick. In later years he still recalled a number of members of the party – Mr. and Mrs. King, Buck, Smith, Taplin, and Dancer (later a member of the Norwich and York companies) and Wills and Reinagle as musicians and occasional actors.[22] What they played and what he saw in the early part of their visit, we do not know, but once more under their influence, Cooke and his friends formed a company, and this time, in a deserted barn and with an improvised motley mixture of costumes and patchwork scenery, they seem actually to have performed before an audience Bickerstaffe's *Love in a Village* and a truncated version of *Hamlet*. It was in the former that Cooke made his first ever performance before an audience as the hero, Young Meadows, and apparently got through two songs. In the latter he played Horatio, and consoled himself for missing the leading role with some kind comments on his performance by some of the Edinburgh players, who apparently, whether out of kindness, or for a laugh, or as a piece of public relations work, or for the lack of anything better to do, attended the production.[23]

Later in the season he saw the Edinburgh company play *Alexander the*

11

Great, Romeo and Juliet, George Barnwell and *The Wonder* and tried to get in to see *Douglas* without paying, by hiding with one or two companions under the stage, only to be discovered by Burke, another member of the company, and thrown out with, in the old phrase, a flea in his ear.[24]

This incident he records himself. Dunlap also has a story which may be apocryphal, but which he applies to this period, of Cooke on another occasion hiding in a barrel for the same purpose, only to discover too late that he was sharing the barrel with two twenty-four pound cannon balls, and that he had in fact got into the theatre's thunder-barrel. When the property man tied a piece of old carpet over the open end of the barrel to prevent the balls escaping he also effectively prevented the departure of the young stowaway, who remained silent while the machine was set in position for its first eruption to usher in the witches in *Macbeth*.

> It would be a hopeless task to paint the agitation of the contents of the barrel. The property man swearing the cannon bullets were so damned heavy, placed the complicated machine in readiness – the witches entered 'midst flames of rosin – the thunder-bell rang – the barrel received its impetus, and away rolled George Frederick and his ponderous companions. Silence would now have been no virtue, and he roared most manfully, to the surprise of the thunderer, who, neglecting to stop the rolling machine, it entered on the stage, and George Frederick bursting off the carpet head of the barrel, appeared before the audience just as the witches had agreed to meet again when "the hurly burly's done".[25]

A splendidly theatrical entrance, and perhaps the climax comes just a little too pat – a tale that, even if founded on fact, may have been embroidered in the telling. But at the very least, it provides a vivid vignette of eighteenth century strolling stage management, and a worthy gloss on Wright's aquatint of the witches performing in a country theatre.[26]

III

The best and worst of schooldays have an ending. For Cooke they ended when his aunts bound him apprentice to a local printer, John Taylor.[27] From their point of view this was doubtless a worthwhile undertaking. The boy would have to earn his living in some way, and for one who could read avidly and write and spell correctly, what better offered in a small country town? It would be surprising if Cooke saw it like that. More likely he saw shades of the prisonhouse closing around him. Apart from local jobbing printing, there cannot have been much scope in the trade; and as he grew up, Berwick must have seemed increasingly limited and frustrating. It was a very healthy town, said the worthy Dr. John Fuller when he wrote its history at the end of the eighteenth century, and its inhabitants lived much longer than their neighbours.[28] But old people tend to be conservative in outlook, and in spite of the fresh blood and outlook brought in from time to time by changes in the garrison troops, in spite of the circulating library and the occasional visits of the players, the world outside must have looked inviting, and the routine daily life of an apprentice printer in a small provincial town stultifying and confined.

One way of escape, by travel, lay on the doorstep; the tides of the North Sea lapped around the little harbour of Berwick twice daily. The other way of escape lay in the mind, and this the theatre fed. If he could not live romantically in the real world, he could in make-believe. Like many an actor before and since, the call to a world of paste-board and tinsel was fed by a frustration and dissatisfaction with the way of life that society was asking him to undertake. And perhaps there was something else. As he sat in the back of the Town Hall, or stood in Marygate outside when he had no shilling for the box-office, and saw the gentry driving up in their coaches, he may have reflected on the difference between their wealth and status and his own. If by then he really did know – or believe – that his father had been a "high Irish Officer", his prospects in society as a jobbing printer must have seemed much smaller and less glamorous. But if he turned from the audience to the stage, there he could see people very little different from himself being high and noble and aristocratic and successful – at least for the two hours traffic of the stage. If he had no status in life, at least he could have it in the theatre.

Whether or not he speculated consciously in this way, his apprenticeship to John Taylor clearly did not diminish his passion for the stage. In the early part of 1770 another strolling company – not the Edinburgh one this time, but a less reputable group under the management of a Mr. Fisher, converted an old malt-house into a theatre and played among other things *The Provok'd Husband*, again, and *The Earl of Essex* and *Oroonoko*. With, of course, the usual result – that in the autumn the local stage-struck youths were performing Addison's *Cato*, and Cooke and the future surgeon of light dragoons, on account of their youth, were cast as the two Roman ladies Lucia and Marcia respectively.[29]

That all this was not to the liking of John Taylor (and probably also of Cooke's aunts) is clear. On another occasion when Cooke with cork-blackened face was performing as *Zanga*

To the delight and astonishment of the canaille of Berwick, the enraged printer dispatched a posse of constables, who rushing in, hurried away

13

the Moorish Chief to bewail at leisure a second defeat and captivity.[30]

It is hardly surprising, then, that he either broke or was released from his indenture, and, according to his own account, in June 1771, when he was fifteen years old, left Berwick for London.[31]

IV

How and why he went there remains something of a mystery. Our only authority for this period of his life is the Ms. Chronicle which he left to Dunlap. This was largely written in 1807 during his months in detention in Appleby, when for a large part of the time all he had to rely on was his admittedly formidable memory. But that memory was also selective, as we have already noted. Where anything occurred which did not fit with his own picture of what he ought to be, Cooke was liable to omit, or gloss over it. So that while at times checking has shown the Chronicle to be reasonably reliable, at other times it can be less than reliable, or even misleading. And dates can sometimes be vague or contradictory.

He left Berwick in June; in October 1771 he was in London, where he went to Covent Garden and saw *Oroonoko* and *Midas*; in November he went to Holland; in the early part of 1772 he was back in Berwick.[32] He recalled that he went to Rotterdam and Helvetsloeys in the *Britannia* – a 200-ton trader captained by one Robert Scott, which regularly plied between London and Rotterdam.

> We had four cabin passengers, two of which I remember were an old Jewess and her son. I remained on shore in Rotterdam several days. I was ill there and after being let blood by a French or Dutch surgeon, attended by an English apothecary of the name of Adams. I lodged at a coffee-house kept by an old woman of the name of Dorothy Stevenson, a native of Carlisle, who had resided many years in Holland, and was well known by the English masters of vessels. I remember after I came home hearing my uncle George, who was at that time Master of the Griffin, belonging to Yarmouth in Norfolk, say he remembered her very well.[33]

Afterwards they had a rough passage back to the Thames, and their Irish cook dislocated his wrist by a fall. The account seems circumstantial enough (perhaps the reference to cabin passengers might suggest he went as a cabin-boy), and it could account for the *Monthly Mirror's* biographical reference to his having served on board merchantmen; his own later assertion that he had been a midshipman aboard a King's ship may have been conversational embroidery.[34] But whether he was trying out a seafaring career, or on a holiday trip organised, perhaps, by his uncle George, we simply do not know.

All that seems certain is that whether or not he had abandoned a second possible livelihood, in 1772 he returned to Berwick, and there, possibly in that same summer, he saw yet another strolling company, this time, he wrote, managed by Holland and Booth, and containing among the actresses Mrs. Browne, who later played at Covent Garden, and her sister Mrs. Mills (later Mrs. Sparks).[35] Perhaps it was this company that applied the final spark to the tinder. At any rate, within a matter of months he was back in London again, and this time with the definite intention of embarking on a theatrical career. He was not yet seventeen.

V

At this point A Veteran Stager takes up the story again. According to his account Cooke did not journey to London alone, but with a fellow printer's apprentice, Colin Mitchell, who had just completed his articles, but who was also determined on a stage career. They arrived in London with seventeen shillings and sixpence between them and made their way immediately to one of the well-known theatrical taverns at that time, the Black Lion in Russell Street, kept by a retired actor called Waters. Here they announced their intention of becoming actors in London. Waters took pity on their innocence, gave them beds for the night, and in the morning

> painted to them in such doleful colours, the misery of a strolling player, together with the impracticability of obtaining a situation on the London boards, as totally damped their youthful spirits . . .[36]

Bad as this prospect may have been, that of returning to Berwick defeated was even worse, and with the aid of the good-natured Waters, Mitchell, an accredited journeyman printer, obtained a place in a printing-office in Gray's Inn Lane. On his meagre wages they both survived for a while, Cooke in his turn helping Mitchell out at work from time to time.

The recognised resort of stage-struck youth in the city at this time was the "Spouting Club", in which young apprentices and the like met together to talk theatrical gossip and to "spout" speeches and scenes at each other.[37] How many of these existed we do not know; they probably grew up and died sporadically as groups of young addicts coalesced and then disintegrated. But many later professional players started their careers in this way; and country managers were not above attending such performances in search of likely talent.

That Cooke and Mitchell would be introduced to such a club is highly likely, though Dunlap remarks that it happened only once.[38] If so, perhaps it was the precise occasion which A Veteran Stager describes vividly and amusingly.

A play was got up, Richard the Third; their theatre a hay-loft; their only scene an old carpet, hung over a line, stretched across the building, to support it; their lights, small candles stuck into lumps of clay, fashioned for the purpose; their seats deal boards, supported by empty beer-barrels; the orchestra had to boast of a Scotch bag-piper, who, from that harmonious instrument "blew a blast so loud", and answered the purpose of drums and trumpets; and when Richard exclaimed "a flourish trumpets, strike alarm, drums," was replied to by a blast from Sawney. Richard's dress was a borrowed vestment of a footman, consisting of a scarlet waistcoat, with sleeves of the same colour; a red cloak, obtained of an ancient dame in the neighbourhood, fancifully decorated with strips of paper embellished with Prince's metal, a star and garter made from the same materials.

Richmond was dressed much after the same fashion, with the addition of an enormous pair of trooper's boots; his head adorned with a grenadier's cap by way of helmet: the other heroes of Bosworth Field, as their characters were not of equal magnitude, did not perhaps adhere so pertinaciously to costume and propriety; the "Dramatis Personae" ran thus, "Richard Mr. Briarly", (since which a respectable manager and good actor in the northern district of Scotland) the "Earl of Richmond Mr. Colin Mitchell", to which he added Tressel: "King Henry by Mr. Cooke", "Buckingham by Mr. Joseph Munden."[39]

How far this can be taken as an accurate account we cannot say. It could well have been told by Cooke to the author during their later association in Bolton and Buxton, when, for a time, they lodged in the same house; and like many an actor's story, it may well have gained detail in the telling. It could equally well contain details recalled by the author from some such experience of his own, or had additional points added to it. But it has the ring of truth in spirit about it. And if that great comedian Joseph Munden did first meet Cooke on some such occasion, it was the beginning of a friendship and association that was to bring them together again in the provinces, and eventually to Covent Garden.

There cannot have been many such occasions. There was hardly time. For though Colin Mitchell was to stay on in London for a time as a compositor, before leaving for Dublin, where eventually he became a professional actor in Ryder's company at the Crow Street theatre,[41] Cooke was more fortunate. By the late summer of 1773 he had obtained his first professional engagement, and was appearing with James Whitley's company at the theatre in Lincoln. His real apprenticeship had begun.

Chapter III

The Apprenticeship – 1773-1784

According to the Veteran Stager, Cooke was engaged at the Black Lion by James ("Jemmy") Miller, the "Northampton and Shrewsbury manager" to join his company at Shrewsbury at a salary of 10s. per week.[1] The Stager typically is here confusing Miller, the Shrewsbury manager, with the other "Jemmy" – James Whitley, who according to Henry Lee, had Northampton as part of his circuit; for in fact surviving playbills for Whitley and Herbert's companies at Lincoln, King's Lynn and Stamford during 1773–5 record some 84 performances by a Mr. Cooke during these years, and there can be no reasonable doubt that this was George Frederick.[2]

Though the earliest surviving bill dates from 15 September 1773, it is likely that this comes from the latter part of the season, since by the 24th benefits had begun; and there is, in fact, a distinct possibility that Cooke had actually joined the company earlier in the summer at Boston, which was also part of the Lincoln circuit. The writer of the Lincoln News section of the *Stamford Mercury* in 1829 recorded that:

> We believe it is not generally known that Cooke, the celebrated trage-dian, made his first appearance on the stage in the Boston company. He was a resident for several years, if not a native, of Lincoln, where he worked as a printer, and the present worthy Manager well remembers him in that capacity calling for proofs at the theatre.[3]

The "worthy Manager" was Thomas Shafto Robertson, whose father was a member of Whitley and Herbert's company in 1773, later to become its manager, and in due course hand the control down to his son, who had clearly talked to the writer.[4] So the link is a direct one. And the use of Cooke's apprenticed trade as an additional source of income – perhaps during lean spells at the theatre – provides further confirmation. There is nothing unusual about this – for example, while Charles Whitlock was co-manager with Joseph Austin in Chester in the late eighties, he continued to

18

practise as a dentist[5] – and in 1781 there is evidence that Cooke returned to his trade as a printer in Nottingham before rejoining Whitley's company.[6]

If then, Cooke did begin in the theatre as early as the summer of 1773, why should Dunlap, and subsequent writers accepting his authority, place that first appearance at Brentford in the spring of 1776?[7] The answer is that Dunlap appears to have been following Cooke's own Chronicle, which is silent on the years before 1776. Yet during this time Cooke was playing leading roles (Young Marlow, Archer, Lord Ogleby, Mercutio) and before long progressed to essays in Hamlet, Macbeth, and Lear. Even allowing for the possibility of poor standards and poorer audiences, it was a notable beginning to a career, and it seems surprising that he should omit to record it.

Perhaps the clue to this lies in the presence of another member of the company at Lincoln and King's Lynn – "Mrs. Cooke". If there were anything connected with her that in later years Cooke felt detracted from his image of himself, then, as we have already seen, he might well drop the episode from the record. The most obvious and likely explanation in terms of eighteenth century theatrical society is that the title was a courtesy one only, and that she was not in fact Mrs. Cooke; that perhaps here was a temporary liaison which broke up in the end in a manner which Cooke preferred not to remember. A more complicated one might be that they were indeed legally married, a marriage which eventually broke up and was never legally dissolved. By the time Cooke came to set down the Chronicle he had been married to Alicia Daniels, and that marriage had subsequently been dissolved in Doctors' Commons. If in fact it had been technically a bigamous marriage in the first place, again perhaps he would not want to recall it, or have it probed by any outside party. At any rate, given Cooke's psychology, it is not difficult to find possible reasons for his dropping her out of the Chronicle.

Who was "Mrs. Cooke"? Like all her later successors except Alicia Daniels, she remains a shadowy figure. After these two seasons we hear no more of any Mrs. Cooke until 1784 in Manchester, and it may or may not be the same person. The Mrs. Cooke of the Lincoln and King's Lynn bills would seem to have been a personable young actress (she played Venus in *Midas*, Miranda in *The Tempest*, Dorinda in *The Beaux Stratagem*, for instance) with a taste for comedy (Lady Bab in *High Life Below Stairs*, Jenny Diver in *The Beggar's Opera*, and the Widow Brady in *The Irish Widow*, which she played for her benefit in 1774). But who she was, or when and where they met, prior to September 1773 when they were living together in Lincoln, remains a mystery.

Whatever the story behind it, however, at Mr. Ealand's, Joyner, near St.

Mary's Church in Lincoln, or at Mrs. Gurling's in Broad street, King's Lynn, they were installed as Mr. and Mrs. Cooke, and from there they went daily to the theatres in the King's Arms Yard or in Checquer Street.

II

As he looked around King's Lynn in those early days of 1774, Cooke may have been reminded a little of his home town, Berwick. Lynn was then a prosperous little sea-port whose later rivals, Hull and Grimsby, had not yet begun to rob it of its trade. Much of that trade was liquid – the importing of wines, and the brewing and exporting of beer to the Baltic countries – and the comfortable way of life and consequent smugness of many of the inhabitants was not to John Wesley's taste. As at Berwick, the old walls of the town were still intact, and with its regular Tuesday and Saturday markets and its ancient fairs in February and October Lynn was a centre of local trading as well as for overseas – a place where, at the right time, the players might expect to do reasonably well.[8]

The theatre in Checquer Street was still comparatively new. It had been built by the Corporation in 1766 inside the medieval St. George's Hall, which had been a regular site for players since the fifteenth century. But the new playhouse was built in what had come to be the standard pattern of the small Georgian playhouse, and boxes, pit and gallery catered for the full cross-section of a provincial theatre-going public.

The managers of the company which Cooke had joined, both Irishmen, were both, like so many of the Georgian country managers, "characters". Dennis Herbert had been associated with East Anglia for over thirty years, and had first led a company in King's Lynn in 1743.[9] By this time he had become a well-known local figure. According to Charles Lee Lewes he was celebrated throughout the shires of Norfolk, Lincoln and Nottingham for his truly astonishing consumption of beer – if Lewes is to be believed, a daily intake of ninety-two half pints between 5 am and 9 pm finishing with the ninety-third for supper.[10] The arrival of the company must have brought a useful modicum of additional trade to the local brewers. Mrs. Herbert apparently looked after the money-bags, and regularly doled out to him two and sixpence a day pocket-money. Even with the purchasing power of those days, this was hardly adequate to such a consumption, and he was reduced to various stratagems (including extracting money from her purse, which she kept under her pillow, before she awoke in the early morning) to keep the supply going. A dangerous precedent for Cooke to be set.

Of Jemmy Whitley a valuable portrait has been drawn in recent years.[11] He, too, had been touring up and down Yorkshire, Lincolnshire, the Midlands and East Anglia since about 1750. By this time he had become a man of substance and power in the theatre, with financial interests in many playhouse buildings, and with more than one company on the road at the same time. He may have seen the Lynn company only occasionally, if at all; if Everard is to be trusted (though he rather made a profession of his misfortunes), Whitley turned up at Warwick a little later, where one of his companies was playing, only to collect all the takings and depart, leaving the players on short commons; and A Veteran Stager, too, has amusing anecdotes concerning his shrewd eye for his own interest, interrupting his declamation of a speech of Richard III, for instance, with the line "that man in the brown wig there has got into the pit without paying"; and making the most singular arrangements on his deathbed.

> While on his death-bed in the town of Sheffield, he sent for an undertaker, and actually made a contract with him for the expenses of his funeral, with this stipulation, he (the undertaker) should take one half the amount in tickets, for his widow's benefit.[12]

The fact that Whitley died in Wolverhampton, not Sheffield, is another example of the Stager's unreliability as to detail; but even if the story is apocryphal it is still significant – this is the kind of anecdote his colleagues of the profession told and were prepared to believe about him.

Whitley and Herbert seem to have complemented each other – Herbert easy-going, convivial, not over fond of exertion (according to Lewes his companies had a reputation for conducting their rehearsals in a very slovenly manner),[13] while Whitley was shrewd, energetic, and determined to raise and maintain the standard of his companies.

> At the rehearsal in the morning Whitley stood before me and after I had repeated the speech asked me significantly if I meant to speak it so. Yes, sir. "Why, my dear, it may do in these companies you have been in, but it won't do with me, my dear."[14]

Which attitude was in the ascendent at King's Lynn we do not know, but whatever may have been the standard of performance, at least Cooke was being given an admirable opportunity to learn his way around the repertory. One of the King's Lynn Fairs, the Mart, took place annually in February; for obvious reasons the company opened its season then, and for the first week played every night except Sunday and followed with five nights in the second week. During that time Cooke played in either play or afterpiece each night; sometimes in both. On the opening night, Monday 14 February 1774, he played Young Marlow in Goldsmith's *She Stoops to Conquer*; the following night Jaffier in Otway's *Venice Preserv'd*. On the

Wednesday he was not in the cast of *The Provok'd Husband*, but sang a cantata after Act IV, and afterwards played Henry, the young romantic hero of Dibdin's *The Deserter*, in the course of which – if they presented it uncut – he sang three songs and took part in a duet and a concerted piece. Thursday saw him as Sir George Hastings in Kelly's *A Word to the Wise*, and as Whittle, the old man fallen in love with the young widow, in Garrick's *The Irish Widow*; a piquant piece of casting, this, since Mrs. Cooke herself played the Widow Brady. Friday brought him Jack Meggot, the young man-about-town in Hoadley's *The Suspicious Husband*, after which he played Paris in *The Judgement of Paris* (presumably Abraham Langford's entertainment, rather than Congreve's earlier masque). Finally on the Saturday he played the young lover Lionel, in Bickerstaffe's comic opera *Lionel and Clarissa*, in which again he may well have sung three songs and taken part in a like number of concerted pieces. An energetic and versatile week's work.

In the second week the only character to be repeated was Henry; he added Granville in Kelly's tragedy *Clementina*, Young Meadows in Bickerstaffe's comic opera, *Love in a Village*, Lord Duke in Garrick's farce *High Life Below Stairs*, Epicene in *The Macaroni*, and Lord Aimworth, the aristocrat in love with the Miller's daughter in Bickerstaffe's *The Maid of the Mill*.

With the end of the fair, the initial burst of activity came to an end; the company advertised that in future they would play only three nights a week, Tuesday, Thursday and Saturday; then tried Tuesday, Wednesday and Friday, and finally for the remaining eight weeks settled down to twice weekly on Tuesdays and Fridays. During that time Cooke added to his repertoire, among other things, Hamlet, Don Felix in Mrs. Centlivre's *The Wonder*, Zanga the Moor in Dr. Young's melodramatic blank-verse tragedy *The Revenge*, Lord Hastings in *Jane Shore*, Alexander in *The Rival Queens* for Mrs. Cooke's benefit, and Posthumus, Macbeth and King Lear (the latter for his own benefit).[15]

He was also to have played Richard III, the role that in the end he made peculiarly his own, on Friday 8 April, for the benefit of Glassington and Mrs. Maddocks, but at noon that day the theatre had to issue a special bill:

Mr. COOKE being taken suddenly ill, and incapable of performing the part of RICHARD, 'tis hoped the play of GEORGE BARNWELL will be accepted in its stead.

There may, of course, have been nothing sinister about this. It might have been a perfectly genuine illness; or it might have been that the pressure of the other major roles he had been learning so fast was beginning to tell, and that he just could not get Richard ready in time. But to the biographer conscious of the real significance of many of Cooke's "indispositions" in later years, there is an ominous ring about it. He was playing again on the following Tuesday for his wife's benefit, and the playbill announces:

N.B. the PUBLIC may rest assur'd, MR. COOKE will spare no Pains or Expenses to render this Night's Entertainment worthy of their attention.

With anyone else one would perhaps take this completely at its face value, an extra advertising flourish to the potential playgoers. It is only from hindsight that one wonders whether there may not be here some element of covering up an indiscretion. To be fair, A Veteran Stager gives him a clean bill at this time:

as they acted but three times a week, he had the others for his own private practice, during which time he applied himself to the studying of such characters as he conceived would one day fall to his lot; every hour, every minute of his time was devotedly employed in close application to study; he was never addicted to card-playing, or gambling of any kind; smoking he abhorred, drinking ardent liquors in those days he never indulged in; it would have been well for his future fame, perhaps, if he had adhered to that determination.[16]

And he has a vivid little picture of the local rector seeing this young man so often walking through the fields studying, that in the end he got into conversation with him,

and finding him a young man of great promise, and highly pleased with the mildness of his manners and conversation, gave him an invitation to his house, the use of his library, from which he improved and stored his mind with much general information, but in a very short time he was deprived of this, his first theatrical friend and benefactor by death; we have often heard him lament the loss of Mr. Strange with unfeigned sorrow and regret.[17]

This, also rings true; we shall find many references to this side of Cooke's character before the story is through.

With this kind of repertory he must have worked hard and long at his "lengths", the forty-six lines which actors at this time used as a unit of a measurement for the size of a role; even though, doubtless, the plays were cut, and the performances at times more rough than ready. Many of the plays, of course, he was familiar with before, either from reading and study, or amateur performance; and some of the roles, like Zanga and

Young Meadows, he had played in his youth. In later years Cooke was as astonished, as we may well be, at the thought of himself as a singer; but the nature of the kind of entertainment demanded by a Georgian audience forced this kind of versatility on the country actor, especially when he was young and in a small company. Charles Macklin, whose work in some respects Cooke was to revere and emulate, was another actor who, in his prime, would not have been thought of as a singer; but he too, had done it – and danced – in his early days.[18]

How successful a season this was is difficult to estimate. According to the Stager, it was not. He says that though Cooke was engaged at a salary of 10s. a week, business fell off, which compelled the managers either to disband the company, or reduce it to a sharing scheme. The company discussed this, and as they were satisfied with the integrity and honesty of the management, and considered that half a loaf was better than no bread, they reluctantly agreed and went on to sharing,

> ... and poor sharing it proved to be, for in seven weeks they obtained but 9s. each, still the ardour of George felt no abatement so long as he obtained good parts to act 'the siller' was but of slight or trivial consideration.[19]

The fact that after the first fortnight the bills suddenly become larger (suggesting that perhaps the smaller hand bills for use in the theatre were not being printed, as an economy measure) and are sometimes printed in red; the inclusion of announcements like that informing the public that the company's stay will be shorter than the previous season (with the implied invitation to come now, while it was still possible); and the dropping to two performances per week, might add weight to his statement. On the other hand, the bills are fully detailed and well got up; this is no "barnstorming" company; and King's Lynn was to remain a regular "date" for some years. Perhaps Herbert, like the peasant, would never admit to a good harvest; this, certainly was his excuse to Everard at Lynn in 1780, when he was unable to offer him a place in the company: at the Mart they had "done £200 less than usual".[20] He gave him half a guinea to help him on his way; but he may, of course, have been glad to see the last of him, and unwilling to employ him for other than financial reasons.

The company in 1774 was of reasonable strength. Besides the Cookes, the men included Herbert, Adcock, Light, Watson, Thornton, Robertson, Tankerville, Sherborne, Maddocks and Glassington; the women Mrs. Read, Watson, Robertson, Light, Reddish, Maddocks, and the Misses Glassington, Lowell and Adcock. Master Robertson, too, appeared when needed.[21] Miss Glassington was the new leading actress (the Glassingtons and the Maddockses were appearing in Lynn for the first time) and she had joined the company from Edinburgh. Which of the many Mrs. Reddishes this was is now impossible to say, though she was advertised as "from the Theatre Royal Drury Lane".[22] Robertson and Thornton had the main low comedy roles; and the full repertory of the season was a representative one for the time. Certainly, for Cooke to be playing leading roles so soon in a company of this kind was a considerable achievement. The "long-nosed raw Scotchman" was proving his mettle.[23] And learning his trade.

III

The season ended on Tuesday 17 May with a performance of Kelly's *The School for Wives*, in which the Cookes played Belville and Mrs. Tempest; and *Harlequin Fortunatus*, in which Cooke, no doubt as gorgeously caparisoned as he could contrive, played Riches. After that, for a time, the clouds close in again.

By the end of October 1774 he was back in London, since on the 31st he went to Covent Garden to see Mrs. Barry's first appearance there as Euphrasia in Murphy's *The Grecian Daughter*[24] and it seems likely that he remained there for at least a month, going regularly to the theatre and watching the leading actors of the day. "Now I began to see acting" says the *Chronicle*[25], and he specifically mentions Garrick as Leon in the Beaumont and Fletcher comedy *Rule a Wife and Have a Wife*. This must have been on 24 November 1774, since that was the only occasion Garrick played it during that season; when it was played a second time on 17 May 1775, Smith played Leon.[26] Whether Cooke was also appearing at this time with any of the smaller "illegitimate" companies in the suburbs we do not know. At some time, however, he rejoined the Whitley-Herbert company; with its reappearance at the King's Lynn Mart on 14 February 1775 we pick up a clear trail again.[27]

The pattern was much as before. Two weeks of nightly performances during the fair, followed by seven weeks at three a week. Herbert seems to have been making a special effort, since he announced considerable additions to his wardrobe; he was also tightening up discipline. "No persons to be admitted behind the scenes, and no livery servants to be admitted to the Box-lobby or Gallery without paying." The company is almost exactly the same, except that Light's name is not mentioned (though Mrs. Light remains) and there is no Mrs. Reddish. There is also no Miss Lowell, though there is now a Mrs. Sherborne; perhaps the one became the other. With these minor exceptions, and Master Glassington to ally himself with Master Robertson, the same company presents a broadly similar programme.

Cooke played many of his main roles of the previous season (Macbeth with Miss Glassington as the Lady, was promoted to the second week of the Mart, so it must have been reasonably successful previously); he added, among others, Hotspur, and Lord Ogleby in *The Clandestine Marriage*; the virtuous ruler Tamerlane, the noble savage Oroonoko, the benevolent merchant Stockwell, the jealous young lover Beverley in Murphy's *All in the Wrong*, and Charles Dupely, the young man-about-town in *The Maid of the Oaks*. To Miss Glassington's Juliet he also played Romeo; and the Richard III that was denied to the solid burghers of King's Lynn in 1774 was un-veiled to them on Tuesday 7 March 1775; if it really was the first perfor-mance in the character that Cooke ever gave, then the date marked a notable beginning. For his own benefit Cooke chose to play social comedy, Marplot – the coxcomb with a passion for knowing about and inter-fering in everyone's affairs, but getting his interventions irretrievably muddled – in Mrs. Centlivre's *The Busybody*; and to sing *The Toast*, a favourite cantata never before performed in King's Lynn; whether it was ever performed after, must remain an open question.

During the last week in March the company departed to Stamford for the Fair Week and gave nightly performances, though Cooke had to work on only four out of the six, and never twice in an evening. The final week in King's Lynn, after their return, was an ambitious one. For Mrs. Cooke's Benefit he announced, from the Crown Tavern, where they were now living:

> Mr. COOKE, ever grateful for the Favours he has received from the Town of LYNN, has made it his Study to get up Something NEW for their Entertainment; and the PUBLIC may rest assur'd, That no Expence or Pains have been spared on this occasion.

There was music, extra scenery, dresses, decorations etc., entirely new. The "something", which had never before been performed in the town, was Dryden's *King Arthur*, with music by Purcell and Arne, and Cooke himself in the title role. Whether it lived up to the promise of the Drum and Trumpet we cannot know, but it was repeated again the following evening for the benefit of Glassington and Mrs. Maddocks. Three days later, with an assault on *Matilda*, Franklin's new tragedy adapted from Voltaire (which had been given its first performance at Drury Lane only three months before), and in which Cooke played Morcar, they ended the season with a flourish. Voltaire's pill was sugared with *The Maid of the Oaks* for an after-piece, and on 28th April 1775 it was as Charles Dupely that Cooke took his final bow in King's Lynn. Whether he ever returned there we do not know. Certainly though the company played as usual in 1776 many of Cooke's roles were taken over by an actor called Vernsberg. Cooke's association with Whitley, by then, was over.

IV

He must have returned almost immediately to London, for his Chronicle records that he was present at Covent Garden on 18 May 1775, when Macklin made his triumphant return to the theatre after winning his court case against those who the previous year had prevented him from acting.[28] Opposition to Macklin in the autumn of 1773, beginning with his new production of *Macbeth*, had culminated on 18 November in a riot in the theatre when he attempted to play Shylock, as a result of which Colman, then manager of Covent Garden, gave in to the pressure of the rioters, and discharged Macklin from the company. Subsequently the old actor brought a law suit against four or five of the ringleaders, accusing them of conspiracy, and in the summer of 1775, triumphantly won his case before Lord Mansfield. He then gave one of the finest performances of his career, in the court of King's Bench, reversing his familiar role as Shylock, and affirming that he had no wish for revenge. Though the judge made clear that he might have sued for, and won, substantial damages, he asked only that the defendants should pay his legal fees, and take £100 worth of tickets for the next benefit performances of his daughter and himself, with a further £100 to compensate the management for its losses.

Judgment was given on 11 May. It was the Benefit performance for Miss Macklin a week later that George Cooke attended, and there he saw the veteran actor, now in his seventies, in his favourite roles – Shylock in *The Merchant of Venice* and Sir Archy MacSarcasm in his own farce of *Love-à-la-Mode*.[29]

For other than theatrical reasons, this was therefore a special performance, which must have produced an extra element of excitement and tension in the theatre. And Cooke, though he was not to know this at the time, was witnessing a grand old actor at the end of his career, playing a double-bill of roles that, a generation later, Cooke was to make peculiarly his own.

How much Cooke based his later performances on those of Macklin is difficult to assess. "These characters two or three times, and Iago once, was all of Macklin's acting which Mr. Cooke ever saw," according to Dunlap,[30] and he never saw Macklin in the other Scottish role, Sir Pertinax MacSycophant, with which, again, he was to become specially identified in later years. What was important was that at this formative stage of his career, Cooke was being given an opportunity to see some of the best work the contemporary stage could offer. Macklin, though old, had the authority of a great teacher and a lifetime's experience. Garrick, too, though again

27

at the end of his professional life, was taking leave of the theatre as its acknowledged master.

Garrick did not retire until June 1776. By that time Cooke, according to the Chronicle, had managed to see his Hamlet twice, and two performances each of his Leon, Benedick and Don Felix. Kitely and Lear he saw once only, and it was as Lear that he saw Garrick for the last time. Whether this was also the occasion of Garrick's performing the role for the last time, on June 8 of that year, we do not know; Cooke must surely have concluded his engagement at Brentford by then (see below), but there were other performances during the times when we know Cooke to have been in or near London. For a rising young actor a Garrick performance must have been a powerful magnet; and we know from Everard that Cooke was an enthusiastic admirer of the great man.[31]

But the young actor had his living to earn, and that cannot have been easy in London, whatever success he may have had in the provinces. Cooke had to wait another three years before his first London engagement. For the present, he must look elsewhere.

V

He returned to Whitley and Herbert for one more period – six bills survive from the Lincoln season of September-October 1775,[32] after which the record is blank until the spring of 1776, when we pick up the trail once more, this time in Brentford, not far from London. There, according to the Chronicle, he played Dumont, the hero of Rowe's *Jane Shore*. The theatre was the large room in an inn, and the conditions were primitive.

> We dressed, male and female in one room: the dressing room was at the audience end of the house, and we had to pass through them to reach the stage, which was no higher than the floor, the whole theatre being a large room in a public house. *I have forgot the sign.*[33]

Beyond this, and the fact that the following evening he played Ensign Dudley in Cumberland's *The West Indian*, he recorded – or could remember – nothing more. The company can hardly have been a prosperous or reputable one. By 1776 much of the provincial circuit system had been set up and theatres had been built or converted in the main towns; that this had not been done in Brentford argues a lack of regularity or financial stability.

And indeed, for the next few years, Cooke was to find himself mostly in companies of this kind, the poorer sort of strollers, living often from hand to mouth. It is impossible to establish a complete chronology. The most that can be done is to reconstruct a few episodes, sometimes dateable, sometimes not.

According to his own account, after a visit to Berwick and Edinburgh in the summer of 1777, he returned south and joined a company at Hastings, in Sussex, under the managership of Charles Standen. There they played in the Town Hall, and after the season there went on to Rye, twelve miles away, where they played in an old school house. This, again, can hardly have been a company of any quality. Standen himself was as deaf as a post, but nevertheless fond of playing major parts like Richard III and Othello. These he could get through reasonably satisfactorily, according to Everard, provided the other members of the company did not play tricks on him; but often they did – changing their cues so that his lines became nonsense, or continuing to move their lips after they had finished speaking, so that for the audience there were long stage pauses while he waited to take up his cue.[34] Nevertheless, he was prepared to attempt almost anything. "He used to have a book or part affixed at the side of the stage, to which he coolly resorted when he was at a loss for his author," recalled Cooke. None of this suggests a high level of competence, to say the least, and the only other member of the company of whom we know anything confirms its eccentricity.

In our company was a little old woman of the name of Woodward, upwards of seventy years of age, who generally appeared in male characters. I have seen her in Sir Francis Grip and the Miser and have seen both much worse acted. She had an excellent comic appearance and dressed the miser after the manner of Mr. Griffin, who belonged to Drury Lane early in the last century, and was, I think, the original.

At Rye Cooke succumbed to a fever and ague, and returned to London in November, leaving behind some of his property, which he never saw again.[35]

Cooke was doubtless glad to be out of that pickle: though Standen, with such assistance as he could acquire, continued to tour and pick up some sort of a living. Three years later, Everard, tramping from Stowmarket to London,

. . . saw an open waggon, with a woman and two or three children at the top, some old boxes, with what appeared to be scenes and a green curtain; and to confirm and crown the whole, a drum at the head; a picture of the parapharnalia (sic) of a poor strolling company. Presently I saw the manager trudging on. I knew him as he had been with me at China-hall.[36]

It was Charley Standen, and being in no better state himself, Everard joined him and went on to Billericay in Essex for a share, plus half-a-crown a night for dancing, and the later addition of 7/- a week for being acting manager.

In the spring of the following year, 1778, came what may have been Cooke's first performance proper in London, at the Little Theatre in the Haymarket. Normally at this time, of course, the Haymarket theatre concentrated on a summer season, but it was also opened occasionally for a few nights, for benefit performances got up by individual actors, with *ad hoc* companies; or for amateur productions. In one of the former, on 9 April for the Benefit of Mrs. Massey, Cooke played Castalio in Otway's tragedy, *The Orphan*.[37] If he had any hope that this performance might catch the eye of the management at Drury Lane or Covent Garden, he must have been disappointed, and we next find him, in the summer of that year, at the China-hall Theatre in Rotherhithe.

Here, about two miles out of London, a large garden whose proprietor sold china, and any liquid from wine or ale to tea, had become for the time a popular summer resort. Perhaps with the thought at the back of his mind of turning it into a kind of suburban Ranelagh, or perhaps with an ambition no more extended than the proprietor of Sadler's Wells, the owner of China-hall had built in the centre of the gardens a wooden theatre, small, but well-equipped, according to Everard; and since it was so near London, with a good company of players. But its popularity was its undoing. Either from commercial or religious opposition (or perhaps even, though this does not seem to occur to Everard, carelessness) a fire was started one evening after a successful performance. It had been a hot, dry summer; the wooden building was soon reduced to its low brick foundations, and all that remained were two or three chests of clothes.[38]

Everard was a member of this company. So, too, was Cooke, and he had acted in whatever play was being performed on the night of the fire.[39] After the catastrophe the manager and some of the company who could obtain country engagements, departed; but the landlord, one Oldfield, conscious of the extra trade the playhouse had brought him, and the fact that some of the actors had nowhere else to go, suggested the making of a temporary substitute theatre. He obtained a carpenter, borrowed sailcloth and canvas, and with the help of the players produced in about a month an adequate tent-theatre. The scheme was run – according to Everard – by a committee which included himself and Cooke, and when they were ready to open, additional players were brought in, including Sparks Powell, later of Covent Garden, and Cooke's old friend Colin Mitchell, with whom he had first come to London from Berwick.

But again, the opposition began to operate. An information was laid before the magistrates, and the company was ordered to discontinue its performances after six more nights. At the end of that time the players pressed their luck too far and put on a further performance of *The Beggar's Opera*, only to have it interrupted by the magistrates' officers, who conveyed several of the players to the lock-up and a court appearance.[40] Whether Cooke was among them we do not know. But it was not the most fortunate of summers. After extricating himself in whatever way from Rotherhithe, he went to play a few nights at The Tennis Court Theatre in the Borough; but that, in its turn was shut up by the Surrey magistrates.

During all these vicissitudes he was playing his usual mixture of roles – Frederick in *The Wonder*, Gayless in *The Lying Valet*, Young Marlow, Lord Hastings, Hortensio, Benvolio, Tybalt, Tressel – and even Edgar, to the King Lear of Everard, of all people. But if he gained little valuable experience as an actor he was certainly gaining experience of the resilience needed if he were to survive in his chosen career.

How he survived we do not know. He had some more occasional performances at the Haymarket – Modeley in Shirley's *The Country Lasses*, Young Belmont in Moore's *The Foundling*, Lovewell in *The Clandestine Marriage*, and Glenalvon in *Douglas*,[41] but by September 1779 he was trying his fortune in the provinces again, this time in Suffolk, at Sudbury and Stowmarket in a company managed by one of the Fisher family.[42]

This time the problem was not opposition from outside, but dissension within the company. They did good business, according to Everard, who was to get involved a little later; but the company was really run not by Fisher but Scraggs, the low comedian, who at any threat of opposition would threaten to leave the company. This in itself would not have disturbed Fisher for a moment; but apparently the situation was such that if Scraggs went, he would have taken Mrs. Fisher with him – indeed, had done so, as Everard found when he arrived at Stowmarket to join the company.

> Their business has been wonderfully great, considering the shameful public misconduct of Scraggs and Mrs. Fisher, who had then twice left the town clandestinely together; but being immediately pursued and overtaken by Fisher and Mrs. Scraggs, their persuasions and entreaties brought them back again.[43]

In these circumstances, Everard found that all the company had left but one – his old companion Cooke, who himself was about to leave for Norwich, where he hoped either for an engagement in the theatre or work as a printer. It is typical of the generous side of Cooke that when he heard of Everard's situation – penniless and with a heavily pregnant wife – he invited them to accompany him to Norwich and offered to share his income with them. Everard stayed on – wrongly, as it turned out – with Fisher; Cooke walked off to Norwich, and for the next twenty months or so into near oblivion.

VI

His own records are a blank for this period. He is not named on the Norwich company bills in the *Norwich Mercury* and the *Norfolk Chronicle* during either 1780 or 1781. This does not necessarily mean that he might not have played a few small parts as an auxiliary.[44] But he was clearly not a member of the company, a tightly-knit one, many of whose members were regular performers over a period of years.

According to A Veteran Stager Cooke at some time joined a theatre at Canterbury, on the recommendation of his old friend Munden, already a member of the company. Munden was a member of the company managed by Hurst and Miell which opened at the Canterbury Theatre on 24 January 1780, and remained there till May.[45] Miell and his wife had been members of the Norwich company in 1774 and 1775.[46] It seems possible that Cooke may have been recommended by former colleagues of Miell in Norwich to try his luck in Canterbury, since there was no vacancy in the East Anglian company, and that on arrival in Kent he found Munden there, and through him obtained some kind of supernumerary work with the company. Again, it can have been no more than that; for unless he changed his name temporarily, the cast lists at Canterbury contain no mention of him,[47] and he seems to have come up against the same old problem of the major roles being pre-empted by other but less talented members of the company:

Hamlet, Macbeth, Richard, Shylock, Romeo, all, all the long list of tragedy heroes, were in possession of a Mr. Penn and Mr. Billy Swords, records the Stager,[48] so at the end of the season, if not before, he must have departed again in search of further opportunity. There is no mention of him in the next Canterbury company – Mrs. Baker's, in August 1781.[49]

However, one further possible confirmation that Cooke may have been in Canterbury during 1780 does emerge. According to the Stager, any flagging of his ambition at this time was recharged at Canterbury by encouragement from a significant quarter.

In this determination (to try his fortune elsewhere) he was warmly seconded by the opinion of the veteran Macklin, who chanced to be starring it for a few nights in Canterbury, and in Cooke's hearing said to the manager, "Sir, the weeds of your garden you seem to cultivate with care and attention; the only root you possess of value, and likely to flourish, you have planted in a barren soil, and in the shade – mark my words, Sir, that young man (pointing to Cooke) will one day be at the head of his profession.''[50]

If this interview did take place, it is a little surprising that Cooke himself should not have recorded it. Perhaps it was merely the embellishment of a convivial conversation years later in Buxton. Nevertheless, Macklin did make a guest appearance in Canterbury in April 1780, where on Friday 7 April he played Shylock, and on the following Monday Sir John Brute in Vanbrugh's *The Provok'd Wife* and Sir Archy MacSarcasm in his own *Love-à-la-Mode*.[51] It is tempting to speculate that here Cooke had a further opportunity of studying at close quarters Macklin's interpretation of two roles which later Cooke was to make his own, and in which he was regarded as Macklin's legitimate successor.

Be that as it may, Canterbury had nothing more to offer him. Perhaps no-one had. So far all efforts to trace him during the next fifteen months have failed. Did he in fact, in a mood of disillusionment, relinquish the theatre and seek employment again in his old trade of printing? It would not be difficult to understand if he did so. He had now spent nearly seven years in the theatre; and after an extremely promising beginning had made little, if any, progress during the last few years. The companies for whom he had worked had been either sub-standard or unfortunate. His attempts to break into the London scene had failed. He must have been aware that he had talent greater than most of the journeymen with whom he acted, yet by the old prescriptive rule of the theatre, many of the parts he could have played successfully were the jealously guarded prerogative of older actors. There was no room for him in the senior London companies or the better provincial ones – only among the rag-tag-and-bobtail such as he had just left, where the theatre was subservient to the squabblings and emotional complications of a group of inadequate personalities. Or so it may well have seemed. Did he, for a time, give up the struggle? Or even more sinister, was this the first of those periods, all too familiar in later life, when he retreated from his inability to shape the world to his own dreams, into a twilight limbo where alcohol blunted the senses, and he could forget for a time the inadequacy and the pain?

It may have been so. On the other hand it may simply be a coincidental blank in all the records at this time. The only clue so far to have come to light does suggest that at some point he made his way back to the Midlands, perhaps in the hope of work with Whitley again, and that either because it was not forthcoming, or out of disillusionment, or while waiting for a vacancy, he did return for a time to the printing trade in Nottingham. According to the Mss notes on the History of Nottinghamshire made by

William Stretton of Lenton Priory, who died in 1828, Cooke was, previous to his first appearance in the Nottingham theatre,

a journeyman Printer or Bookbinder, and worked for Mr. G. Burbage;

and in another entry he refers to him lodging

in a Garrett with Mr. Jos. Ward, Tailor, in Greyhound Yard.[52]

It is hard to know how reliable this is. Stretton makes the date about 1784, says that Cooke began his theatrical career in Nottingham, and refers to him dying in America "in one of the prisons", all clearly wrong. On the other hand these are matters on which his information could only have been hearsay and might easily be inaccurate. On local matters he is presumably more reliable, and it is difficult to see why he should invent the printing episode if it were not a piece of local knowledge. Certainly G. Burbage and Son did exist – theatre tickets could be bought from them. Whatever the truth of it, it is indeed in Nottingham and with Whitley's company that we do at last find Cooke clearly at work again as an actor in October 1781; and this time as a leading member of the company.

VII

The company called itself the Nottingham and Derby Company. Herbert had been one of its managers as late as 1778, and Whitley until his death in Wolverhampton on 13 September 1781, though the latter had not been able to perform during the last year or two.[53] Now the company was being managed by O'Brien on behalf of Whitley's daughter and her husband, Mr. and Mrs. Gosli. Their preliminary announcement for their autumn season opening on 22 October referred to several new performers already engaged, including "Mr. COOKE, from the THEATRE ROYAL, HAYMARKET", and the announcement for the performance on October 29th at the New Theatre in St. Mary-gate gives Cooke a modified star billing.[54] The company contained Beynon, Palmer, Richardson, Curtis, Rubery, West, Keymer, Dunn, Wheeler, Peters, Earl, Robinson, Spragg, O'Brien and Hudson, the Mrs. Beynon, Curtis, Hayes, Hudson, Kell, O'Brien, Sisson, Richardson, Robinson, Huntley, and Miss Stebbing; and the season lasted until the middle of January 1782. During that time Cooke's roles that are known to us were: Pierre, Tamerlane, Saville in *The Belle's Stratagem*, Evander in *The Grecian Daughter*, Sir George Airy in *The Busybody*, the Earl of Pembroke in *Lady Jane Grey*, Young Cape in *The Author*, and an Eastern Magician in *Oriental Magic*, or *Harlequin Sorcerer*. Of these

Lady Jane Grey and *The Author* came at the end of the season for Mrs. Hudson's Benefit, and a newspaper comment which, since no further performances were to follow, may not have been a managerial puff, refers to an elegantly crowded theatre – Nottingham "not only discerns but rewards Merit" – and notes some good performances, especially those of Beynon and Cooke which "would have done great Credit to either of our first Theatres Royal."[55]

For Cooke this must have been a welcome change and stimulus after the obscurity of the last few years, and doubtless he went on to Derby with the company in January 1782 in good heart. The neat little theatre there, in Bold Lane, had been built in 1773.[56] The company was little changed from Nottingham, and the repertory, too, was much the same, including two pantomimes, in one of which, *Oriental Magic, or Harlequin Sorcerer*, Cooke again played the Eastern Magician making a dramatic descent on to the stage in a cloud;[57] in the other he played Salmandore, the Genius of the Peak, perhaps fundamentally a not dissimilar character, in *The Rape of Proserpine, or Harlequin in the Peak of Derbyshire*, a flight of fancy which did its best to exploit local colour and the painting of Mr. Gamble of Derby.[58]

In March the company departed for a fortnight to Stamford for the Fair, returning after Easter with some new pieces in the repertory. During this period Cooke played Joseph Surface, Hotspur, and Clytus, ending up on 10 May with Lord Townly in *The Provok'd Husband* for his joint benefit with Hudson. This seems to have been a second attempt – a previous benefit had failed – and there is a note in the *Mercury* hoping that Derby will reward Real Merit. Whether it did we do not know. After the last benefit on May 17 – again a repeat after a previous failure, the company departed, and though they returned briefly in September for their regular short visit at that time of the year, they made no further attempt at a long season in Derby till December 1783.[59]

Does this suggest that the season had not been a very satisfactory one financially? And was this why Cooke left the company? For though he went with them again to Stamford in June and July[60] he was not in the September company in Derby nor at the re-opening in Nottingham in October. Perhaps after the death of Whitley the management was no longer so effective. Certainly by the time the company returned to Derby in December 1783 Mr. and Mrs. Gosli had sold out their interest and Pero had become proprietor. But by then Cooke was on his way to Manchester.

Where he spent the rest of 1782 and 1783 is again not clear. According to Dunlap he was in London at various times during this period where among other things he saw some of Henderson's performances.[61] There is also the possibility that he may have been in Bath during this time, though not as a full member of the company.[62]

But from his own account Cooke was in Louth in Lincolnshire by December 1783, for it was from there that he left to begin an engagement at Manchester at the beginning of January 1784.[63]

"I come now," he says in his Chronicle, "to a more important era in my theatrical career." He recognised it himself, and we, following in his footsteps, can confirm his sense of a turning point being reached. For a decade as a professional actor his life had been subject to extreme changes of fortune. Periods of great opportunity had been followed by spells of extreme frustration. He had learnt his trade, but had frequently been denied the opportunity to practise it. That time was almost over. From this time forward he was accepted, in the provinces, at least, as a leading actor, and with few exceptions we can henceforth follow his career in much detail. The days of obscurity – unless he himself were deliberately to seek it – were over. The long apprenticeship was complete.

Chapter IV

Explorations in the North – 1784-1787

I left Louth on Saturday the twenty seventh of December, 1783, and arrived at the Lower Swan Inn in Manchester (at that time kept by Dixon) on Tuesday evening, the thirtieth. The next day I went to private lodgings. I made my first appearance on Friday the second of January 1784, in Philotas in the Grecian Daughter, and was received with much applause.[1]

Thus Cooke records his first entrance on the Manchester scene. The city to which he came was as yet only at the beginning of its transformation by the Industrial Revolution from a country trading town to a vast centre of manufacture; the theatre serving the thirty thousand or so inhabitants was the first Theatre Royal, built at the junction of York Street and Spring Gardens in 1775 by Joseph Younger and George Mattocks.[2] They also had a summer company in Liverpool; the Manchester operations, being in the winter, were more directly controlled by Younger since at that time the Mattocks were otherwise engaged at Covent Garden. By 1781, however, possibly as a result of failing health, Younger had to relinquish the direction of affairs in Manchester. For two seasons Austin and Whitlock provided the company, but then, for reasons not now clear, returned to their other circuit operations, and for the winter of 1783–4 James Miller, better known for his management of the Shrewsbury-Worcester circuit, came in for a single season in Manchester. It was Miller who engaged Cooke for his new company.

That company, while containing a number of regular performers from earlier seasons had additionally in leading roles the Marshalls from York, Thomas Grist who had been at Drury Lane, and Mrs. Robinson fresh from Covent Garden. The season had begun on December 3, and according to Cooke's recollections, by the time he joined it personal relations had already begun to be a little strained. He was not altogether happy about his opening performance, feeling that Philotas was by no means his best role,

37

but the tradition of an actor's own choice of character for his first appearance was not observed by Miller, who had been used to smaller companies, and "was really governed by a cabal, not one of whom are now living or ever mentioned in theatrical society."[3]

Grist was the leading man. Cooke played Antonio to his Shylock, Claudius to his Hamlet, Don Alonzo to his Zanga, King Henry to his Richard III; but Cooke also had exploitable roles like Hotspur, Wolsey, Douglas, Young Marlow, Ranger and Don Felix, and played Benedick to Mrs. Robinson's Beatrice.

But to us the most fascinating member of the company, about whom Cooke is predictably totally silent, is the second Mrs. Cooke. Who she was, where she came from (and indeed, after a year or two, where she went), we do not know; nor whether their union had any blessing from the church. Presumably Cooke had acquired her during the last year or so, since there was no Mrs. Cooke in the lists at Nottingham or Derby. By inference from the varied roles that she played she was already an actress of some experience; since many of them were young girls, she too was perhaps quite young. She was also a singer and seems to have had an eye for comedy; her "manual exercises" as Nancy in *The Camp* were referred to in the bills, on more than one occasion, as a positive attraction. Beyond that, tantalisingly, we know nothing.

The theatre in which they worked seems to have been a neat and pleasant one. According to the German, C. G. Küttner, whose letters provide some fascinating glimpses of it at this time, it was small, but warm, comfortable, and well-equipped, and with no spectators allowed on the stage. In the audience he noted the comparative lack of professional and middle-class spectators compared with Germany – in Manchester he felt such people were too busy – and found the gallery during the intervals much more noisy and badly behaved than at home. Nevertheless, during the play itself, the gallery was quieter than he had heard anywhere else, though it had no hesitation in noisily expressing its approval or disgust.

> Of battles and murders they are especially fond, and when the theatre is full of bodies, as at the end of *Hamlet*, there is no end to the applause and trumpeting.[4]

It was the realism of English actors that struck him forcibly, compared with their counterparts in Germany and France. But though it is clear from internal evidence that he must have seen Grist as Hamlet and Richard, Cooke as Claudius, and Mrs. Robinson as Southern's Isabella, Küttner does not mention them by name, or discuss their individual techniques; and since this is before the era of dramatic criticism outside London we are left with little more than expressions of approval or disapproval. One such, towards the end of the season, is worth noting in view of what was to happen a few months later. The performance of *The School for Scandal* on Friday 21 May was commented on. The form adopted was correspondence to the editor of the *Manchester Mercury* by a gentleman passing through Manchester who, familiar with performances in London, was agreeably surprised at the standard of the Manchester players, and in particular referred to the Lady Teazle of Mrs. Robinson, the Charles Surface of Grist, and Sir Peter Teazle by Cooke. Whether this was a totally independent comment or a disguised managerial puff is an open question; Harrop, the proprietor of the *Manchester Mercury*, was the direct lessee of the theatre from the subscribers who had financed the building of it, and so had an interest in the success of the company. But either way, Cooke's performance in the role of Sir Peter seems to have been approved; which would make it all the more galling for him when it was later taken from him.[5]

The season ended on 1 June 1784, and it ended Miller's association with Manchester. Perhaps, as Cooke implies, he found the task of controlling a large and temperamental company too much for him. That there had been dissension is clear. The announcement of the last performance but one, on May 28, was for the benefit of Mr. and Mrs. Marshall "whose dispute with Mr. Miller is now at an end". Perhaps these troubles affected the work of the players and consequently the box-office, which would not please Mattocks. It was too late for Younger to be able to do anything about it, for in September he died; and so for the following season Mattocks had to take on responsibility for Manchester himself. Meantime, there was the summer season in Liverpool to be prepared, and it was to open on June 7.

II

The Liverpool audience at this time seems to have taken some pride in the belief that its company was led by London performers out in the provinces for the summer. In 1778 there had been riots when the management attempted to introduce a company of provincial actors – presumably basically the Manchester company – even though they included Mrs. Siddons and J. P. Kemble, then permanent members.[6] Hence the Manchester company, though it was under the same ultimate management and the seasons were complementary, could not be transferred to Liverpool *en bloc*. The season lasted from June to December, but for the first half, until the metropolitan theatres began calling them back in September, London players formed the spearhead of the company, backed by some of the rank and file members. Only after about mid-September did the composition of the group become recognisably like the Manchester company it was to

39

become in December. Till then, those players not needed probably picked up such engagements as they could with other managers in the region.

Cooke (and presumably Mrs. Cooke, since she was still with him later in the year in Liverpool) took a summer engagement with Austin and Whitlock, first in Lancaster and then in Preston.[7] No bills or newspaper records for this season appear to have survived, but we shall see a great deal of the Austin-Whitlock company later. By September the Cookes had rejoined Mattocks in Liverpool, and there on Monday September 13 Cooke appeared for the first time as Frankly in *The Suspicious Husband* and Young Wilding in *The Citizen*.

The theatre in Williamson Square was now twelve years old, a large and handsome building, elegantly finished and apparently with admirable acoustics. At this time, before the enlargement and remodelling in 1802, the theatre had the usual Georgian single gallery; it appears to have been one of the best positions in the house for seeing and hearing, and so was used in part by more fashionable sections of the audience than was customary.[8]

Performances were usually on Monday, Wednesday and Friday. The season began on 7 June with J. P. Kemble as Hamlet – his first appearance as a leading actor from Drury Lane since those riots of six years before when he was thought not good enough for Liverpool. Other members of the company beside the Cookes included Ward and Banks (later to take over the Manchester management), Grist, Stephen Kemble, Lever and Hollingsworth; the Mrs. Mattocks, Robinson, Langrish, Kniveton and Sidney. In his three and a half months there, Cooke played on 29 evenings – 23 different roles, a fair mixture of leading and supporting parts. One role, however, he did not play. When *The School for Scandal* was produced on Monday September 18th the cast was much as it had been in Manchester in May – Mrs. Robinson as Lady Teazle, Mrs. Cooke as Lady Sneerwell, Grist and Banks as Charles and Joseph Surface. But the Sir Peter was Moss, a managerial decision which clearly hurt Cooke's self-esteem. He continued his work; but the matter rankled.

The season ended in Liverpool on Monday December 27, and the new season began in Manchester on the 29th – a close call, which Mattocks must later have regretted. One additional performance had been scheduled in Liverpool for Tuesday January 11, 1785, for which the company would return from Manchester: a performance of *The Revenge* (for the Benefit of Langrish, who had unfortunately broken his leg towards the end of November) in which Zanga was to be played by a young army officer who some time previously had successfully essayed Hamlet. The performance duly took place, but was less than satisfactory, according to the *Liverpool Advertiser*. The young man appeared to have a cold; the supporting company (Cooke was playing Alonzo, Mrs. Cooke Isabella) worked hard, but were let down by the manager's failure to superintend the production personally.[9]

A week later Mattocks replied indignantly to the criticism. When he left Liverpool the bulk of the machinery and wardrobe were sent off to Manchester, but because of the wintry weather were frozen up in the Canal. This (understandably) caused great difficulties. He had done all he could to help Zanga – had sent the play to him ten days before; had the play carefully rehearsed on Monday morning; made a new costume for Zanga, which he did not use; had sent the prompter off at 6 a.m. on Tuesday to attend Zanga at his lodgings and get his instructions, to prevent if possible any mistakes. Had he – Mattocks – been there things would still have gone wrong, owing to carelessness or ignorance on the part of the servants. In fact, since the prompter was in Liverpool, Mattocks had to do his work in Manchester, or the theatre would have closed, which would not have been fair to the town of Manchester. Mattocks has since written to Zanga and hopes he is acquitted by him of any intentional disrespect. The reproach that he has forgotten his obligations to Liverpool wounds him deeply, and he hopes the facts will vindicate his conduct, who remains, the public's ever obedient, Obliged, and humble servant, Geo. Mattocks.[10]

But more trouble was in the offing. That unhappy Liverpool decision to prefer Moss to Cooke as Sir Peter Teazle rebounded. Moss suddenly left the company in Manchester, and Mattocks, intending to revive the play, sent the part once more to Cooke. Cooke reacted in that impulsive and stubborn way with which later we are to become all too familiar. His pride was hurt. He had been passed over, and was now being turned to as second best. He would not be humiliated in that fashion. He would not play it. And once having made the gesture of defiance, he would not go back on it. Managerial authority and stubborn, wounded self-esteem, clashed head on. There was only one solution. Cooke left the company, and was not to reappear in Manchester for three years, until the management had changed.[11]

III

The break, according to his recollection, took place on February 5, and for over three months he was out of a job. Since after a few days Mrs. Cooke's name also drops from the bills, she presumably went with him. How and where they survived these months we do not know. Fortunately, however, Joseph Austin had already had a taste of Cooke's quality. He was prepared to re-engage him for the summer in Lancaster (and presumably later

Preston as usual); and in the autumn, still with the Austin-Whitlock company, Cooke paid the first of his many visits to Chester, which was to prove one of the most successful of his provincial centres.[12]

He was not without acquaintances in the company. There was his old friend Munden, developing his genius for comedy; Stephen Kemble and his wife, and Mrs. Marshall, the Cookes had worked with in Manchester. It was a short season – less than two months – but it was to enable Cooke to extend himself in several major roles, and it gives us our first glimpse of a contemporary comment on him as an actor.

He played some of his familiar Manchester parts, like Philotas and Lord Raby. In comedy, he had his first opportunity to tackle Captain Absolute in *The Rivals*, and Sir John Melville in *The Clandestine Marriage*. But most important were four roles which were to become part of his major repertory, Lord Hastings in *Jane Shore* and Stukely in *The Gamester*, and – for the first time since those apprentice efforts in King's Lynn ten years before – Macbeth and Hamlet.

It is the latter, which he played first on Wednesday 26 October for his and Mrs. Cooke's Benefit, and was announced to repeat on Monday 7 November for the Benefit of Platt, that gives us our first detailed example of Cooke at work as a leading actor; for by chance his prompt copy for that performance has survived, while at the same time the *Chester Chronicle* printed one of its rare direct comments on an actor.[13]

Miss Byrne's study of the prompt book in *Theatre Notebook* is so detailed that little needs to be added here. As she has pointed out, while the annotations are in Cooke's handwriting, the book is more than just a Hamlet part-book, and so presumably reflects the whole production as the company played it. As such, some of the points which it makes may have been Austin's, as senior manager (indeed, must have been agreed by him, at the very least), and may even have represented at certain points his memories of the Garrick production he had witnessed years before. But in, for example, Cooke's restoration of some traditional cuts, his reflections on the inadequacy of certain traditional pieces of stage business, his quiet playing of the end of the "nunnery" scene, there is clear evidence of the working of an intelligent and original mind, content to take nothing for granted, and concerned to make action emerge from, and be relevant to, the text. (Seventeen years later, when at last Cooke was able to play Hamlet in London, his low-key playing with Ophelia in that same scene was commented on – unfavourably then, in contrast with the fashionable Kemble, but evidence of the consistency of his reading over the years.)

The prompt book gives evidence of careful and detailed preparation – Cooke was working hard at his profession at this time – but it might have been evidence of intention rather than achievement; the writer in the

Chronicle, however, confirms the impression received in the theatre.

> The pathetic situations he played to the heart and in the 'very whirlwind of passion'; in our opinion 'his actions were suited to his words and his words to his actions'. To the *antithesis*, or opposite situations, he gave a marked variety of tones, with the strictest harmony; and his instructions to the players (which ought never to be omitted) were recited with a degree of energy and ease that very sensibly impressed every part of the theatre.

There was criticism, however, of his delivery in the closet scene.

> . . . 'Farewell! and when you are desirous to be blest, I'll blessing beg of you', which, by accenting the proposition *of*, instead of the pronoun *you*, that immediately follows, the meaning of the author was not only destroyed, but the harmony of the verse materially injured. The most finished performance is not, however, without a blemish; and here the beauties are so many, that ill-nature and envy must stand up, and say to all the world, 'This is an actor.'

A splendid accolade as the climax to his season's work. But it appears to have been counter-balanced by another of those personal crises from which Cooke was never to be free for long. When the season ended on November 9 and the company departed to Whitehaven and Newcastle, Mrs. Cooke went with them,[14] but Cooke did not, his roles being taken over by others. So far as we know, they never appeared together again.

IV

For a few months we again lose track of him. But that there was no reflection on his growing reputation as an actor is clear, for his next engagement for the summer of 1786 was with Tate Wilkinson in Yorkshire, as a leading player opposite Sarah Siddons in that first, and almost regal progress she made through the country after her establishment as a London star. She had not been in York since her stock company days in Manchester. Now she was returning bearing the seal of metropolitan approval, and simple curiosity to see what had happened to this young woman, as well as a desire for a great theatrical experience, could be counted on to swell the audiences. Wilkinson, a shrewd as well as eccentric manager, knew how to exploit this situation. Prices were raised, no money was to be returned, free seats for servants were abolished. The advance publicity was cleverly done.

A biography of her appeared in the *Yorkshire Magazine* in July,[15] fulsome puffs in the *Yorkshire Chronicle*. And after it was all over Wilkinson even allowed (or perhaps encouraged) the *Yorkshire Magazine* to publish the receipts of the season.[16] They were remarkable enough. For ten nights in York and four in Hull the box office took in £1,885, of which over £1,000 went to Mrs. Siddons herself.[17]

She played all her renowned parts – Lady Macbeth, Lady Randolph, Belvidera, Mrs. Beverley, Jane Shore; Cooke supported her in many of them – Count Baldwin to her Isabella in York and Leeds, Villeroy in Hull; Philotas to her Euphrasia, Stukeley to her Mrs. Beverley; Gloster in *Jane Shore*, Earl Raby in *Percy*, the King in *The Mourning Bride*.[18]

They opened in York on July 29, moved to Hull on August 14, on the 21 back to York for the Races, and then on the 30 to Leeds and Wakefield for a few performances. For her it was a triumphal tour; Cooke, perhaps subconsciously, sums it up when he writes – "the company went with Mrs. Siddons to Hull and Leeds."[19] It was Cooke's first meeting with her; he had, of course known her brother, Stephen Kemble (who was also in this York company), for some time at Manchester, and with Austin and Whitlock; and in the latter company he had already worked with her sister Elizabeth, who was Mrs. Whitlock, of whom he was to see much more in the future. His acquaintance with the Kemble family was therefore already established. Whether he had yet met his future antagonist, John Philip, does not appear. Perhaps he had seen him in one of his recent London visits; certainly he must have heard a good deal about him. But there is no evidence that as yet they had played together.

Mrs. Siddons ended her tour in Leeds. There Mrs. Jordan succeeded her as guest artist for a night or two, and Cooke stayed long enough to play Loveless to her Miss Hoyden in *A Trip to Scarborough*. But brilliant as Mrs. Jordan was in her own line of comedy, she had not the drawing power of Mrs. Siddons. Prices were back to normal; the comet had exploded across the sky and now vanished below the horizon. In any case, Cooke had an autumn engagement in Chester with Austin. After his last performance in Leeds on 7 September, he started back for the west, where the season was to begin on the 15th.

There, with the end of the previous season in mind, Austin arranged Cooke's first re-appearance on Friday 29 September in *Hamlet*; and five days later he played Macbeth, for his own benefit, to the Lady Macbeth of Elizabeth Whitlock. Though his audience could not be aware of it, this evening must have had a certain piquancy for him. Less than two months before he had been watching her sister Sarah's interpretation of the same role at close quarters – though not so intimately involved. Tate Wilkinson himself had played Macbeth on that occasion, and Cooke had the lesser role of Rosse. The comparison can hardly have been to Elizabeth's advantage. Whether she sensed this and whether in consequence their relationship already was acquiring an uneasy element, of the kind that was to have repercussions later in Newcastle, can only be speculation; but it would be understandable if it were so.

Clearly Cooke had acquired a reputation with Austin. A former member of the company at this time told Dunlap in America,

> As an actor he was in great estimation; his salary was two guineas a week, the highest then given in that company; he was accustomed to have a given time for study, not unusually long, was always very perfect, and had the reputation of being a *correct* actor.[20]

The evidence of the bills in the *Chester Chronicle* bears this out. Ten days after Macbeth he played Lear; again, so far as can be seen, for the first time since those apprentice years in King's Lynn; a fortnight after that Richard III, a week later Shylock, and then Posthumus and Sir John Restless in Murphy's *All in the Wrong*, all for the first time for some years.[21] In between he kept up his more familiar stock roles, Stukely, Frankly, Villeroy, Mr. Belville, and added Raymond in *The Count of Narbonne*; from the actor's point of view, a stimulating range of parts.

And from the company's point of view, one has the impression that the season, a concentrated two months only, was a successful one. The bills are displayed much more fully in the newspapers, as though the managers could now afford to do so. And the company, with the Mundens, the Whitlocks, the Duncans, Austin and Caulfield, Mrs. Sparks and Mrs. Marshall among others, contained a great deal of talent.

In spite of this, when they moved on, Cooke did not go with them. That there was no disagreement is clear, for he was to return within the year. It may be that while with Tate Wilkinson in the summer he had contracted to return to him when the Chester engagement was over. It may be that he knew Mrs. Cooke was returning to the company for their next stand[22] and wanted to avoid her (or, of course, it may be that Austin only re-engaged her because he knew Cooke was contracted elsewhere; she does not reappear with Cooke again). Which ever it was, he packed his bags, and a month later rejoined Wilkinson's company in Hull.

This time he was not taking part in a royal progress but joining the normal stock company on its circuit, and it may have proved something of an anti-climax. Certainly he was playing leading roles, and was able to add Othello to his Shakespearian range. He played Macbeth for his own benefit in Hull, and Sir John Restless in York.[23] Unfortunately Wilkinson's account books, some of which have survived, do not exist for this particular season, so we cannot tell how successful they were with the Yorkshire audiences. From the names of the players it would not seem to have been as talented a group as either that of the previous summer, or the Chester company he had just left. Moreover there was trouble in the company. In April Mrs. Belfille wanted to do Mrs. Inchbald's new play *Such Things Are* for her benefit, and had obtained a copy from Norwich; but Wilkinson wanted it, too. Mrs. Inchbald decided that Mrs. Belfille should have it, but Tate insisted on his managerial priority. Whether there was a genuine misunderstanding or not (and Wilkinson's announcement for the performance on Easter Tuesday 10 April 1787 may suggest there was), it led to a quarrel between him and Mrs. Inchbald that was not made up for some years.[24] The ill-feeling engendered by this was contagious. Knight objected to being third in the bills in his role of Twineall, and in spite of Wilkinson's obtaining and showing him a bill from Bath in similar terms, refused to play, and Betterton had to play instead. The quarrel seems to have been patched up, but Knight and Miss Farren, who was shortly to become Mrs. Knight, left the company and in the autumn joined the company at Bath and Bristol.[25] Others left, too.

Whether Cooke took sides we do not know. He played the Sultan for Wilkinson; four days later he played Sir Clement Flint in *The Heiress* for Mrs. Belfille and recited part of Garrick's Ode on Shakespeare. But the atmosphere in the company must have been uncomfortable; and during the last part of the season he was clearly not getting such interesting parts to play. He stayed with the company until May 12. Thereafter, though the season continued until the 26th, his name does not appear again in the bills; he did not work in York again until nearly the end of his career, when he made a guest appearance in 1808.

Chester, clearly, had been much more congenial to him; and there he made his way, to rejoin Austin. When he did so in the autumn, he was to remain with that company for four years – the longest period of stability in his career so far.

Chapter V

The Austin-Whitlock
Companies – 1787-1791

Joseph Austin, the senior manager of this company, had been with Garrick at Drury Lane from 1758–61, part of the time as his assistant prompter.[1] Subsequently he had gone to Ireland where he played in Cork, and at the Crow Street theatre in Dublin. In Dublin he seems to have joined up with Michael Heatton, and from about 1766 they began touring with a small company in the north west of England and north Wales. Like all provincial companies at this time their touring pattern was exploratory and eclectic, but by the time Cooke joined the company, nearly twenty years later, they had settled down to a fairly regular, and presumably reasonably prosperous, circuit routine. Chester, which they had first visited in June 1767, provided a regular autumn season, Newcastle a winter one.[2] Lancaster and Preston, sometimes Warrington and Whitehaven, seem to have occupied the summer months. Sheffield, too, provided winter seasons, though not so regularly. We have noted also Austin's forays in Manchester from 1781–3. Heatton left the joint management in 1777, and the following year Charles Whitlock took his place, though with Austin retaining some seniority and privilege.

This was a widely stretched circuit; according to Winston Austin's companies travelled "eleven hundred miles each year in addition to the constant weariness and fatigue of studying and acting"[3] and by the eighties their affairs were organised in an efficient and business-like manner, a far cry from the hand-to-mouth sharing companies of thirty or forty years before.

In one of Austin's collections of playbills in the British Library has survived a copy of the printed agreement drawn up for use by Austin and Whitlock and their players. It legislates for rehearsal discipline, benefit procedure, behaviour during performances (and in public generally), casting rules, payment of shares and salaries, notice of resignation or dismissal, and so on; since there are XXXI articles, a great deal of detail is covered.[4] That the managers were endeavouring to concentrate authority

47

in their hands is clear; but it is probably fair to say, in part, at least, from a sense of responsibility. Austin was determined to do all he could to make and maintain a respectable company; he regularly advertised in the local newspaper at the end of a season asking that all creditors should present their bills to the theatre before the company's departure. The concentration in the Agreement on details relating to Benefits clearly reflects a desire to avoid dissension within the company and between them and the management; probably each clause related to some specific issue that had arisen in the past.

It is interesting to note that at this date the sharing system still survived, but alongside a salary system, and that performers might be on either – but presumably not both. It is not clear whether the choice was the performer's or the managers', or whether perhaps it was the result of mutual negotiation. But the whole document is interesting evidence of an attempt to regulate the working of a touring company and to legislate on behalf of efficiency and harmony. No legal document, unfortunately, can prevent an individual feeling disgruntled or discriminated against, if he is determined to do so; it was to happen to Austin himself, after he relinquished his management.

In his heyday, Austin was a popular actor with provincial audiences – better, it would seem, in comedy than in tragedy. According to the *Rosciad* he loved to "glisten in French silks"; Lord Ogleby and Sir Peter Teazle were two characters in which he excelled. His own list of parts which he was prepared to perform on either Stock nights or Benefits contains 29 characters, ranging from Shylock and Benedick, Scrub and Colonel Oldboy to Richard III, Hotspur, and Hamlet. The latter was a mistake, according to Ryley – he would have been wiser to stick to comedy.[5]

Perhaps his greatest achievement, however, was the company and itinerary that he built up. That he was proud of it is clear. Bound in with the printed agreement already quoted, is a double sheet of Ms. in Austin's own hand, entitled

Well known Theatrical Performers of Abilities, well known to the Public (some of them *first introduced*) under the management of J. Austin at the Theatres in Lancaster, Whitehaven, Sheffield, and at the Theatres Royal in Manchester, Newcastle upon Tyne and the City of Chester.

He then lists 53 players, among them the Mattocks, Edwin, Murray, Munden, "Gentleman" Lewis, the Popes, Miss Chapman, and, of course, Cooke, of Covent Garden, the Kings and the Sparks and Miss Hart (Mrs. Reddish) of Drury Lane; Blisset, Knight, and Miss Mansel (Mrs. Farren) of Bath; and, of course, the Kemble Family – Sarah and her husband,

Elizabeth and hers (she was with Austin before she became Mrs. Whitlock), Fanny, and Stephen and his wife. But he also lists others who never became known nationally but who were good and versatile and reliable provincial players, the backbone of the circuit system – the Marshalls, the Duncans, the Hunns, the Kennedys, Banks and Lovegrove. A not undistinguished list for its time.

A number of them were in the company which Cooke rejoined in Chester in the autumn of 1787 – the Whitlocks, the Sparks, the Hunns, the Duncans, the Mundens, and Mrs. Belfill.[6] The Marshalls joined the following year, the Duncans left. Others came and went, at least one, Hodgkinson, leaving some havoc in his wake. Some of them, like Platt and Mrs. Leister, stayed with the company for years – journeymen rather than artists, no doubt, but knowing all the tricks of their hazardous trade.

Ryley tells a story of Platt, in Newcastle, in a performance of *George Barnwell*, that, exaggerated as it may be, can stand for the resource as well as the unscrupulousness that their life bred in the corps of supporting players, an instinct for improvisation and survival that was often tested. Ryley was playing George Barnwell for the first time, Platt was playing Thoroughgood after, doubtless, times innumerable. He was an actor of the old school, says Ryley,

In declamation he was pompous, and well versed in all the crossings and recrossings necessary to impose upon the million. Pointing the toe, and standing erect like a fugle-man, he called *the line of beauty*. A cocked hat drawn over his right eyebrow, gave a fierceness to his appearance, which he endeavoured to support both on the stage and in private life, by never giving up an argument, or suffering, if he could help it, a dissenting opinion. Mossop was the criterion by which he judged of stage excellence, and any deviation from that bombastic actor was a crime against the sovereignty of eminence … The first four acts went off smoothly enough; but in the prison scene, poor Platt, having taken too much of the '*creature*', his favourite word, was embarrassed, and made frequent applications to the prompter. At length there was a total stand; I had not experience enough in the profession to cover the mistake by speaking out of my turn, and Platt, pretending to be much affected at our parting scene, covered his face with his tragedy handkerchief, to give time for recollection. Vain was the effort – his grief could no longer be continued; upon which he hurried to the side of the wing, and said, 'Give me the word b——t you!' The prompter nettled at his intemperance, instead of obeying this imperative command, very coolly closed the book, and walked away. This drove Pomposo to the last extremity; and continuing his strut around the stage, he took me by the hand, and said in a whisper, 'Don't be alarmed, I'll bring you off, my boy.' Then, leading me down, he thus addressed the audience: 'Ladies and Gentlemen – As there is no accounting for the timidity of young actors, especially on their first appearance, this gentleman I hope, will experience that lenity you have so often shown on similar occasions. His fears have caused some little inaccuracy, which I trust, will not be repeated.' He then made his bow and his exit.

Taken by surprise, not at all expecting the imperfection would be placed to my account, I was in reality, now 'at fault'. Platt had left the scene unfinished – I knew not where, nor how to take it up. My embarrassment was visible to the audience; but they took the good-natured part – they applauded, I bowed, and *Trueman* came to my relief.

When the curtain dropped, Platt seized me by the hand, and giving it a hearty shake, exclaimed, 'I told you my dear boy, I'd bring you off, b——t me!'[7]

Even without applications of the *creature*, in those days of three and more changes of programme a week, with at the most one brief rehearsal for a stock play, that kind of situation must have been all too frequent; and the skill at covering up which they learnt – and which is often attested – was as important to them as the ability to declaim, or to build up a character. One hopes it was not always so egocentrically used.

Mrs. Sparks was the young comedienne – Lucy Lockit, Phoebe in *Rosina*, Catherine in *Catherine and Petruchio* (Cooke played Petruchio), Flora in *The Wonder*, Moggy MacGilpin in *The Highland Reel*; but the great comic genius of the company, then "remarkably good-looking and in the full possession of buoyant spirits and exuberant humour"[8] was, of course, J. S. Munden, now approaching the maturity of his art. His Touchstone, his Launcelot Gobbo, his Dogberry, his Autolycus, his Filch – even his Shilty and Tim Tartlet, to say nothing of his innumerable comic songs were already the joy of his audiences. The great comedian transcends his material; he can make a thing of joy and wonder out of the trivial as well as out of great comic writing. But of its very nature his art is evanescent – even more, perhaps than that of the tragic actor, for it is less easy to describe. Munden was more fortunate than many of his fellows, in that he caught the eye and the imagination of Charles Lamb, who in six or seven hundred words caught the comic genius of the man and the insight of the artist.[9]

There can have been no doubt in anyone's mind as to who was the leading lady of the company. Elizabeth Whitlock was not only the second manager's wife; she was also a Kemble, and the sister of Sarah Siddons. She it was who had a prescriptive right to the big Shakespearian roles – Lady Macbeth, Portia, Hermione, Imogen, Rosalind – and also to the heroines of more recent tragedy – Monimia, Belvidera, Mrs. Beverley. She had the Kemble face and figure; she resembled her sister Sarah "in her commanding figure, dignified attitude, and expressive intonation, but she was not handsome".[10] She seems to have had much more vivacity in her manner than her sister – Campbell described her in later life as "just what Mrs. Siddons would have been had she swallowed a bottle of champagne", and Sarah herself described Elizabeth as "a noble, glorious creature, very wild and eccentric".[11] Perhaps the best and most vivid description of her that has come down to us is by her niece, Fanny Kemble, who knew and described her in later life.

She was a very worthy but exceedingly ridiculous woman, in whom the strong peculiarities of her family were so exaggerated, that she really seemed like a living caricature of all the Kembles. She was a larger and taller woman than Mrs. Siddons, and had a fine, commanding figure at the time I am speaking of, when she was quite an elderly person. She was like her brother Stephen in face, with handsome features, too large and strongly marked for a woman, light grey eyes, and a light auburn wig, which, I presume, represented the colour of her previous hair, and which, together with the tall cap that surmounted it, was always more or less on one side. She had the deep, sonorous voice and extremely distinct utterance of her family, and an extraordinary vehemence of gesture and expression quite unlike their quiet dignity and reserve of manner.[12]

In 1785 she had married Charles Edward Whitlock, Austin's co-manager. Whitlock, originally a dentist (a profession he continued to advertise and practise for some years, alongside his acting), had joined Heatton and Austin's company in 1774, becoming co-manager after Heatton's departure in 1778.[13] He played what might be called "second leads" – Bassanio, Claudio, Faulkland, Sir Oliver Surface; though he had managerial authority, he knew his place – or was it that Austin's seniority and experience and judgment kept him in it? Later events might well imply that. What ever the reason, he it was who played Horatio to Cooke's Hamlet, Clytus to his Alexander.

In this group, Cooke was Leading Man – and on his mettle. With all their eccentricities, they were good enough to bring out the best in him. Indeed, if Munden's recollection is to be trusted, he was at this time at the peak of his powers,

superior to those he afterwards evinced, and a voice as mellifluous as it became, in the end, hoarse from intemperance.[14]

51

And according to Tate Wilkinson, at the time of these three or four seasons in Newcastle he was extremely popular with audiences. The ladies swooned over his love-making on stage, and many of those who knew both preferred him to John Kemble.[15]

Certainly Austin and Munden gave him enough scope. He had all the major Shakespearian roles – Macbeth, Othello, Hamlet, Romeo, Richard III, Shylock, Iachimo, Posthumus, King John, Henry V, Hotspur, Leontes, Wolsey, Jaques, Falstaff, Petruchio, Benedict, Prospero; and there is an even longer list of leading parts in eighteenth century comedy and tragedy, the standard repertory of his day, and new plays as they were introduced. Only during the 1790–1 seasons in Sheffield and Newcastle, after Munden had left and the company began to disintegrate, does the quality drop. Even then he is rarely required to play in an afterpiece.

Independent comments are still too few to enable any confident generalisations about standards to be made. Ryley, after his early nervousness and confusion, found the Green Room atmosphere congenial and thought the company a very competent one.[16] One rare assessment of *Inkle and Yarico* and *The School for Scandal* from Newcastle in 1788 mingles praise and censure in such measure as to assert its independence – this is no managerial puff – but since it is the only one, it is impossible to make any assessment of the prejudices and assumptions of the writer, who found Cook "too stiff and solemn" as Inkle, and not equal to Austin as Sir Peter Teazle.[17] But that the part of the shipwrecked merchant's son Inkle should sit uneasily on Cooke's shoulders hardly surprises us; he was clearly not happy about it himself, played it rarely, and when the play was revived later changed over to the more congenial role of Sir Christopher Curry.

But with all its limitations, their professionalism was missed when occasionally the amateurs took over. In Chester in 1789 *Venice Preserved* was performed for Whitlock's benefit. Mrs. Whitlock, of course, played Belvidera, but Cooke, who normally had Jaffeir or Pierre, was confined that evening to Farmer Freehold in the afterpiece, *The Farmhouse*. In his place two local gentlemen appeared, Major Halliday (who appears to have had some talent – Austin includes him on his list of players) as Jaffeir, and A. N. Other as Pierre. The *Chester Chronicle* was driven to comment:

It is hardly necessary to say, Major Halliday, in Jaffeir, was pathetic, judicious, and chaste. – The gentleman who performed Pierre (for *his own* amusement) play'd the part in a *manner* that will not *soon be forgotten*: His *dying* scene was so *universally approved of*, that the audience felt themselves more than half inclined to have wished, the author had kill'd him at the end of the *first act*.[18]

Outside his professional activities, how well was Cooke behaving himself at this time? According to Dunlap's informant in America who claimed to have been with him at about this period, his problem had already begun to make itself felt, but intermittently:

his habits of living were pretty much the same as when in America, only he would sometimes abstain from excess for three months, and behave with the greatest propriety; but when he broke from this restraint, he was not to be heard of for several days.[19]

A Veteran Stager confirms this[20] and has two very circumstantial anecdotes from this period which illustrate it. But they contain such a mixture of verisimilitude and palpable inaccuracy that it is difficult to know what weight to give them. The matter is so curious as to be worth some analysis.

The first concerns the opening of a season in Newcastle, Cooke's first appearance there. According to the Stager's story, it was in 1786, and Cooke was advertised to perform as Othello on the Monday but did not appear. At 2 p.m. a man on horseback arrived with a letter addressed to the Managers from Cooke asking them to send him £10 as he was detained in Chester-le-street for lack of money to pay his expenses. The property man was immediately sent with a post-chaise and the money, but when Cooke, in his cups, learnt who had come for him, he was indignant, and refused to return with so lowly an emissary. As a result the play had to be changed at the last minute, to general disappointment. After the farce his friend Munden went to the watch-house in search of him.

The instant he beheld Munden ... he sprang from his seat, and with stentorian lungs, vociferated "The property man, sir – the property man, sir! – tell that tooth-drawing reptile (Mr. Whitlock was a dentist) and his coadjutor Austin, George Frederick Cooke will annihilate them; one look of mine, sir, will cause them to shrink into their original nothingness, but eagles war not with sparrows"; when he had exhausted his imagination in invective, threats and abuse, he suffered himself to be taken from his confinement, and was conveyed to his apartments prepared for him by Munden. As when in a state of intoxication no man could be more abusive or insulting, so also when in his perfect senses no man could with more elegance, more seeming contrition, atone for errors past –

he was easily able to make his peace with the managers, but it was expected that the disappointed audience would be less easy to placate. However,

Othello was once more announced, and when Cooke appeared, to a mixed reception, he stepped forward and addressed the spectators.

> Ladies and gentlemen; I stand before you self-accused, self-convicted, self-condemned; should your displeasure be added to my own, my punishment, though just, will be more than I shall be enabled to endure.

His audience was won over, and the performance was a great success. For the rest of the season he behaved impeccably,

> his society was courted by the first circle in Newcastle and neighbourhood, Sir Matthew White Ridley, Mr. Foster the banker, Sir Thomas Liddel, and many others of high respectability, honoured him with their patronage and friendship, which, notwithstanding some occasional irregularities, he continued for several seasons to enjoy.[21]

The tale is very much of the kind we become familiar with in later years – an assumed insult to his dignity called forth an exaggerated and irrational reaction, followed by contrition and a period of reform. It could not have happened in 1786, for Cooke did not make his first appearance in Newcastle, according to the bills, until 1788. But it is true that for the opening of that season (a rather special occasion, since on January 21 the new Theatre Royal in Mosley Street was being opened for the first time), a bill appeared for the opening performance, Murphy's *The Way to Keep Him*, containing "Mr. Lovemore, Mr. Cooke (*sic*) (his first Appearance on the Newcastle Stage)"; and both the *Newcastle Courant* and the *Chronicle* confirm that the performance took place. But presumably without Cooke, for a week later another bill announced a performance of *Othello* with "Othello, Mr. Cooke, (his first Appearance here)".[22] So far, apart from easily explicable errors of detail, the facts as we know them could fit in with the story. But the Stager follows with an equally, if not more, circumstantial account of a guest appearance by Mrs. Jordan in Newcastle, in which she was to open as Lady Bell in Murphy's *Know your Own Mind* and Priscilla Tomboy in *The Romp*. In the Murphy play, Cooke was cast as Dashwood

> – a character certainly as opposite to his general style of characters as it is possible to imagine; a gay, lively, volatile young man, constantly playing upon the follies and eccentricities of all around him; such a part was totally unfit for Cooke: this, perhaps, the managers were aware of, but as he was a decided favourite, they were well assured the town would be satisfied.

Cooke, however, was unhappy with it; at the final rehearsal he still had to read the part, but the managers were confident he would perfect his lines during the day. In this they were disappointed, for Cooke then disappeared and could not be found. The performance began with the farce, while searches for him were still being made, but in the end the play had to be performed with Hodgkinson, a promising young actor, reading the part. Mrs. Jordan, good-natured as she was, was furious and declared often in the Stager's presence that she would never forgive Cooke. Searches were made in Sunderland and North and South Shields, but without effect. Eventually after about ten days Duncan discovered Cooke, delirious from drink, in an obscure public house in the village of Swalwell, near Newcastle. He was returned to his lodgings and eventually sent to Buxton to take the waters, which enabled him to recover and he returned to the company in Chester, where he was received back willingly by the managers, and later by the audience in Newcastle when he returned there. No one asked for any explanation,

> but we have heard him since declare, he did not like the part, as it was quite out of his way, and could not brook the idea of disgracing himself before his generous friends and benefactors – 'as well, sir, might they have allotted me Darby or Lingo'.[23]

All very circumstantial and plausible. Unfortunately there is no evidence whatever from the records to show that Mrs. Jordan ever visited Newcastle during the years that Cooke was there, and every probability that she did not – though she did visit Chester in 1789.[24] Nor were Hodgkinson and Duncan ever there together; Hodgkinson was at Newcastle only in 1789, and by that time Duncan, who was there in 1788, had left the company.[25] What is more likely is that the Stager is here confusing with Mrs. Jordan the basic events which led to Cooke's departure from Newcastle in 1791.

Meanwhile two other Newcastle matters in 1789 to which the Stager refers can be more safely recounted from other sources. They began some months earlier. At the end of the Chester season in 1788 Joseph Austin, after some twenty years in the city, retired from management. In a number of ways it marked the end of an important era in company history; Austin had begun at a time when there was no tradition of circuit touring, and the life was haphazard and uncertain; he left, the senior manager of a regular circuit, with a legal establishment, a company of quality and a recognised social position; he retired also, it would seem, with more than a modest competence, and his final bill was presented with a flourish – a far cry from the bare titles of advertisements two decades before.[26]

Though he was retiring from the cares of management, it appears that he still hoped to perform from time to time; he was to live in Chester, where he had been a great favourite, and he seems to have had at any rate a verbal understanding that he would rejoin the company as a sharer when it returned to the town. Meanwhile he sold his share in the management to Munden, who borrowed money to buy it; Whitlock seems to have been angered by not being consulted about this; he would, apparently, have liked the opportunity to become the sole manager.

The new season in Newcastle, Munden's first as co-manager, opened in January 1789 in a spell of severe, wintry weather, and with a background of some discord in the direction of the company. Nevertheless, as far as Cooke was concerned, it was to be, professionally, his best season yet. One observer described him as "the sole support of the Theatre during the whole season",[27] and while this was probably partisan exaggeration, it is clear from his list of parts that a good deal of responsibility was being placed on him. It is all the more sad, therefore, that towards the end of the season he should unwittingly provoke an incident that was to cause even greater dissension within the company. An anonymous pamphlet – *Thoughts on the late Disturbance at the Theatre Royal Newcastle* (1789) – tells much of the story, with the local newspapers adding additional detail.

When it came to his Benefit, which he had drawn for March 23, Cooke decided to do, for the first time, Addison's *Cato*, and approached Mrs. Whitlock, as leading lady of the company, to ask her to play the leading female role, Marcia. Whether because of a genuine dislike of the part, or whether Cooke's success had been greater than hers that season, and had aroused a certain amount of professional jealousy (a reaction not unknown in theatrical circles), she refused the part. Cooke seems to have accepted this without any fuss, and approached Frances Butler instead. She agreed, and it was her name, therefore, which appeared in the bills in the *Newcastle Advertiser, Chronicle*, and *Courant*.

So far this was purely a matter within the company, but information about it seems to have leaked out to supporters of the theatre, and some of the ladies, disapproving of her attitude, withdrew their support from Mrs. Whitlock's benefit. She then, with astonishing lack of tact, issued an advertisement:

Mrs. WHITLOCK having been informed the Ladies and Gentlemen of Newcastle are very much incensed at her not performing for Mr. Cooke's benefit, she hopes to be pardoned for thus endeavouring to exculpate herself from such unmerited displeasure. Mr. Cooke chose a play where no one could appear to any advantage but himself, I therefore thought it was no more than what I owed myself, and the station I hold in the

Theatre, to refuse a character where I had no opportunity of exercising my abilities, and indeed he himself seems perfectly satisfied that I had no right to act such a part; I should even now be very happy to take any character on his night, where the author has allowed me an equal claim to the attention of the audience.

After this I hope to stand acquitted in all impartial minds; and to prove *that* is my utmost wish, I publicly renounce all pecuniary motives, and return those Ladies and Gentlemen my thanks, who have kindly patronized my night, and beg they will withdraw their names from the box-book, as I intend to resign my benefit this season.

ELIZABETH WHITLOCK.[28]

Though perhaps unintentionally, it could hardly have been more provocative. The arrogance of the attitude would doubtless irritate many audiences today; in the eighteenth century, when in spite of the increasing social acceptance of many of the players, there was still the assumption that actors were servants of the public, and had to be prepared to pay deferential lip service to them, it was like a blow in the face. Moreover, the last paragraph, though doubtless designed to avoid a débâcle and a half-empty house, was phrased in such a way as to make matters worse – a petulant "I don't want your patronage, thank you. I can do without it."

The affair now became the talking point of Newcastle society. Sides were taken and attitudes adopted. It must have been clear even to Mrs. Whitlock that her approach had left something to be desired; perhaps pressure was brought to bear on her within the company as well as without. In the event, she changed her mind, and on the Sunday evening, twenty-four hours before the performance was due to take place, she issued another statement.

HAVING been informed that my Apology is deemed insufficient, and that it is still thought I ought to perform the character of *Marcia*, – whatever my own sentiments may be on the occasion, respect for the public has induced me to undertake it, even at this short notice, and I shall certainly tomorrow night exert the utmost of my abilities, to prove I am their

most obedient servant,
ELIZ. WHITLOCK.[29]

Had it come earlier, instead of the previous statement, it might perhaps have been accepted. Now it was taken as being no apology at all; she was persisting in her opinion, and was prepared to play only under pressure, and as though the very fact of her deigning to appear was enough to cancel any offence.

She and Munden now took advice from some respected outside party, who counselled that the only way to save the situation was for her to make an unreserved apology before the play began, and this she agreed to do. When however, Munden led her forward that evening to "say a few words" she was received with a good deal of hostility. Whether this angered her and changed her intention, or whether she had still intended to try to stand on her dignity as leading actress and the manager's wife, the effect was the same. Her explanation was seen not as an apology but as an attempt at vindicating herself, and part of the audience became more clamorous and violent. She stood her ground; others in the audience noisily supported her. When she was able to be heard again she angrily told the audience that "if they did not choose to receive her, other Theatres were open", and stalked off.

IMMEDIATELY on her retiring, Mr. *Cooke* came forward; – and in a few words, prompted by the impulse of the moment, returned thanks to the town for their support; – and generously added, "could he have imagined his request of Mrs. *Whitlock*'s performance on his night, would have been productive of so much uneasiness to her, he would not have made it". – He received the loudest marks of applause from the whole house, – disturbed by only one single, solitary, unsupported hiss. – I AM happy in the opportunity afforded me of paying a slight tribute to the modest merit of a man, whose abilities as an Actor do not need my praise; and whose conduct, throughout the whole transaction, has been irreproachable.

After a little more disturbance, Mrs. Whitlock was eventually allowed to play Marcia, but gave further offence by cutting out large parts of it – nearly a half, according to the same account.[30]

All this inevitably increased the controversy. In the *Newcastle Chronicle* Mrs. Whitlock was supported by "Nathan", who had written the occasional critical report there during the previous season. He was present that evening, and subsequently wrote fulsomely about her performance, the inequity of asking her to undertake it, her abilities – far greater than those of anyone else in the company, and deserving of better opportunities than could be provided by a "country company"; – and finally, comparing her with her sister Sarah, to find her "in some parts confessedly equal, and in Comedy infinitely superior".[31]

This was too much to take, and out came the pamphlet to argue differently and to suggest a more critical balance in the controversy.[32]

Without taking sides in the contest at this distance in time, one can nevertheless feel that this must all have made unhappy reading for the

Whitlocks, and that it was a very great pity that the situation had been allowed to escalate as it did. For it was surely something of a storm in a teacup. Or was there a good deal more behind it than appeared on the surface? The pamphleteer has a tantalising final paragraph.

> I HAVE abstained from touching upon Mrs. *Whitlock*'s private conduct in this transaction: – I have not drawn aside the veil of the green-room. – I have suffered all that more particularly disgraced her understanding, to remain unnoticed, – nor do I intend to hold it up to view now; as I hope I have already said sufficient to leave only one opinion in my readers. – BUT should Mrs. *Whitlock*, or any of her friends, think I have said too much, I will open a further scene to the eyes of the world; – and shew, that if I stop here, it is not for want of materials; – but because I do not wish to step out of the common course of my narrative, to introduce any circumstances, which are not immediately under the cognizance of the public, – though nearer allied to the question, than any panegyric of her abilities can be.[33]

And with that genteel piece of blackmail, the pamphlet ends, and with it, so far as we now know, the paper war. But what *did* he know? And, indeed, who was the pamphleteer? There is no indication, though the fact that the printer was M. Brown may turn out to have some significance. The Whitlocks almost certainly believed that Austin was connected with it in some way.

Though on this occasion Cooke's reputation has a clean bill, the whole episode was an unhappy one. The atmosphere in the Green Room must have been very strained for some time, and it must also have had its repercussions on their support for the following season. But more Green Room trouble was to follow.

The season ended on April 29. At that performance, for Whitlock's Benefit (as senior partner he seems to have taken over Austin's prerogative of the final performance for his Benefit), Hodgkinson, who as well as playing young male parts, was also the company's Harlequin, was billed to deliver a prologue as Harlequin, and then take a flying leap through a cask of blazing fire. Shortly after that he took a flying leap of a different kind, away from the company, taking Mrs. Munden with him.

In fact, legally speaking, she was not Mrs. Munden at all. She was Mary Jones, but she and Munden had lived together as man and wife for some years, and he had four daughters by her. She seems to have been beautiful, but, according to one account, vulgar and illiterate.[34] She played small parts with the company, but was in no sense a leading player. Perhaps their relationship was getting strained in any case; perhaps Munden's new

59

managerial responsibilities were taking time and energy that she thought ought to have been devoted to her. If the Stager is to be trusted, Hodgkinson had already at least one elopement to his credit.[35] At any rate, they departed for Bath, where in the autumn he (but not she) joined the Bath and Bristol company for the next three years.[36] There he and Miss Jones were married; but three years later, history repeated itself, and he left her in Bristol, departing for the United States of America with Miss Brett, another member of the Bath company.[37]

How far the episode was an emotional shock to Munden does not appear. If it was, he soon got over it. At Chester in October he married another young and attractive member of the company, Frances Butler, who remained with the company until Munden's removal to London, after which she left the stage.[38] But coming hard after the *Cato* affair, it must have helped to unsettle the company further.

The routine of the circuit went on – Chester, Sheffield, Newcastle, Lancaster – but further trouble was brewing. Relations between the two managers seem to have been less than cordial; there are indications, too, that Whitlock was less flexible and benevolent than Austin had been. For instance, at the end of the autumn 1789 season in Chester, Hurst and Griffith, the Box-keeper, advertised a performance of Collins' Evening Brush for their Benefit, because "they could not get any other benefit". In the previous season, the company had played for Griffith. A similar situation seems to have arisen in Newcastle.[39] At the end of that season of 1790 in Newcastle, Munden decided that the worries and tribulations of management were not for him, and offered to sell out to Marshall, and then to Whitlock. Both declined initially, but Munden having made clear that he would dispose of his share at the first opportunity, Whitlock decided to take it while they were at Lancaster in the summer. It is not clear exactly when the agreement was signed; it was drawn up but not completed for some weeks. However, before they returned to Chester in the autumn, the deed had been completed, and Whitlock was the sole proprietor; at which point, and only then, did he learn that it was to be his last season at Chester – that for the following season the proprietors of the building had leased it to Banks and Ward, the Manchester managers.

His consternation is understandable. He had just become completely responsible for the company, to find that its best and most reliable support had been suddenly removed. What had been going on?

A three cornered correspondence of between four and five thousand words in the local newspaper, between Whitlock, Austin and Munden, enlightened the local populace.[40] The gist of all the prolixity can be simply told. Austin, when he retired, had understood that he would be invited to return to the company as a sharer in Chester, but Whitlock, in fixing the repertory up in Newcastle had contrived, deliberately or otherwise, that there was nothing for Austin to do, so no invitation was sent. A guest engagement of King at Newcastle in 1790 (presumably instead of an expected one for Austin) had also given offence. Austin saw this as ingratitude and deliberate slighting; he bombarded Munden with letters about it, which Munden, in the interest of peace and quiet, kept to himself and did not show Whitlock, since he was sure they would exacerbate the situation.

In the end Austin seems to have decided that Munden, too, was culpable, and that if they were going to behave like this to him, he would see that they did not do it in Chester. Whether he approached Banks and Ward or they him, does not appear, but the notion of a circuit consisting of Manchester, Liverpool and Chester seems to have been canvassed, and its attractions in terms of ease of operation and potential profitability were obvious.[41] The Liverpool end of it never in fact emerged, but an approach was made to the proprietors of the Chester theatre. It seems to have been customary for the lease to be renewed at the end of each season, so that the outgoing company had the option of renewal, and Whitlock had taken this for granted. In some way (possibly the influence on the shareholders of Austin living in Chester) this custom had been bypassed, and when Whitlock arrived in October, the theatre had already been let for the following season.

In his anger Whitlock unfairly saw Munden as another conspirator, aware of all this, and unscrupulously arranging to off-load his financial responsibility on to Whitlock before the blow should fall. He also brought up the subject of the *Cato* affair which still rankled, and blamed Austin for it.

You cannot, sir, suppose I could be over anxious for the society of a man who had made it a peculiar point to injure me and mine in the estimation of the Newcastle audience; I need not remind you of the late Dr. Brown, or of the gentlemen present at his table.

(It will be recalled that the publisher of *Thoughts on the Late Disturbance* was M. Brown.) In fact the only one of the three to emerge from the correspondence with any dignity at all is Munden. Austin is irritable, querulous, and full of self-pity. Whitlock is egotistical and arrogant, devious and full of injured dignity. Caught between them, Munden was in an intolerable position. When, at the end of the season he and his wife left for London, he must have gone with few regrets and much thankfulness.

Meanwhile, Whitlock ended the season with his Benefit, as usual, and made his farewell speech, but this time taking good care to see that a copy of it went to the press. Its unction and its anticipation of Uriah Heep formed an appropriate coda to a most unhappy affair.

> ... Tho not very old in years, I am old in your service, a period of not less than twenty seasons having elapsed since I had the honour of first appearing before you; thirteen of which were in the capacity of manager – Whatever my defects have been, during that time, I shall leave for *others* to determine; for *myself*, it is sufficient that I feel the pleasing consciousness of having, on all occasions, and under every circumstance, *done my best* to render the stage (what I conceive it *ought* to be) at once a rational and intellectual source of amusement. To this intent, no expence, or exertion, within the scope of my power, has at any time been wanting. If I have ever fail'd, I trust even my *enemies* will do me the justice to believe, that it has been an error of the *head,* and not of the *heart*; having the unspeakable happiness to say – I feel no accusation *here*. [42]

And with much more verbiage, and his hand still clutching his heart, Whitlock took leave of Chester. There is no indication that Cooke took any public part in this controversy, but there can be little doubt where his sympathies lay. Munden was a friend of long standing, who had always supported him, and in management given him opportunities such as he had never previously had. Austin, too, had backed him, and been understanding when he had transgressed. Moreover Austin was a living link with the Garrick whom Cooke revered as the great master of their profession. (Years later he told J. P. Kemble on one occasion that if the pair of them were ground together they would not make so much as an arm of Garrick.)[43] The Whitlocks, on the other hand, had behaved intolerably to him over the *Cato* affair, and perhaps in other matters. For Munden his new London engagement offered him release from the situation and an exciting future. For Cooke, with no other engagement opening, there remained what must now have seemed the treadmill of a company whose leading figures were at best uncongenial, and from which most of his friends were departing.

He went on to Sheffield, where Stephen Kemble joined his brother-in-law Whitlock in the management. That it was a poor season is beyond doubt. The *Sheffield Register* put the lack of support down to "the influx of business which has left our manufacturers but little time to devote to pleasurable calls".[44] The *Advertiser* put part of the blame on the weather, and thought the company respectable and deserving of better encouragement; but it added a significant rider:

> we will take the liberty of thinking that the plays might have been made more strong and attractive by a little difference in the disposal of

parts – One gentleman in particular has not come forward when he certainly should have done: but we hope he has seen his error, and will think differently in future. His interest, we conceive, behoves him to do so.[45]

Was the oblique reference to Cooke, and was there being trouble about allocations of parts under the new regime? It would seem very likely. When *Macbeth* was put on, Stephen Kemble took over the leading role, and Cooke had to be content with Macduff. For some of his spectators

Mr. Cooke made more of Macduff than we ever saw before. His acting of it was the effect of just conception and superior abilities, made a due impression on the audience, and was as judiciously applauded.[46]

But this must have been cold comfort for what can only have seemed to him demotion. Cooke was obviously understandably unhappy at what was going on. His own records are scathing:

Among other strange modes of entertaining the town, Mr. Kemble introduced a travelling Jew in the dress of a North American Indian, who pretended to shew the method of scalping, and to add to the amusement of the spectators, the savage Israelite devoured raw mutton, for the gratification of their appetite and his own.[47]

That he went on at all to Newcastle is perhaps a little surprising. There, where memories of the *Cato* affair must have affected business, and where in previous seasons he had played Macbeth and Falstaff with acclamation, he was now to play supporting parts to Kemble in precisely those roles. It must have been galling. Perhaps he could see no alternative engagement at the time and needed the money; perhaps he wanted to see again some of his old friends there; perhaps he thought things would get better; most likely he was going through one of those periods of drifting and indecisiveness in which he avoided the responsibility of a decision, and which usually ended in one of his alcoholic collapses.

The break came. He was announced to play Dorimant in Holcroft's new play *The School for Arrogance* on 6 April. He "disappointed" the audience, and Kemble had to read-in the part.[48] Though the season continued till the end of May, that was the end of Cooke's part in it. He may, of course, simply have packed his bags and left in search of more congenial colleagues. In June we find him briefly in Manchester, and later in the summer with a company in Buxton. Or, shorn of its Mrs. Jordan–Hodgkinson–Duncan detail, could his departure from Newcastle have been the origin of the Veteran Stager's tale we have already referred to? Dorimant could well have been an uncongenial piece of casting for him, and coming as climax to a period in which he was being replaced in many of his main roles, in a town where his reputation had been at its highest, it may well have precipitated an emotional crisis, which he resolved in the usual way. (The fact that later in the year he did end up at Buxton may be additionally suggestive.) We have no means of telling. All that can be said is that psychologically it would be much more likely at this point than in the context of Mrs. Jordan's performances in earlier seasons, and the confusions of the story might well be the same kind of muddling and telescoping of incidents which we have found in the Veteran Stager's statements about Cooke's earlier life.

Whatever the truth of it, Cooke left the company. An association which had been the best and most satisfying in terms of work and reputation in his professional life, had collapsed in ruins and some ignominy. As he made his way back over the Pennines to the west he may understandably have felt bitter and angry and disappointed – perhaps with himself as well as circumstances. Some of that bitterness must have been associated with Elizabeth and Stephen Kemble, whose actions had much to do with the disintegration of his hopes and ambitions. Was this to prejudice his relations in the future with those other Kembles – Sarah and John Philip – with whom he was later to have to work? If so, it would be hardly surprising. But in the spring of 1791 he can hardly have envisaged working in the future with either of them. He must have wondered whether and where he was going to be able to work at all.

Chapter VI

Banks and Ward – 1791-1794

So far the happiest and most successful part of Cooke's professional life had been associated with Chester; to return there again in the autumn if possible, under the new Manchester management, must have seemed eminently desirable. To Manchester then, he made his way. Connor and Sidney, the managers during his earlier stay, had gone; their successors, Banks and Ward, were in residence there until the end of April, spending their first winter in the new Theatre Royal, built on the same site to replace the old one which had been burnt down in the summer of 1789. Whether Cooke approached them by letter or went in person does not appear; in any case it was too late in the winter season for him to be taken on immediately. But when the theatre reopened on June 13 for Race Week, the first performance was of *Romeo and Juliet*, Juliet by Mrs. Powell from Dury Lane, making her first appearance in Manchester; and Romeo a favourite actor making his first reappearance in the city for three years – George Cooke. The managers had not hesitated.

They certainly made the most of his return. There were seven performances in eight days, and in them he played Romeo, Dumont, Young Marlow, Sir George Airy, Colonel Tamper, Don Felix, and Lord Townley.[1] If he had indeed left Newcastle after a prolonged alcoholic bout, he must have recovered in the intervening months, and he must have coped successfully, or the extended engagement would not have followed.

The rest of the summer, until the autumn season in Chester, he spent with lesser companies in Bolton and Buxton, and it seems to have been in Bolton that he first made the acquaintance of A Veteran Stager. Cooke arrived to join Welsh's company there, dressed in

A grey frock-coat, scarlet vest, buckskin breeches, white silk stockings, long quartered shoes, and an enormous pair of buckles according with the fashion of the day; his hair fashionably dressed and powdered.[2]

He was to play Petruchio in the afterpiece – typically he did not arrive until after the play had begun, and had made no arrangements for lodgings. The Stager was able to get him a room in the same house as himself, and thus their acquaintanceship began. They seem to have found each other congenial, and as well as working together spent some of their free time in each other's company. They lodged together, too, when the company went on to Buxton, and it is presumably to conversations during this period that we owe much of the Stager's recollections of Cooke's early life.

Clearly they drank many convivial draughts of Rhenish, or its equivalent, together. While at Bolton they spent a bibulous night with Bates, of the Manchester company, listening to Cooke repeating passages of Macbeth, and demanding to know if Black Jack (Kemble) could do them better. "I will shake the black rascal on his throne before I die" he thundered: it suggests already an awareness on Cooke's part that this was the only rivalry that mattered. Kemble had already had eight years at Drury Lane while Cooke was still travelling the provinces, so that Cooke could only come up from behind; but the sense of rivalry was there, to have its repercussions a year or two later in Dublin.

There were other lively sessions in Buxton. One at Darby Logan's tavern put him to bed for ten days afterwards. Another might have had more serious consequences had not humour kept breaking in. One Cartwright, a noted performer on the musical glasses, had arrived in Buxton, and Cooke, attending his performance and being delighted with it, especially by the Scottish airs he had played, invited the musician to a tavern supper afterwards. It was a convivial occasion, and as the glass went round suddenly they heard from the kitchen the sound of Scottish pipes, played by another itinerant.

Now, though George was not a Scotchman, he had all the prejudices of one; he sallied into the place where the piper was, and ordered him something to drink, then returned to us; the brandy and water had by this time sensibly affected him, and forgetting all the praise he had but a short time before bestowed on the performance of Cartwright, exclaimed, "Sir, I have received from that poor piper more pleasure than for all your humbug glasses:" this, poor Cartwright took with seeming good humour; Cooke proceeded to abuse, which provoked from Cartwright certainly a becoming reply, when Cooke very deliberately walked to the corner of the room where stood a certain pewter utensil, which he instantly seized and emptied the contents on Cartwright, leaving the vessel on his head, who, as soon as he could extricate himself from the encumbrance which George had honoured him with, proceeded to inflict condign punishment on the delinquent:

66

poor Cooke's eyes soon bore ample testimony of the prowess of Cartwright. We forced Cooke out of the room and with considerable entreaty got him to bed; in the morning we found him full of wrath and valour, and nothing would satisfy him but an ample apology from Cartwright, or honourable satisfaction from the explosion of a pistol; fully aware of Cooke's disposition, we felt a little dread as to the result: having obtained an interview with his opponent and delivered our message, he laughed heartily at the remembrance of the circumstance, and expressed his concern of being obliged to disfigure the face of Cooke, but at the same time positively declined any thing in the shape of an apology, but would willingly over a friendly glass, bury in oblivion all that had occurred. The more unwillingness Cartwright exhibited towards ending the quarrel in the way proposed by Cooke, the more anxious the latter seemed to proceed; however, by a little skill in our negociation, we prevailed on Cooke to make the first advances towards a reconciliation, which was effected by an if, "if you said so, then I said so; oh! oh! did you so," as Touchstone says "there is much virtue in an if." We left them together in perfect harmony and friendship.[3]

The swing from benevolence to belligerence as the alcohol takes effect is a characteristic of Cooke with which we become all too familiar; so too, is the inability, however much he tries, to avoid the kind of situation in which his weakness takes hold of him. Another of the Stager's stories exemplifies this. Before he left Buxton Cooke was invited by his colleague of his previous Manchester days, Tom Grist, to travel over to Sheffield and make a guest appearance as Iago to Grist's Othello for the latter's benefit. Since Grist was appearing there with Stephen Kemble's company, from whom Cooke had parted so recently in such dubious circumstances, Cooke could hardly expect his reception at Sheffield to be other than embarrassing, and a refusal in the circumstances would have been understandable. But Cooke sober could never deny benevolence to a friend, and since Welsh his manager was prepared to release him, and Grist to send a chaise for him, he agreed to go. When the time came Grist was ill and unable to play, and so the Stager was asked to substitute, and he and Cooke travelled the twenty or so miles to Sheffield together. So far so good. But as they got near Sheffield, Cooke

felt assured some of his old friends would be upon the watch for his arrival, and perhaps induce him to do that he should be sorry for; he said he would leave the chaise and enter by another route, to avoid temptation. We offered to accompany him, this he resisted; he left us with an assurance of his arriving in half an hour.

Prudence may have been one motive here, but one suspects that also at work was the desire to postpone any embarrassing encounter with Kemble or others until the very last moment; and to steel himself against such an encounter it would be very much in character to seek the help of a glass of brandy on the way. So, of course, the inevitable happened. Grist was surprised at Cooke's non-arrival but accepted the Stager's explanation.

This was at four o'clock: we proceeded to the inn: five o'clock, no Cooke: another hour elapsed and no tidings: messengers were dispatched in various directions to find him out; they returned without obtaining the least information. Grist from indisposition was unable to make the proper apology; the manager volunteered his services, and explained as far as he was able to do, the cause of disappointment, and requested Mr. Cunningham, many years a member of the Bath theatre, might be allowed to perform the character of Iago; the request was reluctantly complied with, and we were suffered to proceed; when about the commencement of the 5th act, in staggered Cooke, his cloaths torn and covered with filth, his face marked and bloody, his entire person exhibiting the utmost state of derangement, and in that condition was laid on a chest behind the scenes, until the play concluded, when he was conveyed into the same chaise that brought us to Sheffield, nor did he once awake until we were within a short distance from Buxton, when he inquired with much eagerness how the audience received him through the part of Iago, as he believed he was devilish tipsey. We did not at that time conceive it necessary to state all that had occurred, but in due time he was informed the particulars, nor could he by any possible means call to his recollection, how or where he had passed the time, or what he had done with his money, eight pounds being gone.[4]

Yet the paradox remains that in spite of these squalid incidents Cooke retained an enormous sense of his own dignity and was ready to rise immediately to any affront to it, imagined or real. (Or was it that he was hypersensitive about his own dignity since he himself compromised it so often?) The Stager has another anecdote of this kind. Cooke's performance of Shylock had greatly impressed a gentleman visitor to Buxton that summer, one Alderman Skinner, who invited him to dinner. Cooke contrived that the Stager should be included in the invitation.

We attended the great alderman, and on our arrival found the table prepared for three; after a short delay a gentleman appeared, not our host, but our host's valet, who apologised for the absence of the alderman from indisposition, but he was deputed to do the honours of the table; George surveyed him with a look of anger and contempt, and seizing his hat, said, "Sir, tell your master, we were invited to sup with a gentleman, and not with a gentleman's gentleman!" We then left the house.[5]

Professionally he was getting the opportunity of plenty of leading roles – Richard, Shylock, Iago, Faulkland, Joseph Surface, Moody are among those mentioned either by the Stager or in his own records at this time; but the supporting company may not have been of a very high standard, or the public support very good. His own notes show him to have been unhappy with the "mean, ill-constructed, thatched building" that was the theatre, and the performers who seemed to him appropriate to it.[6] Perhaps this was one of the reasons why he repaired so frequently to Darby Logan's, or Cummins, the landlord of the St. Ann's Hotel, or James Hall's hotel in the Crescent. He must have been relieved when, with the end of August, he could escape and rejoin the Banks and Ward company in Chester, where on Monday September 5 they opened their first season with *Tancred and Sigismunda*, and *All the World's a Stage*. And when they did, Cooke was leading the company as Tancred.[7]

II

Both management and company needed to be on their mettle. Whitlock's departure and the row with Austin and Munden was a very recent memory. Comparisons with the previous company would inevitably be drawn; there would be supporters whose loyalties to the previous players would make them positively antagonistic to the new, as would be those who felt the previous management had been ousted by sharp practice; doubtless there would also be friends and supporters of Austin who would positively welcome the new regime. But for the most part the welcome was probably a warily sceptical one. The new players would have to justify themselves by their deeds.

As a popular member of the previous company, Cooke was an asset, and Banks and Ward must have been well aware of the fact; but he was a lonely one. The only other survivor of the Whitlock-Munden days was the supporting actor Grice. Betterton had also hoped for a place, but there was no room for him.[8] The rest of the company was basically the Manchester one, and the core of it was to remain unchanged for the next three years of Cooke's stay. For that 1791–2 season they were Banks and Ward, the joint managers; Bates, Barrett, Cooke, Congdon, Davis, Errington, Francis, Griffith (prompter), King, Merchant (alias Tom Dibdin the Younger), Richardson, Tyrrell; the Mrs. Banks, Bates, Davis, Francis, Pitt, Powell, Simpson; and the Misses Webb, Errington and Valois.[9]

There was a family connection between Banks and Ward, the managers – Mrs. Banks, Mrs. Ward, and Mrs. Powell were all sisters, and for some years in Manchester they kept a joint household at 19 Falkner Street.[10] Ryley regarded Banks as an excellent manager – he was "a complete man of business and suffered nothing to interfere with this duty"[11] and as an actor the anonymous author of *The Thespian Mirror* thought much credit was due to him.[12] *The Thespian Mirror, or, Poetical strictures on the Professional characters of* [members] *of the Theatres Royal, Manchester, Liverpool, and Chester*, by C. Censor, was a 40-page pamphlet of rhymed couplets providing sketches of the chief members of the company. Its comments can be fulsome or savage so, though doubtless subjective, it is no managerial "puff". It referred to Banks' partner as "respectable Ward", a good comedian, though with the traditional comedian's unfortunate desire to play Hamlet from time to time. Barrett was the Munden of the company; Tyrrell an Irish character comedian, rather too fond of stock gestures. Davis seems to have been a jack-of-all trades: Congdon, primarily a singer, who, though "blest with a vocal harmonious treasure", as an actor was something of a liability. Francis was a dancer, and the company's Harlequin; Merchant another gentleman of many talents – something like the equivalent of the modern A.S.M., playing small parts, painting scenery, prompting, writing small pieces, and generally learning his trade, as Dibdin's *Reminiscences* make clear.[13]

Of the ladies, Mrs. Simpson did not stay long enough to reach C. Censor's pages. She had joined the company in the summer from Bath and Bristol, where for the last four seasons she had been a popular leading member of the company; small in stature, but a "pleasant, elegant actress both in tragedy and comedy" according to Tate Wilkinson, whose company she went on to join after a year in Manchester.[14] At Chester and Manchester she had roles like Beatrice, Portia, Gertrude, Imogen, Belvidera, Mrs. Sullen; and the *Chester Chronicle* found her an actress of merit.[15] Mrs. Ward was at this time still playing at Drury Lane, though she was later to be associated with the Manchester company until well past the turn of the century. Of her sisters, the best that C. Censor could say of Mrs. Powell was that she meant well, but that her intentions were inhibited by her physical attributes. She seems consciously to have exploited this by playing such eccentrics as Mrs. Malaprop and Lady MacSycophant. Mrs. Banks played low comedy – but in C. Censor's view she had made a great mistake in taking to the stage in her youth. As for Miss Valois, though she was primarily a dancer, and regularly played Columbine to Francis' Harlequin, she too was fighting a losing battle with nature, if our versifier is to be trusted –

> Could her agile, and Fairy like tread,
> Prove *Mercury's* heels compounded of lead,

Yet cannot she alter the work of the fates
Or stem the aversion her person creates,
To the temple of *Fortune* she never can *jump*,
For the noble dimensions and weight of her R–p,
Besides, other causes too obvious to mention,
Has laid an embargo upon her ascension.

The other causes may have been all to obvious to C. Censor, but he has left posterity speculating.

There were a few changes in the company during Cooke's stay. When Mrs. Simpson left some of the leading roles were taken over by Miss Cleland and Mrs. and Miss Cornelys. The latter, though young, showed considerable promise. But it was Mrs. Taylor, who joined the company in 1792, who caused C. Censor's adrenalin really to flow. Nature had not let her down, and she sent him into raptures.

With mild condescension, and dignity blended,
See Taylor advance by the graces attended,
Ye sisters of Helicon hither repair,
And gaze with delight on the elegant fair;
For trust me she highly your charms can embellish,
And give to your dainties an exquisite relish: . . .
As cupids disportively play in her eyes,
Morality sickens, and chastity dies:
Religion suppresses her impotent rigour,
And age is supris'd with a temporal vigour;
Tumultuous responses for passion provides,
And drives the hot blood in impetuous tides:
Quick fancy regales on her exquisite charms,
And constancy meets with unusual alarms,
Precautions consum'd by unquenchable fire,
And reason is lost in a flood of desire.

Whether either Mrs. Simpson or Mrs. Taylor had that kind of effect on Cooke – susceptible as he was – does not appear. But with them he was given plenty of major roles. During that first season in Chester and Manchester from September 1791 to June 1792 among other roles he played the following: Shylock, Claudio, Jaques, Posthumus, Othello, Wolsey, Prospero, Hamlet, Hotspur, Richard III and Petruchio, from the Shakespearian repertory; in tragedy Tancred, Earl Douglas, Beverley, Jaffeir and George Barnwell; and in eighteenth century comedy Young Marlow, Aimwell, Captain Absolute, Joseph Surface, Captain Plume, Sir

George Splendorville, and Dick Buskin. Enough to keep the most avid actor happy. This was where he had been at the peak of his spell with Munden and Whitlock, before the Sheffield-Newcastle debacle.

The company survived that first testing season in Chester in the autumn of 1791, but there are hints that it was not altogether an easy passage. On 23 September the *Chester Chronicle* had notes on the company comparing them sometimes unfavourably with "our old theatrical servants"; the following week it refused to publish Theatricus' comments on *Midas* and carried a note about Kemble's company now at Sheffield — "the first provincial company in this kingdom". On October 7 it sat uncomfortably on the fence, referring to Cooke as "the lofty poplar among underwood", but printing two squibs, one referring pejoratively to Bates' performance in *The Lying Valet*, and the other implying a "shirtless season" — poor support and little money at the box office.

£20 were given to public charities; old Mrs. Leister, who had been a member of the Chester company for more years than anyone cared to remember and who now lived in retirement in the city was brought back to perform, as was Austin himself, and in a shared Benefit performance of *The Clandestine Marriage*, on Friday 4 November, she played one of her former popular roles, Mrs. Heidelberg, to Austin's Lord Ogleby. Three days later on the Monday Austin took his own Benefit, playing Sir Anthony Absolute, with Cooke as Captain Absolute, Mrs. Powell as Mrs. Malaprop, Mrs. Davis as Lydia and Mrs. Simpson as Julia — a judicious mixture of the old and the new, that may have helped to ease the strains; though Austin took pains to announce that he was only engaged as a performer and had no share in the management — he did not accept any salary, and his only emolument was his benefit. We can only hope that it was a successful one.[16]

In the following season further steps were taken to heal the breach. In October 1792 Elizabeth Whitlock (but *not* her husband) was engaged for five guest appearances, and Cooke played Dumont to her Jane Shore and Evander to her Grecian Daughter, a professional duty he can hardly have enjoyed. But the *Chester Chronicle* noted that the Managers had consulted the public wish in bringing her back, and were to be congratulated, so presumably the object of the exercise was attained.[17] A year later, in November 1793, her greater sister, Sarah Siddons came for three nights to Chester, with a similar engagement the following week in Manchester. In both Cooke played Biron to her Isabella; in Chester Stukely to her Mrs. Beverley, and in Manchester Shylock to her Portia;[18] and in both she gave extra performances to provide flannels for the English soldiers fighting in France.[19]

The execution of Louis XVI and the Revolutionary Wars had raised patriotic and royalist feelings throughout the country, and the theatre reflected them. At the last performance of the 1792 season in Chester the orchestra and company sang God Save the King twice, and the *Chester Chronicle* wondered whether this theatrical fashion of the moment was really necessary; it referred to the "confounded politics" of the times.[20] And in Manchester in February 1793 the company put on the patriotic *Henry V* (for the first time ever, according to their computation) and had to repeat it at least four times within a month – and Cooke found himself playing it again for his Benefit.[21]

Playing Pistol on that occasion was Cooke's old friend Tom Grist, who had joined the company that season, and who began to share the leadership with him; but it seems to have been on an amicable basis. Cooke played Iago to his Othello while he played the Ghost to Cooke's Hamlet; they did Beverley and Stukely together, Brutus and Cassius, Falstaff and Hotspur. In that same Benefit performance Cooke spoke Collins' *Ode on the Passions*, a favourite set piece, and in between that and the farce was a song by Miss Daniels, who a few weeks before had played Ariel to his Prospero.

At this time Alicia Daniels was only fifteen; she joined the company as a singer in Manchester during a brief three-week season in September 1792, and remained with them for some years. She had been born in Amsterdam in 1777, the daughter of Solomon Daniels, who practised as a dentist, and she had only recently come to England, so that according to Dibdin she had a completely foreign accent.[22] C. Censor found her inexperienced, affected and vain, and said so firmly:

> Her vanity often mistaking the cause,
> Interprets encouragement into applause,
> The portion of favour she's thought to inherit,
> Is more the effect of her youth than her merit;
> And certainly both would be better protected,
> Was her vocal abilities more unaffected;
> Of reason altho it may seem the perversion,
> Her efforts are weaken'd by over exertion;
> Her artless appearance and infantile face,
> Forbids the idea of masculine grace:
> Her notes when essayed to be sonorous and full,
> Are tedious, unpleasant, insipid, and dull . . .

He then proceeded to give her some advice:

> . . . For why so affectedly wrinkle your face,
> When music consists not in jest or grimace,

73

If transport you would to the senses apply,
Delight not the ear by offending the eye;
As nature inclines you to love and to languish,
So never assume the appearance of anguish;
Renounce the superfluous quaver or strain,
That gives every feature the semblance of pain.[23]

Clearly she had, as yet, much to learn. She was heavily chaperoned by her mother, Elizabeth Daniels, who – if Dibdin is to be believed – suffered as much anguish as the daughter during her performances at this time.

> The old lady took so strong an interest in the nightly reception of her daughter at the theatre, that while the young lady was singing, the mother, from mere nervous affection, while standing at the side of the scenes, was in the habit of pulling all the pins out of her dress, and letting them fall on the ground: thus, if Miss Daniels happened (as was frequently the case) to be *encored* in a tolerably long song, mamma was very nearly undressed before her daughter arrived at the end of it.[24]

As yet any interest that Cooke took in her can hardly have been more than benevolent. But when she sang Rosina for her Benefit in Chester in November 1792, the main piece that evening was a performance of Macklin's *The Man of the World*, with Cooke in the chief part of Sir Pertinax MacSycophant. Two landmarks, one in his personal, the other in his professional life, were symbolically brought together.[25]

In fact, so far as can be ascertained, he had first played Sir Pertinax earlier that year in Manchester for Errington's Benefit.[26] Though it was repeated from time to time, usually on benefit nights, there is no indication yet of the great drawing power that characterisation was eventually to possess; but in his professional career it was a milestone. So, too, in a retrospective way, was that performance in Chester on 16 December 1793 when he played Jaques to Austin's Touchstone for the latter's benefit.[27] Cooke had received his first engagement from Austin nearly ten years before, and Austin had taken a large part in the building up of Cooke as a leading actor. Now an old man, he was still to be playing occasionally in Chester for another ten years or so, and during that time they may well have met on Cooke's return visits, the later ones as a visiting London star; but it does not appear from the available records that they ever played together again. Cooke's living link with his revered Garrick was broken. And in the circumstances – though this, of course, was purely fortuitous – it was not inappropriate casting.

III

During these four years Cooke remained – apart from the summers – with Banks and Ward. In 1792 he had a three-month season from June to the beginning of September at Liverpool, under Aickin, a mixed company of local players and leading players from London. Among these latter was Munden, and they must have enjoyed renewing their friendship. Cooke played the Ghost to Holman's Hamlet and Banquo to his Macbeth, but later in the season he was given the opportunity to play Prospero and Iachimo, and for his own Benefit on 15 August he played Lear – with what success, unfortunately, we do not know.[28]

The summer of 1793, after the end of May, and until Chester in October, is a blank. The summer of 1794 he spent again in Buxton, playing a selection of his usual leading roles, and keeping, from July to September, one of his journals which has survived, some portions in the original, others as abstracts printed by Dunlap.[29]

Though some of his powers were still to develop, there is no question that by this time Cooke had achieved a leading position professionally in provincial theatrical circles. How was he behaving in his private and public life?

Sadly, it must be confessed that the pattern of his later life appeared now to be set. There are those ominous announcements from time to time, in the press or on playbills, that begin to seem so familiar. In Manchester over Christmas in 1791 "Mr. COOKE's Indisposition still continuing the TRAGEDY OF KING CHARLES the FIRST, is obliged to be POSTPONED". In the following December he did not arrive in Manchester from Chester for the opening of the season, and a week later the playbills announced:

The MANAGERS having received letters acquainting them that Mr. COOKE was taken dangerously ill at Chester, the Evening previous to his intention of appearing at Manchester; and will, as soon as his health permits, attend his duty.

Four days later he did so; but just over a month later there is a Ms. note on the playbill for his performance as Harry Dornton in *The Road to Ruin* and the King in *The King and the Miller of Mansfield*:

Mr. Cooke happening to meet with a Misfortune this Evening, he could not perform; *Richardson* read his part of Harry Dornton – The Farce was exchanged for the Quaker. Mon. Jan. 21st 1793.[30]

To the uninitiated these "indispositions" might well be taken at their face value, but we have independent evidence from both Dibdin and Ryley, who were members of the company during this period, to indicate their real meaning. Dibdin says:

> Cooke was perhaps a greater favourite in Manchester than in any other town in England: his powers of acting were at this time in their zenith; his love of conviviality still superior to his powers of acting. Many an hour have I passed with him in his penitential days; when, in the moment of sickness, induced by intemperance, he has sworn amendment: he lodged next door to me; and on all differences between him and the managers, as agent and counsel for both parties, I have often experienced the sincere pleasure of reconciling quarrels where reconciliation had seemed almost hopeless.

He goes on to recount a sample of the kind of thing that could happen. On an occasion when Cooke was due to play Lord Townly he had not arrived at the theatre at eight o'clock. Apologies were made to the audience, and little Barrett was sent on to sing comic songs to keep them happy; when Cooke did eventually appear –

> rather (as sailors say) a few sheets in the wind, he was received with three deafening rounds of applause; and began his part by saying, with an accompanying hiccup, –
> Why did I marry, especially a woman?
> and then he stopped, and staggered, and laughed, – and that with an air of so much drunken independence, that John Bull could hold no longer, indignation came down in torrents, and George was quite as indignant; which was not half so extraordinary, as that the audience were rather subdued by it. "Go on, George!" "Never mind them, lad!" and "Bravo, Cooke!" were heard on all sides; so that the whole of his first scene was inaudible, and he was suffered to make a parenthesis of all but the last, which he played with every appearance of sobriety; went home out of humour, and left word at the door that he never would set foot on that stage again. "Where's Merchant?" was the manager's inquiry; and in half-an-hour I was at Cooke's bedside, for he had wisely, for once, retreated to his chamber; and in case mere argument might fail of effect, I was armed with an unpaid note of hand for forty-five pounds; but this I determined not to present even as a *derniere ressource*; I knew the feelings of my man too well: I had the good fortune to heal the breach (as far as regarded the managers) without it; and, on Cooke's merely commencing an attempt at an apology two nights afterwards, the audience reinstated him in favour as firmly as he had ever been.[31]

As Dibdin says, this "may truly serve for an *ex uno disce omnes*"; it contains so many of the familiar ingredients – the initial indiscretion, the pride and indignation, the financial embarrassment (though how wise Dibdin was not to use that lever – it would simply have provoked a further storm of injured dignity and obstinacy; he did indeed know his man) and the extreme tolerance of both managers and audiences. To have earned this, Cooke sober must have had extraordinary power over them, both professionally and privately.

And this is born out by C. Censor. His comments could be savage on occasion, but for Cooke they are almost fulsome. Cooke is the first sitter for his series of portraits –

> When virtue and talents unite on the stage,
> Precedence they claim on the poetic page

he says, and goes on to reassure anyone afraid of the ordeal of criticism, that:

> Serene and secure, on their darts you may look,
> If clad in the unconscious worth of a Cooke,
> Of Cooke whose deportment, spirit, and ease,
> While merit's regarded, must certainly please,
> For long had the muses lamented their state,
> Long sigh'd for an actor whose worth was innate,
> Who the secret possess'd of improving their charms,
> Whose judgment informs and energy warms,
> Who gives to each feature the tint it requires,
> Who even the bosom of apathy fires,
> Whose efforts are govern'd by genius and taste,
> Who dignifies speech with action that's chaste.

And he argues that Cooke's faults should be condoned: his weaknesses are the co-relative of his virtues, and his benevolence is real.

> . . . Not so honest Cooke who to prudence a stranger,
> Most wishes to serve where he sees the most danger,
> Those subtle distinctions to virtue unknown,
> That shakes the foundation of charity's throne,
> He leaves to the learn'd casuistical tribe,
> On their properties merits or ills to decide,
> While prompt to relieve or revenge the oppress'd,
> He proves the real worth that inhabits his breast . . .[32]

77

It was only when alcohol released the devil of injured dignity that trouble could be expected. Ryley's story of the "grimy buck", which also dates from this period, illustrates this; it also highlights another characteristic of the man – his dislike of pretentiousness and hypocrisy.

The incidents occurred in a public bar in Manchester, where Cooke was the life and soul of the party until he reached that alcoholic level at which perversity and irrationality began to take over. Ryley recounts how first an attempt to persuade him to go home led to a challenge to a fight; how this was then diverted to his making legitimate fun of a grubby and scruffy creature aping the manners and dress of a fop; but how finally it ended in his taunting and provoking Perrins, a noted pugilist of the time – modest and good-natured as a man, but possessing remarkable strength which Cooke in his normal senses would have treated with considerable respect.

Perrins was of a mild disposition, and knowing Cooke's character, made every allowance, and answered him only by a smile, till aggravated by language and action the most gross, he very calmly took him in his arms, as though he had been a child, set him down in the street and bolted the door. The evening was wet, and our hero, without coat or hat, un-prepared to cope with it, but intreaty for admission was vain, and his application at the window unattended to. At length grown desperate, he broke several panes, and inserting his head through the fracture, bore down all opposition by the following witticism.

"Gentlemen, I have taken some *pains* to gain admission pray let me in, for *I see through my error*."

The door was opened, dry clothes procured and about one o'clock in the morning we sent him home in a coach.[33]

Making all allowances for the "improvements" a good *raconteur* may have given the tale in the telling, it is the manner of Cooke's apology that speaks volumes as to why his friends persisted in putting up with his boorishness in his cups – something that Dunlap appears to have been quite unable to understand. He reprints the whole incident from Ryley, but it is typical that the only comment he can find to make is – "This is a good characteristic story, but I cannot see much to admire in the 'witticism which bore down all opposition'."[34]

IV

Whether Cooke was himself feeling the need of a change, or whether the patience of Banks and Ward was wearing a little thin, when an invitation to join Daly's company in Dublin came in the early summer of 1794, he accepted it. While not of the quality of Bath at this time, Dublin was one of the better provincial theatres: moreover if Cooke had any curiosity about his origins, he might there be able to find the answers to some of the questions. So when he went to Buxton again that summer he knew that, for the time at least, he had broken the links with Manchester and Chester.

From the fragmentary journal he kept he seems to have been trying to keep some sort of control over himself. He studied Octavian in *The Mountaineers* and played it for the first time.

> The piece done decently – drank some rum and water during the performance, which I found took hold of me. Afterwards went to the Angel with Williams, and played some games at drafts and took a few throws at hazard: in some situations I feel the spirit of gaming. – Came home, supped, and sat tiring my landlord with talking to him. Went to bed some time early in the morning, but precisely at *what* time I know not.
>
> The next day lounged and sauntered much indisposed all day, a weariness and lassitude attending it – I suppose from the night before – mind wandering and very confused – Hope and will endeavour not to stain paper with the account of another such day.[35]

But almost immediately, going over to Macclesfield to sit to Slater, a local drawing master, for his portrait, he was caught up in a dining party of local gentlemen.

> The glass circulated very freely – adjoined to Mr. Langford's, drank some more wine, and joined by more company – went to the Angel (an Angel in every town) and drank some more there, what I know not, and a little before dusk walked with Williams to the skirt of the town on our return to Buxton – my horse so skittish and I so tipsy, I could not mount him. Rode Williams's a little way, when alighting, and endeavouring to bestride my own again, he got away from under me, and set out for home. Williams rode on, and I returned on foot to Macclesfield, and went immediately to bed at the Angel.[36]

There is a wealth of bucolic comedy behind that sparing account, and in what condition he finally got back to the Angel is a matter for speculation; but there is also an element of tragedy, too. Cooke was really trying in Buxton. He rehearsed regularly and played two or three times a week, including one evening in which he performed a series of scenes from Shakespeare – two each of Hamlet, Macbeth, Mercutio, Falstaff and Shylock – "damned bad in Falstaff" was his own comment.[37] He read an enormous amount, and wrote long comments on his reading. Struggling with ill-health, he took long walks in the country, often on his own; but once he was invited to a party, it would have been churlish and unsociable to say no, and that he could not do. But equally, once the bottle began to circulate, he could not stop at one glass, or two; and the inevitable followed.

There is a sense almost of the inevitability of tragedy about it. Was he aware of it himself? There is a moving entry in his journal for Wednesday 13 August 1794.

> Arose about one P.M.; dined. Walked with Mr Wentworth to Fairfield. Drank some porter at the Swan. Set out from thence, and took a long walk upon the hills, and among the rocks, gathered some mushrooms, and returned to Fairfield. Called at the Bull's Head, and drank some brandy and water. Among some other persons there was a certain clergyman, who is said to be a man of literature and abilities; certain he writes A.M. after his name. He was dirty, drunk, and foolish. Some of the company, though they all professed a respect for him, seemed to use him as an object of their mirth. I could not help viewing him with pity; – not that sensation that approaches to contempt, but a real, sorrowful feeling, as I cannot to please myself otherwise express it. In viewing him, I thought of others. Drunkenness is the next leveller to death; with this difference, that the former is always attended with shame and reproach, while the latter, being the certain lot of mortality, produces sympathy, and may be attended with honour. From the general temper of the world it is too probable, with respect to the gentleman I am writing of, that a long and faithful discharge of the duties of his office will be almost forgotten, while the hours of his frailty, or to speak stronger, the periods of his vice and folly, will be clearly remembered, and distinctly related. I think and hope I shall never forget him. Went to Wentworth's lodgings. Looked into a 'Gentleman's Magazine' for 1793. Supped with him and Mrs W., the fruits of our afternoons labours making part of it. Took leave of them a little after eleven, went home, and to bed. Before I put out my candle, read some pages in the 'Monthly Review' for last month.[38]

If only he could have kept that day with him. Cooke was too intelligent not to realise that he was seeing himself in a reflecting mirror. And the most tragic irony of it all is that within a year of writing that entry he was himself to reach his deepest state of degradation so far.

Chapter VII

Dublin – the Army – Marriage – 1794-1797

Early in November 1794 Cooke embarked at Holyhead for Dublin.[1] After its social and political troubles in the seventeenth century Ireland in the eighteenth century had gone through a period of more settled conditions and increased prosperity. Dublin was now a handsome city, rebuilt in Georgian style, the best of it a kind of red-brick Bath; the leading members of its society were absentee landlords or wealthy tradesmen, many of them with time on their hands and the desire to be thought part of a cultivated society. But their resources were more limited than London and their isolation greater than Bath. Since the Act of Renunciation of 1783 Dublin was in theory a capital city; in practice, culturally it was another provincial centre. It had Trinity College, the only university in Ireland, with fine buildings, a great library, and gardens open to the public. It had the Rotunda, for concerts, and in Crow street it had the playhouse, now the Theatre Royal.

This was the fourth theatre to be built in Dublin. There had been one before the Commonwealth, which did not survive Cromwell. After the Restoration the famous Smock Alley, or Orange Street theatre had been built, with its heyday in the mid-century when Quin and Woodward, Garrick and Woffington appeared there and Thomas Sheridan was manager. Later there were the little theatre in Fishamble Street, down by the River Liffey, and the Crow Street theatre, opened by Spranger Barry in 1758. By the nineties, this had become the only public theatre.

The management was in the hands of Richard Daly, with Thomas Hitchcock as some kind of associate manager and talent scout. He it was who had engaged Cooke in the summer, and Charles Mathews, a young member of the company at this time, whose letters home to his friend John Litchfield give us a valuable insight into the company, refers to his journeys to augment the players.[2] Hitchcock seems to have been well liked in the company, though somewhat ineffectual, but regarded as Daly's tool. Daly, if Mathews is to be trusted, was a good deal disliked, was guilty of sharp practice in the way he handled the players, and equally sharp practice in the way he paid – or sometimes did not pay – their salaries. There seems to have been a curious practice known as "play-house pay" – that is payment according to the number of times a person played during the week – so that if he was engaged at three pounds, but only played three nights of the six the theatre was open, he would only receive half his salary. There were also deductions for benefits, which they were obliged to take if on "play-house pay". Only those on the basic minimum salary of a guinea a week were in theory paid in full however little they played; and they were bound to take benefits, which might have cost them more than they brought in. Leading players, of course, were paid more, and seem to have had their salaries more regularly.[3] The stock company usually opened its season about the beginning of November and played through till May or June, ending with a summer season led by guest stars from the London theatres. From July to September they would migrate to Cork and Limerick, with perhaps a few of them going elsewhere, to smaller places like Kilkenny.

The theatre itself was a little larger than the Haymarket in London and when Cooke joined it it had just been repainted.[4] Mathews wrote that:

> The wardrobe and conduct of the theatre are much better than I expected to find them. They dress their plays in general very well. *The Grecian Daughter* was dressed entirely in "shapes", all belonging to the theatre; and the dress of *Gloster* in "*Jane Shore*" was equally elegant with that worn by Harley at Covent Garden.[5]

But perhaps Mathews being young was easily impressionable; the more experienced (and perhaps jaundiced) eye of Cooke recorded that the theatre was at a low ebb:

> . . . the performers were ill paid, and the house, scenes, and dresses, very mean and bad.[6]

The company consisted of Daly ("Tall and corpulent", "good in genteel comedy"), Hargrave ("a good actor, his voice very pleasant. The only man in tragedy that is decent now"), Palmer, Smith, Stewart, Duncan, Barret, Callan, Hurst ("decent in tragedy"), Cunningham ("a very good actor in fops"), Owenson ("has played all the Irish characters for many years past"), Kennedy, Meadows, Dawson, Parker, King (the harlequin), Gaudry (singer), Cherry (from York – "a very good actor, but extremely short"), Bowles, Mathews, Davis (from Edinburgh), Holland (from Norwich), the Mrs. Hitchcock ("a tolerably good actress"), Parker (the Columbine), Kennedy ("the principal lady in comedy"), Kelly, Murray, Coates, Bateman (from Drury Lane), Callan, Cherry, Davis, and the Misses Brett ("a very good singer and very pretty actress"), Parker, Duncan, Cherry, Williams, Bowles, and Miss Campion ("a great favourite"). Richer performed periodically on the tight-rope, and a lady who called herself the Chevalier d'Eon gave fencing demonstrations.[7] It was a company stronger in comedy than in tragedy; Cooke therefore was designed for the leading classical roles.

The season began on November 10. By the 15th *Othello* was in rehearsal, and on Wednesday November 19 Cooke made his first appearance in Ireland as Othello, to the Iago of Daly and the Desdemona of Miss Campion, with Cherry as Roderigo and Miss Brett as Emilia. The *Freeman's Journal* hailed him enthusiastically, finding his Othello "in many respects the best we have seen for years. He possesses a good figure, a powerful and commanding voice, and delivered several of the passages with peculiar judgment". The writer records Cooke's success, but does not really tell us much about his performance. Mathews is much more interesting. For one thing, he makes it clear that it was not Cooke's choice for a first appearance (presumably the popularity of Daly's Iago was what mattered) – and since they were lodging together at Mrs. Byrn's in Temple Bar, presumably he had first hand information about that – nor did Mathews think it was one of his best characters. Nevertheless, he thought Cooke played it most "delightfully".

> Othello was dressed in a modern suit of scarlet and gold, which I do not think has half as handsome an appearance with a black face as a Moorish dress. His address to the senate was spoken in a different manner from what I have heard it before, being more familiar, and indeed more natural, than the customary mode of delivering it. The more impassioned parts were wonderfully fine; nor do I think the second scene with Iago was ever better played.[9]

Two days later Cooke appeared in Macbeth, with Miss Campion as Lady Macbeth, Duncan as Banquo, Hurst as the King, Palmer as Macduff, Cherry, Barret and Davis as the speaking Witches, and a great chorus of Singing Witches from the rest of the company that very much impressed the *Freeman's Journal*. But it was the Macbeth that impressed Mathews; he thought it certainly superior to his Othello, and records that he played it "to very great houses".[10]

For the next three months – to be precise from 19 November to 3 March 1795 – it is possible, by putting together the announcements from both the *Public Register* and the *Hibernian Journal*, to document almost every performance given at the Crow Street theatre, and so for the first time it is possible to make with some accuracy a statistical analysis of Cooke's work during this period. There were 88 playing days (only two possible additional days are unaccounted for); Cooke performed on 62 of these, playing a total of 26 different roles. Eight of these were Shakespearian – Richard III (seven times), Macbeth (five times), Othello (three), Shylock (three), Friar Laurence (two), and Lear, Prospero, and the Ghost in *Hamlet* (once each). In tragedy he played Addison's Cato (twice), Zanga in Young's *The Revenge* (twice) and Stukely in Moore's *The Gamester* (twice), with single performances of Pierre in Otway's *Venice Preserv'd*, Horatio, in Rowe's *The Fair Penitent*, and later Sciolto in the same play, and Clytus in Lee's *The Rival Queens*. For comedy, far and away his most popular role was Harmony in Mrs. Inchbald's *Everyone has his Fault*, which he played no less than 12 times. The nearest runner-up to that was Sir George in Frederick Reynolds' new play *The Rage*, which had its first performance at Covent Garden on 23 October 1794, and within three months (16 January 1795) was being done in Dublin. There were two performances as Col. Talbot in Pilon's *He wou'd be a Soldier*, and single performances as Sir Anthony Absolute, Sir Oliver Surface, Stockwell in Cumberland's *The West Indian* and Frankly in Hoadly's *The Suspicious Husband*. In addition (drama or melodrama) there was Haswell in Mrs. Inchbald's *Such Things Are*, Columbus in Morton's play of that name, and Eustache de St. Pierre in George Colman the Younger's *The Surrender of Calais*.

It was a demanding programme, especially in January and February, when Cooke performed practically every night each week. The newspapers give us very little information about his performances. His Friar Laurence was "judicious, correct, and nervous", and his Cato "displayed an extended comprehension, and a chastity of action rarely blended in any individual; he almost wrought us into a love of his (Cato's) mistaken philosophy".[11] But again Charles Mathews is more helpful. Writing to Litchfield in December 1794 he describes Cooke both as Richard and as Harmony.

Richard, he felt, was the masterpiece of the characters he had so far played in Dublin.

His figure and manner are much more adapted to the villain than the lover. His countenance, particularly when dressed for *Richard*, is somewhat like Kemble's, the nose and chin being very prominent features, but the face is not so long. He has a finely marked eye, and upon the whole, I think, a very fine face. His voice is extremely powerful, and he has one of the clearest rants I ever heard. The lower tones are somewhat like Holman's, but much harsher, and considerably stronger. The most striking fault in his figure are his arms, which are remarkably short and ill-proportioned to the rest of his body, and in his walk this gives him a very ungraceful appearance.

In comedy, Harmony

... I think was as fine a piece of acting as I ever saw, and I like it much better than Munden's. He played it as a plain gentleman, not at all *outre* in his dress or manner. He delivered the sentiments in a natural and easy style, and his whole delineation of it is so chaste, that it becomes a much more interesting character than it appeared to be before. After playing *Harmony* the first night, he came forward at the end of the play to make the usual announcement, and he had six successive rounds of applause.

Mathews was convinced that Cooke would be a very great favourite in Dublin, and notes that "Mr. Daly is very much pleased with him, and he draws money every time he plays".[12]

The auguries, then, were excellent. Yet, by the beginning of March, Daly and Cooke were having a major dispute, and Cooke was walking out of the company at a minute's notice. What was going on?

Cooke's own comment is succinct and factual.

On the second or third of March 1795, I quitted the theatre; I was heartily sick of it; and being appointed to act Don Felix in the Wonder, and no dress provided, I embraced the opportunity of taking my leave. From this period until March 1796 I ceased to be an actor.[13]

Dunlap regards this as an insufficient explanation and typically uses it as an opportunity for a homily on intemperance, genius degraded by weakness and brought to shame, poverty and disease; quotes a shortened version of Mathews' story of a drunken evening they both had at Mistress Byrn's, where they lodged together, and goes on to assert that "the disgrace attending the notoriety of this transaction drove him on to further intemperance, and he abandoned the stage".[14] This is much too simple.

The story of the evening at Mrs. Byrn's is an amusing and not uncharacteristic one, and there is no need to doubt that something of the kind took place. Cooke and Mathews had played together in the theatre one evening, and as they walked home together afterwards Cooke invited Mathews into his room for supper. Mathews at this time was on short commons, and the invitation was accepted with alacrity. The evening began pleasantly. After supper, whisky punch, for which Cooke was acquiring a taste, was introduced, and they set to work on several jugs. After the sixth Mrs. Byrn was allowed to go to bed in the room beneath – they were contented and well supplied for the rest of their party. Cooke lectured Mathews about the need for industry in his profession and sobriety in his private life, and then began a series of demonstrations or delineations of the various passions, asking Mathews to identify them. The effect of the whisky punch on both of them made both demonstration and interpretation hazardous; "Fear" was mistaken for "Anger", "Sympathy" for "Jealousy", until Cooke determined to express a passion Mathews could not possibly mistake. But the passion Mathews then recognised as "Revenge" had been intended by Cooke as "Love"; and when he presented it again to make the point, Mathews was injudicious enough to laugh – which inevitably called forth one of Cooke's outbursts. Eventually Mathews managed to pacify him, blaming the effects of the punch on himself; whereupon Cooke began demanding another jug in which to drink to their peace again. At which point the riotous part of the evening began. Mrs. Byrn reasonably demurred, considering the lateness of the hour and the fact that she had gone to bed. The stubborn Cooke would not take no for an answer, and began first banging on the floor, then breaking the jug, throwing down chairs, poker, tongs and shovel, and finally beginning to throw them out of the window. This attracted a watchman; when he came to inquire what was going on, Cooke attempted to give Mathews in charge, on the grounds that he had murdered the character Mathews had been playing earlier that evening in the theatre. Mathews, who had been trying to get away for some time then managed to escape upstairs to his own room followed by the candles which Cooke threw after him; he locked himself safely in, and then enjoyed himself listening to Cooke trying to explain away the "murder" to the uncomprehending watchman.[15]

It is a good story, and Mathews must have told it afterwards, at many a dinner table at which his wife must have been present, so that though she it was who eventually wrote it down thirty years later, there is no reason to suppose that she did not get down the essential truth of it. Details are palpably wrong (she makes it occur after a performance in which Cooke had played Sir Archy McSarcasm and Mathews Mordecai in Macklin's *Love à la Mode*, for instance, though in fact there is no evidence that Cooke ever played the part in Dublin that season); and the dialogue is recorded in a detail that would be impossible to recall at such a distance in time. But Mathews was the only person present, and it seems reasonable to accept the general truth of his account; so that when he makes no mention whatever of Dunlap's final episode – that after Mathews' departure "the wretched man sallied out – and was brought home next day beaten and deformed with bruises", and makes it the beginning of a sustained drunken orgy, Dunlap's version seems open to some suspicion.

Both accounts are, in fact, hearsay, with Mrs. Mathews a stage closer to the original than Dunlap. Much more direct evidence comes from Mathews' letters to Litchfield, written down at the time.

> He is one of the most intelligent men and agreeable companions I ever met with, and I think myself extremely fortunate in getting in to the same house with him,

he writes in December, and as late as 9 February 1795 –

> He is increasing rapidly in the favour of the Irish audience, and very deservedly.[16]

Moreover, there is not the slightest hint from any other sources of the kind of indiscretion affecting his public performances that began to be noticeable in Manchester; and Mathews himself described Cooke's excesses as "not habitual".[17] It seems reasonable, therefore, to conclude that, whatever may have happened afterwards, the reason for the break on March 3 was not primarily alcoholic.

In fact, another of Mathews' letters to Litchfield, written on 31 March, confirms and amplifies Cooke's own reason for the break. The situation as it emerges from Mathews' letter and the newspaper announcements is as follows; for nearly two months Daly's wife had been seriously ill, and was not expected to live. Daly was "extravagantly fond" of her, and one night (probably Thursday February 26) he was just going on stage as Sir Robert Ramble in *Everyone has his Fault*, when he was given a note telling him that she was dying. He went on but was able to speak only three or four lines and then left the stage in tears. An apology was made and someone else took the part for that evening. Mrs. Daly did not die immediately, but Daly withdrew himself from the theatre. He had already been announced to play in *The Rage* on March 2 and as Don Felix in *The Wonder*, for Mrs. Parker's benefit, on Tuesday March 3. The Monday play was changed to *Richard III* and Cooke played it; he was also asked to take over Don Felix, and agreed, provided he was given a new costume – but without it he would not play. When the night came, the costume did not, so he kept his word and refused to perform; the part had to be read. Cooke was furious and swore that he would play no more with the company, and did not. The newspaper announcements confirm this; by Thursday 5 March his name is dropped from all advance publicity, and does not appear again. Presumably also he did not appear as Stukely on the 4 for Miss Campion's benfit as previously announced.

Mathews' account confirms that Cooke has not played since that date, and goes on:

Mr. Daly, thinking himself the injured person, has never attempted to make it up. Cooke expected entreaties. Daly is too proud to make them. And both are too proud to make up the breach; though, I believe, both wish it. Daly was by no means in fault. He was shut up, and would see nobody. The tailor would make no dress without his orders. It is a misunderstanding which ten words would make up. But obstinacy and pride prevent it. So the town is deprived of an excellent actor. Daly could arrest him for 200£ breach of articles, but would not distress him for the world. Daly likes him much. Cooke likes Daly. Does not say one word against him. Says he has treated him like a gentleman. Lays the blame on poor Hitchy. Cooke is a great loss. The benefits suffer much for want of him. He knows his own consequence in the theatre, and when he is at all slighted he is the most resolute man, and most to be dreaded in his resentments.[18]

There is an unhappily familiar ring about it all. This is, *mutatis mutandis*, the Manchester Sir Peter Teazle situation of 1785 all over again. "It is a misunderstanding which ten words would make up. But obstinacy and pride prevent it".

It is, sadly, much in character; hurt pride, followed by inflexible stubbornness, however much to his own detriment. The only odd characteristic about it is that Cooke should fail to make allowances for Daly's emotional situation, for as we have seen he was normally sensitive and kind. Mrs. Mathews recorded her husband's opinion of him at this time.

In his natural mood he was most refined, bland in his manners, simple and gentlemanlike in his habits, full of kindness to everybody, and ready to do service to all who required his aid; charitable to imprudence, if it is possible so to be.[19]

On this occasion something seems to have over-ridden his natural benevolence. Perhaps it was the culmination of a series of pent-up irritations. We have noted his feelings that the company was underpaid and badly organised; living with Mathews he was aware of that young man's severe financial problems, and had offered to lend him the money to return to his family, if he were prepared to give up the stage – which in spite of his trials, Mathews was not. Cooke had also, as we have seen, been working extremely hard during the last few weeks; tiredness and worry were as likely to send him to the brandy bottle as conviviality; if at the crucial moment his alcohol content had just tipped the danger mark, the damage would be done, and Cooke would never go back on a decision, once made.

Whatever the ultimate cause, it happened. Unfortunately, Cooke tangled with an Irishman as stubborn as himself; and so, at the height of his opportunity in Dublin, with his reputation and drawing power at their peak, and when the company needed him desperately – for not only were they temporarily without Daly, but also Miss Campion's engagement had expired and she had to leave for another in Belfast – Cooke dropped out into oblivion.[20]

II

For about four months we lose track of him completely. The next positive information comes from Mathews. Writing again to Litchfield on July 5 he reports:

> I am extremely sorry to inform you that Cooke has enlisted. The regiment went to the Isle of Man about a week past. Daly would have been glad to re-engage him, but such was his pride that he would rather turn soldier from real want than come to terms. If he does not get out of that situation, he certainly will be a great loss to the stage, for he is really an excellent actor. Many of the performers saw him in his military garb when he was going off; but he seemed to wish rather to avoid speaking to them, appearing quite melancholy. He was drunk when he enlisted.[21]

A Veteran Stager's account, though he gives a patently erroneous account of the causes of the quarrel with Daly, does suggest that in the final desperate situation Daly was prepared to help, but Cooke's pride was still not prepared to let him. While Cooke was waiting

> on board a tender that lay opposite the Custom-House for the reception of recruits: the circumstance was communicated to Daly, who applied to the Mayor for a warrant to search for the person of George Frederick Cooke, which was granted, but the search proved fruitless, as by some means he contrived so to conceal himself as totally to evade their vigilance, and in a short time sailed with his regiment . . .[22]

As to the sequence of events that led to that last desperate departure, we can only conjecture, but our knowledge of Cooke's psychology enables us to do that with a fair degree of confidence. He had made his gesture, and his stubbornness would not countenance going back on it. Yet he must have known in his heart (though nothing would let him admit it openly) that he was behaving foolishly, childishly, badly. In such circumstances, as we know, alcohol enabled him to hide unpalatable truths from himself. Perhaps he deluded himself into thinking that if he waited long enough the company's need of him would overcome Daly's stubbornness, and some form of accommodation for them both would be arrived at. But the call never came.

Instead there came John Philip Kemble, engaged as the visiting star for a month of the after-season in late May and June. And Kemble's season was something of a theatrical royal progress. He had not been in Dublin for six years; his former popularity there was now enhanced by the clouds of glory he trailed from London's Drury Lane. So that when he opened with *Hamlet* on May 25,

> If twenty guineas had been offered for a ticket of a place in the boxes, it could not have been purchased. In all my life I never saw people more anxious to get into a theatre. Every avenue was crowded at an early hour; and after the theatre was filled, I may safely assert many hundreds went away . . . Kemble's reception was quite rapturous. Everyone seemed delighted – those who had seen him, at the return of their former favourite, and those who had not seen him, at his figure and appearance. The applause was continued to six or seven peals.[23]

During the month Kemble played a cycle of his major roles – Octavian, Othello, Penruddock, Coriolanus, The Duke in *Measure for Measure*, Richard III, Macbeth, Shylock – and when he left at the end of five weeks, he had made £718. Moreover he was living in style and much in Dublin society; in his memoranda the names of the Earl of Milltown, Lord Llandaff, the Earl of Meath, the Guinness family crop up periodically; he dined with them and they with him (even though the Earl of Milltown found his wine so bad that he sent him a supply of excellent port and claret the next day); and he was sufficiently sure of himself socially that when he was invited to dine with the Jephsons, and Mrs. Kemble was not included in the invitation, he

> made her call for me at Jephson's about nine o'clock, that they might recollect I had a wife.[24]

Whether Cooke's pride and circumstances would allow him to witness any of these performances we cannot say; but in the little world of Dublin he must have known, he must have heard, what was going on. And it must have galled him. Here was a man, his only real rival in his profession, in his own view, who had reached the kind of pinnacle, socially and professionally, to which Cooke aspired, but which had so far eluded him. They were more or less contemporaries (Kemble was in fact a year or so the younger) but Kemble had for some years achieved metropolitan recognition, while

Cooke still went the rounds of the provinces, a big fish only in the small ponds. And now he was not even that. He was nearly forty; was there any hope, or was it now too late? And all the time, however much he might try to run away from it, there was the consciousness of the galling fact that it was largely his own fault. He knew, in his sober hours – who better? – what his weakness was doing to him. The exhortations to others to be sober and industrious, which his contemporaries found so amusing, were seriously meant; the reflections in his diaries, like those at Buxton, or the relevant precepts that he copied out into his commonplace book[25] are evidence of his self knowledge. Now the situation could hardly be more symbolically dramatised. Kemble prosperous, courted, lionised. Himself out of work, his reputation shattered, and by now, doubtless, as drunk and consequently as obstreperous and squalid as he could afford to be. What money he had cannot have lasted long – it never did – and while in England he might have escaped from the trap on foot, from Dublin he had to cross the Irish Sea, and that too, cost money. It is not difficult to see Cooke, in an hour of honesty, disillusionment, and self-disgust, and desperation, deciding to abandon the theatre, and to take the King's shilling. At least it would get him away from Dublin, and the constant reminders of his degradation and folly. No wonder he avoided his fellows, no wonder he appeared melancholy. But if he was drunk when he enlisted, sooner or later he would have to sober up and take stock of what he had done. The future looked bleak indeed.

III

Was it purely a drifting and an escape, or was there any rational element to it? Did he, like T. E. Lawrence a century and a half later, feel the need for some form of discipline? Did the romantic in him see a great new career opening for him in the army? If so, he must have been quickly disillusioned. The non-commissioned ranks of the British Army in the seventeen nineties were no place for anyone with any spark of sensitivity. Ten years earlier the young William Cobbett had enlisted to escape the drudgery and depression of his life at the time, only to find the recruiting poster's invitation to riches and glory a chimaera and a disillusionment.

I remember well what sixpence a day was, recollecting the pangs of hunger felt by me, during the thirteen months that I was a private soldier at Chatham ... Of my sixpence, nothing like fivepence was left to purchase food for the day. Indeed, not fourpence. For there was washing, mending, soap, flour for hair-powder, shoes, stockings, shirts, stocks and gaiters, pipe-clay and several other things to come out of the miserable sixpence! Judge then of the quantity of food to sustain life in a lad of sixteen, and to enable him to exercise with a musket (weighing fourteen pounds) six or eight hours every day ... I remember two (recruits from Norfolk) that went into a decline and died during the year, though when they joined us, they were fine hearty young men. I have seen them lay in their berths, many and many a time, actually crying on account of hunger. The whole week's food was not a bit too much for one day.

And life off-duty provided no escape. The young Cobbett was determined to study, but the odds against him were almost superhuman.

I had no money to purchase candle or oil; in winter time it was rarely that I could get any evening light but that of the fire, and only my turn even of that. To buy a pen or a sheet of paper I was compelled to forgo some portion of food, though in a state of half-starvation; I had no moment of time that I could call my own; and I had to read and write amidst the talking, laughing, singing, whistling and brawling of at least half a score of the most thoughtless of men, and that, too, in the hours of their freedom from all control.[26]

Cobbett survived. But Cooke was nearly forty, not sixteen. And he lacked Cobbett's iron will and determination.

According to Dunlap, the regiment was destined for the West Indies, but illness prevented Cooke from sailing with them.[27] The Stager confirms this, and adds that he was court-martialled at Southampton for insolence to an officer, and sentenced to receive 200 lashes – a not unlikely outcome, Cooke being the kind of man he was. Whatever did happen to him during those miserable months he reappeared eventually at Southampton. Dunlap's account seems on the whole the most likely, and tallies in general with other ascertainable facts.

According to it Maxfield, a leading actor with Collins' circuit company, then in Southampton, was one day approached by a soldier, who appeared to know him, and whom he recognised as Geoge Cooke. Cooke asked his help in procuring a discharge, and Maxfield agreed to get in touch with Banks and Ward at Manchester. This must have been sometime in September–October, when we know the Collins company to have been in Southampton.[28] Banks and Ward agreed, and Maxfield heard no more until one day in Portsmouth (the company had moved there in January–February 1796) a boy came to him to ask him to visit a poor sick man at his mother's public house, who wished to see Maxfield before he died. This was Cooke. Maxfield got a doctor to him, saw him taken care of, and later decently clothed; once more got in touch with Banks and Ward, and when Cooke was eventually fit again saw him off to London by mail coach, where he was met by a friend of the Manchester managers, and seen on by coach to Manchester.

These are the basic facts. Dunlap colours them by asserting that Banks and Ward had procured his discharge and sent him money to pay his way to Manchester, but this was spent or thrown away, and he had eventually "crawled from Southampton to Portsmouth" and "sunk exhausted on his arrival at the public house."[29] This may or may not be true. The implication of the delay for Dunlap is that Cooke had spent the money sent him on a long bout of dissipation. But the process of obtaining a discharge cannot have been a speedy one in 1795, nor was the mail, or the processes of making money available. It is unlikely that Cooke would be discharged much before the early part of 1796; if he were discharged suffering from illness or the physical privations of army life, or from severe disciplining by court-martial, his travel-money might soon have legitimately been used up. And the care taken of him over the journey might have been due as much to solicitude for a recently very sick man, as to a desire to prevent his escape into a tavern.

What is significant is that Cooke either asked for, or accepted help. What this cost him in terms of personal humiliation can only be guessed at. His pride must have suffered an overwhelming defeat. The leading actor in Dublin of a year ago, who knew "his own consequence in the theatre" and who would not countenance an assumed slight, was now a suppliant whose grand gesture had been publicly shown up for the folly that it was. That he had given in at last was something; that his friends rallied to his aid was an indication, in spite of everything, of the value they put on him as man and actor. In a sense he was fortunate to be escaping the worst consequences of his folly. But however brave a face he could put on it, the jungle drums of the theatre would be beating out the message; all his colleagues would know what had happened. He was going back to Manchester a beaten dog, with his tail between his legs.

IV

It says much for Cooke's resilience that he survived the experience, both physically and psychologically, but his own comment shows how much it marked him. "From this period until March 1796 I ceased to be an actor." That, and no more. It was too searing an episode to be recalled, or even admitted to himself.

Dunlap, the Stager, and the *Monthly Mirror* all agree that he made his return to the Manchester stage as Octavian in *The Mountaineers*, but precisely when cannot be confirmed.[30] For some reason the Manchester collection of playbills contains none for 1796–7, and the *Manchester Mercury's* announcements do not cover every performance. He was, however, announced as Sir Pertinax MacSycophant on Tuesday 15 March, so that he must have reached Manchester earlier in the month.

The Manchester correspondent of the new *Monthly Mirror* welcomed him, but added to his appreciation of him as an actor public comments about his private life that must have galled Cooke, but that from now on he would have to get used to, and accept. It was another of the penalties of the Dublin affair.

> Reinforcements have arrived – Cooke, whose absence we have so long deplored, made his appearance in Octavian a few weeks ago to a crowded house, and was received in a very flattering manner. His irregularities while in Dublin, procured for him a *private* situation in the army, – he was brought over to England, and confined to his bed at Chatham Barracks some time. Nothing but his indisposition could have saved him from the West-Indies, where his regiment was ordered. He has had plenty of employment since his return, for we cannot live a night without him. His Sir Pertinax M'Sycophant, Macbeth, Mark Antony, etc, etc have received their usual tribute of applause. "A London performer", says Tate Wilkinson in his Wandering Patentee, "will scarcely credit how much sterling merit Cooke possesses", and nothing, I suppose, but his ungovernable spirit, and his attachment to the bottle, have prevented the London managers from engaging him: – They will have performers upon whom they can, at all times, depend; and this is a requisite which, unfortunately for himself, Cooke does not possess.
>
> He has a piercing, pleasant voice, a flexible countenance, and a judicious deportment, without any of that unnecessary *rant* so much in use upon the stage.

It was all perfectly true, and doubtless it had been said privately many times before. The difference was that now it was being written about openly in the public press. The reason for the "indispositions" was no longer being covered up. It cannot have made comfortable reading to see stated thus baldly, the main reason why he and Kemble were in their respective situations. It remained to be seen whether or not after that traumatic year he could gain control of himself, or whether it was already too late.

Meanwhile it is clear, from the performances we can document from the *Manchester Mercury* that the *Mirror's* correspondent was right and the managers were working him hard; doubtless this was enabling them to get back some of the money they had advanced him during the crisis. But the company he was working with was very different from the one he had left in 1794. Gone were most of his friends – Grist, Ryley, Dibdin and Bates – and little Barret had died the previous year. Gone, too, were Mrs. Taylor and Mrs. Cornelys and her daughter; though Mrs. Powell and Miss Valois were still there, as were Tyrrell and King; and, of course, the Wards and the Bankses.

But one other survivor from that previous company had grown up since he saw her last. Alicia Daniels was no longer a girl of seventeen, but a young woman of nineteen, and when, after the end of the Manchester season in June, the company departed to Shrewsbury, she seems to have caught his eye, and they began spending a lot of time together.

Cooke was always discreet about his relations with women, nor is there very much evidence from his contemporaries; their anecdotes concentrated on his drinking. Tate Wilkinson suggests that while in Newcastle he had the ladies swooning after him, and as we have seen, there were at intervals of ten years two ladies who, with or without benefit of clergy, called themselves Mrs. Cooke; but in the flexible and constantly changing society of the provincial theatre no marriage certificates were asked for, and a convenient arrangement could easily be arrived at. Cooke's appetites were normal; and perhaps after the privation of the previous year, sharpened; the pleasures and comforts of female society and companionship must have seemed very desirable after the harshness of the barracks. But Miss Daniels had been carefully brought up, and, as we have seen, carefully chaperoned in the hard world of the theatre by her mother. No casual liaison would be possible here. It had to be marriage or nothing.

What happened has to be reconstructed from the Divorce Proceedings at Doctors Commons in May 1801. It should be borne in mind that what was being sought then was not, strictly speaking, a divorce, but an annulment under an act of 1753 "for the better preventing of Clandestine Marriages" whereby when either of the parties was under the age of twenty-one and the consent of parents or guardians was not obtained, the marriage could be pronounced absolutely null and void. So it was to the interest of the petitioning parties to emphasise that the parents knew nothing about it. In fact they may not have been so ignorant, and the fact that the Cookes lived together afterwards for about eighteen months in Manchester, Dublin, and elsewhere, suggests that, at the very least, the marriage was condoned by Mr. and Mrs. Daniels, until it broke up for other reasons. With this reservation, the story that emerges from the various depositions is as follows.

Daniels, who was in business as a dentist, lived in Manchester, but while Alicia, who had been a member of the Banks-Ward company for about five years, was on tour, her mother accompanied her and lived with her "as a protection to her, she being very young".

After Shrewsbury, in the autumn of 1796, the company played its usual season in Chester, and there, unknown to Mrs. Daniels, George and Alicia agreed to marry. On the day before that fixed for Alicia's Benefit she, under the pretext of going to visit a lady in Chester, went and dressed for

95

going out. While she was doing this, to Mrs. Daniels' surprise, George Cooke called. When asked what he wanted Cooke, "to conceal the real cause of his Visit, which was to hurry the Deponent's Daughter" said that he would like a dozen tickets for Miss Daniels' benefit, "which he would put off for her". Mrs. Daniels gave him these, with pleasure, but to her surprise Cooke still lingered. At length he asked if Alicia was not going to attend her rehearsal. When told that, no, she was going visiting, Cooke recommended that she should attend rehearsal "for that unless she attended her own rehearsal she would never get anybody else to attend". This struck Mrs. Daniels as being reasonable comment, so she hurried her daughter up, and said that she had better pay her visit afterwards, which Alicia dutifully agreed to do. Cooke then proposed to accompany her to the theatre,

But the Deponent being always fearful that her Daughter's Character might suffer if seen walking with Gentlemen she prevented their going together and the said George Cooke went out first and was shortly afterwards followed by the said Alicia Daniels.[31]

Having played out their little comedy for mother's benefit, Alicia and George then went to St. Peter's, the old church at the crossroads in the centre of the town, where in the presence of Jacob Hammerton and Edmund Monk, the rector, Thomas Mawdesley, duly pronounced them man and wife. This was on December 20. About an hour later, Mrs. Daniels was told what had happened, "when to her very great surprise and concern she found that the said parties had gone in a carriage to spend the day at Parkgate". What happened to the rehearsal we are not told, but it must have been a very festive Benefit performance on the following evening.

Looked at objectively, they seem an ill-matched pair; it would take a very remarkable nineteen-year-old to cope satisfactorily with the formidable forty-one-year old Cooke. No doubt he could be an imposing fascinating figure; but she must have known – and perhaps seen – something of his previous conduct. Perhaps she saw herself, romantically, as a Good Influence, redeeming the Errant Sinner and holding him henceforth to the Paths of Virtue. Perhaps he did, too. Perhaps he felt that all he needed was the Love of a Good Woman, and all in the future would be well. One can see them walking away from St. Peter's up Northgate Street on the Parkgate road, hand in hand like two naive children, and one shudders at the thought of what might happen to them. Cooke could be the gentlest and kindest of men, as we know; but involved in a night like that at Mistress Byrn's, what would happen to Alicia?

And indeed, as early as March 1797, within four months of the marriage, the *Monthly Mirror's* correspondent was reporting from Manchester, where the company had been since the beginning of January,

> Mrs. Cooke has been indisposed for some time – report says, her husband has lately given her too many *striking* marks of his affection for her; but the honeymoon is scarcely over – when he returns to his *sober* senses, he will surely be less *rapturous.*[32]

The following month the writer apologised and contradicted the report "from very good authority". There may have been nothing in it – it may have been simply a malicious rumour; but that it could be believed is ominous. The future was not auspicious.

Cooke played his usual selection of leading roles, with success. Richard III on Monday January 16 "exhibited Cooke to great advantage – What indeed, does not?" asked the *Mirror* rhetorically. Mrs. Cooke played with him from time to time – Jessica to his Shylock, and more ironically, Constantia to his Sir Pertinax, though she was always a better singer than actress.[33] And at the end of May Mrs. Siddons came, as she had done in 1796, to provide a climax to the season, and Cooke played Hastings to her Jane Shore and Osmyn to her Zara.[34]

Little Cherry and his wife had joined the Manchester company from Dublin that season, and Cooke must have heard news of changes there. Daly had relinquished the management, and Frederick Edward Jones was taking over. Perhaps also Cherry passed the word to Dublin that Cooke was back and amenable to an invitation. There had been no doubt of Cooke's drawing power in Dublin. If he really had learnt his lesson, Jones must have felt he would be an asset. At any rate, an invitation came.

Why did he accept? Was it wise to return to the scene of his humiliation? Perhaps he saw it as an olive branch – he would have gone back to Daly if only Daly had asked him; perhaps, too, he saw it as a challenge. This time he would show Dublin what he could do. And, doubtless, he felt it would be a good thing to get Alicia away from the influence of her mother; the Irish Sea was a better barrier than the Chester turnpike. There was room for Alicia as a singer in the Dublin company; together they would conquer Hibernia, and themselves.

In the previous summer Cooke had spent some of his time with Stanton's company at Huddersfield, Lancaster and Preston. After the end of the Manchester season, the Cookes joined Stanton again, leaving him at the end of the Lancaster stint.[35] From there they went to Whitehaven, and in October took ship once more for Dublin. The crossing was stormy and the boat diverted instead to Waterford, where they remained for five days before going on by road. On the last day of October 1797, Cooke set foot, for the second time, in Dublin.

Chapter VIII

The Second Visit to Ireland – 1797-1800

Cooke found much changed in the theatre. After eighteen years on the Irish stage, much of that time in management, Daly had decided that enough was enough, and sold out to Frederick Edward Jones, who had recently been effectively running a rival company at the playhouse in Fishamble Street – technically a "private theatre", since it had no Royal patent. Jones also agreed on generous terms to take over Daly's interest in the theatres at Cork and Limerick, which he operated in the summer using his Crow Street company.[1] Jones planned to move his operations to Crow Street, and when the Cookes arrived alterations and redecorations were in progress there to mark the new era. But they were already running up against a well-known Irish characteristic, and it soon became clear that the delays were such that it would be quite impossible for the theatre to be ready for the usual mid-November opening. In the event, therefore, it was at the Fishamble Street theatre, down by the river, that on Monday 20th November 1797 the company opened its new season with *Othello*, the title role played by Middleton, Cooke as Iago, and Mrs. Yates as Desdemona.[2]

There were few survivors from the company Cooke had known in his previous Dublin season, and those who remained were largely supporting players like King, and Callan. Miss Brett, who had now become Mrs. Chapman, was another whom Cooke would remember. There were, too, Miss Cornelys and Eastmure from Manchester, and Mrs. Berry, the daughter of his old friend Tom Grist, who himself was to join the company later in the season, as was Jacob Hamerton, the Cookes' best man at their wedding in Chester. But there were many new faces.

The other leading man was Middleton (he played Othello, Beverley, Antonio, for instance); in his early thirties, but already past his best. Writing of him in 1800, after his death, Cooke recalled:

He possessed a pleasing, harmonious voice; genteel person and address; but his abilities then were much upon the decline, particularly his

98

memory. He seemed good-natured and facetious, a pleasant (perhaps for his own good too pleasant) companion.

Cooke saw much of him during that season, but at the end of it he was not re-engaged, and he seems to have died in poverty and misery in Westminster in 1800.

> But for the humanity of a poor mechanic, he would have perished in the streets. When his forlorn condition was known at the theatres, some among the actors hastened to his relief, but their humane endeavours proved in vain.[3]

A sadly familiar story in the world of the less successful provincial players.
Another of the 1797 company who was to die before Cooke left Dublin was Lamash, who, though much older, still played light comedy leads (Charles Surface, Gratiano, for instance). He had been with Garrick at Drury Lane;

> was the original Jessamy in Bon Ton, and Trip in the School for Scandal; and trifling as those parts may seem, his manner of playing them was sufficient to stamp him as an actor. In the fine gentlemen (such as fine gentlemen *were*) he stood unequalled by any actor I ever saw.

Lamash was more fortunate than Middleton in that he remained with the company, and during his final illness Jones continued to pay his salary and saw to the expenses of his burial in the churchyard of St. Mark. "Would Richard Daly have done this?" asked Cooke.[4]
A younger actor, in his early twenties, playing juvenile leads, was Montague (Lothario, Bassanio, Macduff); actually Montague Talbot, who two decades later was to become manager of the Cork theatre.[5] Eastmure had much of the low comedy (Launcelot Gobbo, Touchstone); Thomas Ludford Bellamy, primarily a singer, was also the Acting Manager for that season.
Of the ladies, Mrs. Yates had the "heavy" roles – Portia, Lady Macbeth, Desdemona; Lady Randolph, Mrs. Beverley, Calista – with lighter leads going to Mrs. Berry (Lady Teazle, Rosalind, Nerissa, Peggy in *The Country Girl*); Alicia Cooke and Mrs. Addison were the chief singers, Lassells, Laurent, Miss Cabanells and Mrs. Parker the dancing team.
Throughout December and January 1798 the company continued to perform in Fishamble Street, while the work at Crow Street went slowly on. But by the end of January it was complete, and a special committee of Jones' friends, under the Chairmanship of J. Monk and Charles Powell

Leslie, was set up to plan the gala re-opening. Elaborate instructions were issued about the taking and keeping of places, the arrangements for carriages and chairs, nothing under full price, and "No Gentleman to appear in Boots, or wear his hat on, in Lower Boxes".[6] It was to be a social occasion, without doubt; and at seven o'clock on Monday January 29, Cooke stepped forward on the refurbished Crow Street stage to speak a special address for the occasion, a large augmented orchestra under the leadership of Sgr. Bianchi struck up Handel's Occasional Overture, and the re-opening was under way.

The play was *The Merchant of Venice*, with Cooke as Shylock, Middleton as Antonio, Montague as Bassanio. Walcot played Salanio; King, Salarino; Lamash, Gratiano; Byrne, Lorenzo (with songs); Eastmure, Launcelot Gobbo; Barret, Tubal; Callan, Old Gobbo; Mrs. Yates, Portia; Mrs. Berry, Nerissa; and Miss Davidson, Jessica (again with songs). The afterpiece was Bate's *The Flitch of Bacon*, with Fullam as Major Benbow, Lee as Justice Benbow, Byrne as Captain Greville, Walker as Captain Wilson, Eastmure as Tipple, Barret as Kilderkin, King as Ned, and Mrs. Cooke as the heroine, Eliza Greville. The Scenery, Machinery and Decorations were new and splendid, and there was provision for the dispensing of Tea, Coffee, and Fruit in all parts of the house. The full resources of the company were clearly being deployed (and had to be seen to be deployed) in all directions. It must have been a hectic occasion for all concerned; and perhaps the date had been chosen with care and forethought, for there could be no performance on the Tuesday (January 30, the anniversary of King Charles' martyrdom), so they could all celebrate afterwards, and sleep off their headaches.[7]

As in 1795, because of the good newspaper coverage it is possible to document almost the complete repertory of the season for some six months. The company normally performed six nights a week and we have records for 140 playing days, so that allowing for holidays, the calendar is virtually complete. Of these 140 days, Cooke performed on 72, about three times a week on average; compared with his 1795 tally of 62 out of a possible 88, this is a more civilised proportion – either Jones and Bellamy were more considerate of their leading players, or Cooke, mindful of the strain of that previous season, had stipulated a limit to his involvement. Seventeen of his main roles were repeated more than once; the most frequent of these were Stedfast in Colman the Younger's *The Heir-at-Law* (seven) and Sir William Dorrillon in Mrs. Inchbald's *Wives as they were and Maids as they Are* (five), both of which had been introduced in London in the previous season, as had Haswell in Mrs. Inchbald's *Such things Are* (four). Penruddock in Cumberland's *The Wheel of Fortune* (five) was only a year or two older. There was a good proportion of the standard tragic roles – Iago (five), Richard III (four), Macbeth (four), Shylock (three), Stukely (three), Zanga (three), Octavian (three) – but comedy had a fair representation also – Joseph Surface (four), Moody in Garrick's *The Country Girl* (three), Sir George Touchwood in Mrs. Cowley's *The Belle's Stratagem* (three) and Harmony in Mrs. Inchbald's *Everyone has his Fault*. He played twelve other roles during the season, only one of which was in an afterpiece (Midas).[8] No objective critical comment has survived, but clearly in the context of its time it is a repertory of good quality; the new popular pieces are naturally well represented, but there is also a good proportion of the classical repertory.

To which department Cooke found himself in most sympathy there can be little doubt. Of Mrs. Inchbald's *Wives as they Were* he wrote in one of his journals:

> The fable is in most places improbably conducted. The circumstance of Sir William changing his coat with Bronzley is absurd in the highest degree, nor are we to suppose the fashion of their clothes to be anything alike. Lord Priory's character is contradictory. And Sir William, while under the disguise of Mandred, expecting his daughter to pay him particular respect, while, as a stranger, he is taking extraordinary, and I may say improper liberties with her, is extremely ridiculous.[9]

Sir William was a professional chore that he had to put up with, in order to keep his hands on the classical repertory.

The season seems to have progressed satisfactorily, and by the end of April and the early part of May, the benefits were well under way. Normally about the middle of May the main season would have ended, and after a short break the summer after-season would begin. But in the Ireland of 1798, things were not quite normal. There was discontent in the agricultural areas; there had once again been failure to achieve Catholic Emancipation, and parliamentary reform had proved a disappointment. Over in France the heady ideas of the Revolution inspired in Ireland the formation of a movement calling itself the United Irishmen, dedicated once again to driving the English out of Ireland. A French expedition to help in the cause miscarried, but a rebellion blazed out in Wexford in the south, and for a time Dublin itself seemed in danger. A state of emergency was proclaimed and a curfew put into force; there were arrests of conspirators for high treason. The theatre season came to a sudden and premature end and the after-season had to be abandoned; nor was it possible to see when, if at all, it would be possible to carry out the touring plans for Cork and Limerick. For weeks the company was without visible means of support and salaries could be paid only irregularly and perhaps on a reduced scale. Credit for some ran out before the situation clarified. Cooke himself was arrested by his butcher; though he was able to obtain bail, he felt the situation was desperate.

> "In the whole of my theatrical life" he wrote, "and I have had my share of ill fortune, I never was placed in a more painful and uncertain predicament. Suspense, of all things, is certainly the worst to be endured. A civil, but pressing creditor has just called in. Oh, the misery of being in debt! How I am to set out on my journey [to Cork], I mean with respect to settling accounts in Dublin, I know not."[10]

Nor do we know how the situation was resolved, but it must have been in some way, for by mid-September he had managed to make his journey to Cork and the company was able to re-open there.

But by then, Mrs. Cooke had made another journey. She was still with the company until the enforced closure, but after that we hear nothing more of her in Ireland. Whether she ran away, whether they agreed to separate, or whether, in the straightened circumstances of the time it seemed sensible for her to return home to mother for a holiday, from which she was persuaded not to return, we do not know. Characteristically, Cooke says not one word about it. All that we know for certain is that by the autumn of 1798, along with the Cherry family, among others, she joined Dimond's Bath-Bristol company, and it was from Bath in 1801, where she was living with her parents in Orchard Street, near the theatre, that she sued for and obtained an annulment of her marriage.[11] They had been an ill-matched couple from the start, and only something akin to desperation, one feels, could have persuaded Cooke that their relationship could be a permanent one. Yet she may well have been precisely what he needed at the time, and his rehabilitation emotionally and physically after the army disaster may have owed more to Alicia than perhaps she herself was aware of.

II

The summer visits of the Dublin company to Cork and Limerick were timed to coincide with the Assizes in both towns. Both were late this year. Cooke arrived in Cork on Friday 14 September, where the *Cork Evening Post* had advertised the opening of the season for Saturday 15th, with Cooke as Shylock, and the afterpiece of *The Wicklow Mines*. In the event, if another of Cooke's journals which he began on the 16th is to be trusted, he did not play Shylock till Monday 17th. There may have been difficulty in getting the theatre ready in time, or there may have been problems regarding the curfew which was still in force in the town. But the officers of the garrison were great supporters of the theatre, and later during their stay the players were able to inform the public, by order of Major-General Myers himself, that

> the Patroles and Centries have received orders not to interrupt any persons 'till after 12 o'clock at night, excepting only Bodies with Arms.[12]

It was Cooke's first performance in Cork, and after it he supped with a party, returning to his hotel at about a quarter to one. It proved to be a slightly disconcerting experience.

> The room I occupied at the Hotel passed through another, and an Officer, who had been shewn into the outer room, had so barricaded the door within, that there was not any forcing an entrance, and he slept so sound, that our efforts to wake him were ineffectual. While the chambermaid was preparing another room, I stood by the Kitchen fire, and the rats frisked around me like young kittens.[13]

Understandably, he did not remain long in that particular hotel, moving out to lodgings and boarding out (with Mr. and Mrs. Lee, Fullam, Rawlings and Mrs. Blanchard) at another place he refers to as "the messroom", and which seems also to have served as a kind of green-room or club.

After Shylock he played a sample of his more recent roles – Sir William Dorrillon, Stedfast, and Delaval in Holcroft's recent comedy *He's Much to Blame*.[14] Much more significant than his performances at this time is his journal. He was making another attempt at self-discipline, but equally important he was trying to understand himself.[15]

Apart from the business of the theatre, he read (*Tom Jones*, for the third time, with much approval), he took exercise by walking, he wrote letters to his friends (Montague, who had left Jones' company and gone to Liverpool; Williams, his companion of Buxton days, who was to join him in Dublin at the end of the year); he enjoyed the company at the mess, without losing control. They played cards there, to pass the time, though without gambling; but Cooke reflected what a waste of time it all was, and that though he might truly say that he had frequently wasted time in a worse manner, that was no excuse.

> When a man reconciles himself to himself by making degrees of sin, he is in the utmost danger of advancing to, instead of receding from, the utmost depth of iniquity.[16]

This section of his Journal is clear-sighted, temperate, and incidentally often a balanced and elegant piece of prose, though it be intended for no eye but his own.

After their fortnight in Cork the company had to move north to Limerick for another two weeks there, returning afterwards to Cork for the rest of October, to complete their season. Cooke records that Sunday journey on September 30 in his journal; it is a vivid picture of the kind of travelling conditions he and his companions had to take in their stride, and, if possible, enjoy; but it also illustrates Cooke's lively interest in the world around him – people, social conditions, antiquities.

About five in the morning Lee came into my room to rouse me. Soon after Rawlins called. I arose, packed my trunk, and went to Mrs. Garvey's lodgings, and about six she, with Rawlins and myself, set out in a post-chaise for Limerick. Mr. and Mrs Addison, and Mrs. King were in another, and Fullam with Mrs Blanchard and Mrs de Volney in a third. The whole company were on the road in some travelling manner. At Mallow (14 miles) we stopped to breakfast. King, with Mrs. and Miss Day, was there before us; Mr. Addison's party and mine joined them. We had passed the extensive ruins of an abbey, and at a small distance those of a castle, and while breakfast was preparing Addison and I went to view a large building, which lay upon our right as we entered the town. Although Sunday, it seemed to be a market day, as the town was very full, and there were several articles exposed to sale in the streets. Mrs. Garvey informed us, that in many small towns in Ireland, after morning service in the chapel, a market was opened for the accommodation of the country people, who were collected from the various parts adjacent. While we were at breakfast, a part of the Dorsetshire militia marched into the town. We proceeded in our journey five miles further, to the town of Buttevant, where Mr. Addison and myself, followed by several others, went to view the remains of a once magnificent abbey, which, an old woman who attended us said, was dedicated to Saint Francis. The remains of the building give an idea of its great extent and former importance. Several altars are still in good preservation, which are much resorted to by the inhabitants of the neighbourhood. We saw two or three empty coffins, which our conductress informed us were used to convey the bodies of certain devotees to the abbey, who were permitted to be attired in the habit of St Francis, and in that case were always interred without a coffin, the *blessed habit*, as the old woman styled it, being deemed a sufficient covering. Having returned to our companions, we proceeded nine miles further, to Charleville, where we were to remain for the night. The town was full of military, as indeed was every place between Cork and Limerick.

For that reason, they had great difficulty in finding lodgings for the night. Eventually two beds were found into which the females of the party were crammed; the males had to make do without.

> After a disagreeable and almost sleepless night, between 5 and 6 o'clock in the morning we proceeded to Killmallock, in the same order as we had travelled the day before. At the end of five miles we reached this town, which from the many ancient ruins, seems once to have been a place of strength and grandeur. We entered at one gateway, and proceeded along a street terminated by another. As it rained we did not alight. Three miles further we reached Bruff, at the entrance of which we met a part of the Louth militia, with their baggage, etc. Here we breakfasted in a dirty incommodious inn; indeed the whole place seemed very filthy. Twelve miles more of good road and pleasant country brought us to Limerick.[17]

In the town they found a ten o'clock curfew in operation, but again they were able to get permission to play, and a guard to protect them from interruption, so that Limerick, too, was able to see Cooke as Shylock, with Mrs. Garvey, his latest Portia. Bellamy arranged appropriate thanks to the establishment in due course, when as the climax to his benefit he disclosed a "Grand Emblematic Transparency" representing the Viceroy, Lord Cornwallis, supported by Justice and Mercy, while the company (and doubtless the audience) sang "See the Conquering Hero", "Rule Britannia", and "God Save the King".[18]

By 19 October they were back in Cork, and on Tuesday the 30 they ended their short but eventual season with a performance of *The Country Girl* and *The Hotel*, bespoken by General Myers and the officers of the Garrison. They had got away from Dublin for six or seven weeks, and presumably escaped from their financial entanglements, since they were able to travel by post-chaise; they had seen something of the campaign against the rebels; and they had enjoyed the Irish countryside in early autumn. It must have been almost as good as a holiday.

III

It is not untypical that after a few weeks of detailed diary-keeping, we are plunged immediately into a period of doubt and uncertainty. Cooke kept no more of his journal for over a year. And for six weeks or so we lose track of him. *The Public Register* announced the opening of the new Dublin season for November 5, and then postponed it to the 12th because of the non-arrival of some of the principal performers. On 12 November the *Hibernian Journal* announced *The Merchant of Venice* for Thursday 15th and on the 14th dropped it. *A Cure for the Heartache* was played instead. On the 19th it announced that *The Castle Spectre* would have to be held back on account of the absence of certain performers not yet arrived. By the beginning of December *The Castle Spectre* was in rehearsal, but Cooke's name is still not mentioned for any of the plays being announced. He was down to play Sir Christopher Curry in *Inkle and Yarico* on December 8, but seems not to have done so, for when eventually he did appear as Shylock on December 20, it was announced firmly as "his first appearance this season". What had been happening we simply have no means of guessing. It may have been nothing sinister at all. Whatever the cause of his absence, he must have returned in good form, for he played Macbeth on the 21st and again after Christmas on the 26th, and on the 28th and January 5, Richard III. It is to be hoped that he enjoyed them for he was not to play another Shakespearian role till the benefits began two months later.[19]

Lewis' *The Castle Spectre* was the reason. After vast preparations, and new scenery, machinery, dresses and decorations, it made its long-delayed entry on Monday 14 January, and it took the town by storm. Osmund was played by a gentleman of Dublin, Cooke played Reginald; Hamerton, Percy; Mrs. Williams, Angela; and Mrs. Yates, the Spectre. The full musical strength of the company was deployed on the glees and chorusses, and on the following day the *Public Register* gave it half a column, an almost unprecedented length. It approved the Gentleman, and mentioned Hamerton, Fullam, Stewart, Mrs. Williams and Mrs. Hitchock with approbation. Cooke

> rendered Reginald truly respectable and interesting; we had only to lament that the author had not alloted (*sic*) a scope equal to his judgment and powers; in what he did he was impressive and pathetic.

Mrs. Yates' appearance, though silent, was impressive; no expense seemed to have been spared to present the piece as lavishly as the original;

> the hall, armoury, prison, and subterraneous caves were well-designed and masterly executed; the transparencies, with the two views of Conway Castle, particularly that by moonlight, were equal to any ever beheld in this kingdom.

The house was crowded, the boxes remarkably fashionable, and the applause unbounded.

Reginald may have been – indeed was – well below Cooke's judgment and powers, but he was to have to play it another twenty-nine times before the season was out. Compared with the previous season, his repertory (through no fault of his own) makes depressing reading. He played about the same amount – 70 nights out of 185 known performances (134 in the main season, 51 in the summer after-season) – but thirty of them were of Reginald, nine of Baron Wildenheim in *Lover's Vows*, eight of Dr. Specific in *The Jew and the Doctor*; the remainder were all single, double, or at the most treble performances, only six of which were Shakespearian – Shylock, Macbeth, Richard (two each) and single performances of Iago, Benedick and Friar Lawrence during the benefits. For a classical actor, what a falling off was here? This was what the public wanted, but Cooke deplored it, and it depressed him. He wrote of *The Castle Spectre*:

> I hope posterity, if they read it, will not believe it could repeatedly attract crowded houses, when the most sublime production of the immortal Shakespeare, even for one night, would be played to empty benches, at least to empty boxes:– But it certainly is the best treat for empty skulls.[20]

The core of the company remained the same, but there were a few changes, some of which Cooke must have approved. Hamerton replaced Bellamy (of whom Cooke thought little) as Acting Manager, and his old friends the Williamses from his Buxton days joined the company, Mrs. Williams to take over some of the roles previously played by Mrs. Berry; Mrs. Berry seems to have become Mrs. Bellamy. Grist, too, had gone, and Miss Cornelys, Montague and Middleton. The Cresswells, like the Williamses, were new to Ireland; Mrs. Cresswell to some extent replaced Alicia Cooke. Mrs. Garvey and Mrs. Bellamy, though not new, were getting more scope in the company, while Herbert arrived in place of Middleton; later, in the after-season, Huddart and Miss Gough joined.

An interesting innovation in May 1799 was the institution of a new Irish Theatrical Fund, for the support of actors and their dependents in difficulty. The London Fund had been started more than thirty years before; the Irish Fund, when sanctioned by Act of Parliament on March 3rd 1799, was to be financed by one benefit performance a year, together with voluntary subscriptions from the nobility and gentry, and weekly contributions from all performers according to their salaries, at a rate of 6½d. in the £. This was all to be banked for five years, and then the first claims to be admitted – the lowest £30 per annum, the highest £60; for widows £18–26 per annum, plus occasional relief. It was thought to compare fairly with similar schemes elsewhere, and the opening benefit performance was given on

17 May; it was an important, though all too limited, step towards providing some kind of social security for the provincial players.[21]

Incledon was the star visitor in July – his first appearance in Dublin for three years – and he went through his usual round of popular singing roles – Macheath, Young Meadows, Lionel, Tom Tug, Wilford in *The Woodman*, Alphonso in *The Castle of Andalusia*, Don Carlos in *The Duenna*. Mrs. Inchbald's *Lover's Vows* was the other great success of the summer season, and when from late July to early September the company went on its travels to Limerick and Cork it was that play, together with *The Castle Spectre*, that were again the popular successes.

In Cork, a further ominous note was struck for the coming winter season in Dublin; another new piece was introduced for the first time in Ireland – an anonymous adaptation of Kotzebue's *The Birthday*.[22]

And when the new season opened in Dublin in mid-November, it was *The Birthday, Lover's Vows*, and *The Castle Spectre* that kept the audiences happy while a new production of the other Kotzebue success, *The Stranger*, was being mounted. When it eventually emerged on Tuesday 17th December, with Miss Gough as Mrs. Haller and Cooke as The Stranger, it became the popular play of the winter. "We draw audiences by no other" Cooke recorded in his Journal on 17 January 1800. Out of 108 performances Cooke gave that season (rather more than in the two previous years) 25 were of The Stranger, 13 of Osmund (he had changed over from Reginald in *The Castle Spectre*, which may have reduced the boredom a little) 10 of Captain Bertram, 10 of Las Casas in *Pizarro*, 8 of Baron Wildenheim, and 6 of Sir Philip Blandford when *Speed the Plough* was introduced during the after-season. He was allowed only two performances of Richard and one each of Shylock and Macbeth; but one half-penny worth of quality to an intolerable deal of fustian.[23] For a man to whom the great plays of Shakespeare were the staff of life, it is little wonder that he became frustrated and depressed, and in the usual way sought escape from time to time with some of his colleagues in Kearney's public house.

In January and February 1800 he again kept a journal; during most of that time in the theatre he was ringing the changes on Captain Bertram, Baron Wildenheim, and The Stranger; but he was unhappy about the company – "very ill-assorted and arranged" he called it, and referred on more than one occasion to their "slovenly rehearsals"; he noticed more cordiality and fellowship among Astley's equestrians when he visited them, than was to be found in a company of actors "unless it might formerly be said to have existed in small communities, which the knavery and rapacity of country managers frequently interrupted".[24] In his free time he was reading a number of travel books (Pennant's *Tour in Scotland in 1769*, Johnson's *Tour to the Hebrides*, *The Complete Irish Traveller*) on which he commented; there were critical notes on plays (those on *Wives as they Were* and *The Castle Spectre* have already been noted), and a feeling obituary of Lamash; he looked again at the long poem on *The Stage* which he had begun to write in June of the previous year, and of which had now achieved about two hundred lines; but none of these were enough to subdue that nagging instinct that here he was wasting his time. And when he was not needed in the theatre, Kearney's beckoned. After a Sunday session there on January 5 that went on well into the night, he had to stay in bed until six in the afternoon of the Monday and fortify himself with black coffee before he could tackle The Stranger that evening. A fortnight later much the same thing happened.

This day I dined at Kearney's where I remained until near daylight the next morning. The society, if I may profane the word, with whom I join at this place, is disgusting at the least. Some individuals I could wish to select, & the time we might be together would, I believe, pass tolerably; but there are others it shocks me even to think of. It may seem strange why I do not withdraw from it. Local convenience, and the foolish habit actors possess of unaccountably associating with each other, though contrary to inclination, must be my plea; however, I shall make my visits rare and shorten their duration. As the morning was far advanced when I got home, and the voice of reason drowned in a confusion of intellect, I did not go to bed, but sat until near ten o'clock, when I went to the Commercial Coffee House, looked over the papers, & breakfasted. Called in at the Theatre . . . Dined at the tavern & remained there until it was full time to go to business. Played 'the Stranger' for the ninth time; felt weak, low, and in the last act very hoarse, or rather a failure of voice, from the preceding day and night. I will not affront myself with any reflections upon the matter, as it seems, if I may so express myself, to have the appearance of *self-hypocrisy*.[25]

There is a sanctimoniousness about Dunlap's comments on this period of Cooke's life that is more than a little unpleasant; he sees it all in an over-simplified way, through the eyes of the writer of a temperance tract. He seems to have no conception of the almost intolerable psychological pressures that Cooke was trying to cope with. Of course he ought to have kept away from Kearney's – who knew better than he did? – but in the tightly-knit, closed, hot-house world of the theatre, the Kearneys of this world are an occupational hazard. The great actor lives by dreaming, and translating those dreams into a vivid emotional experience for the less well endowed. When the ability and opportunity to dream and to communicate are soured and frustrated in the playhouse, they demand an outlet in other directions. Cooke understood himself better than Dunlap.

> To use a strange expression, he wrote, I am sometimes in a kind of *mental intoxication*. Some, I believe, would call it insanity; I believe it is allied to it. I can then imagine myself in strange situations and in strange places. This humour, or whatever it is, comes uninvited, but is nevertheless easily dispelled; at least generally so. When it *cannot* be dispelled, it must, of course, become madness, at least be termed so. It is not always preceded by some fortunate or pleasing circumstance, for in that case, although it might still be said to come uninvited, it came with pleasing company. On the other hand I am sometimes as much dejected and depressed, without any sensible or apparent cause. Both, I imagine, proceed from the frame of thought, or temperament of the body, and both may be driven away most successfully, by some immediate application to pleasure or employment.[26]

The tragedy is that Cooke could rarely find a harmless way of coping with the problem.

Sometimes the horror of having to work on what he knew to be third-rate material became almost insupportable, and he behaved badly and tried to run away.[27] Yet fundamentally he was sensitive and kind; if he could be made to realise how much others were depending on him, he would respond.

> Called in the morning to the rehearsal of "Wives as they were and Maids as they are", one of the *delicate* Mrs. Inchbald's comedy's. Having no "devotion to the deed", and much unnerved, I sent word I could not attend either morning or evening. A little before one, Hammerton called: he seemed much indisposed and assured me there was not any piece he could substitute that evening. I promised to play, and he left me. From him I was informed of the death of Mr. Lamash, which happened the evening before . . . Arose, dined at home; went to the Theatre and played Sir William Doriland (*sic*). My knee pained me, I was out of spirits and also out of humour; but, towards the conclusion of the play, the natural acting of the charming little Bellamy, in Miss Doriland, roused me, and I was ashamed not to endeavour seconding her in the best manner I was able.[28]

But too often he sought escape through alcohol, which in turn blunted that sensitivity and prevented that response; it was then that trouble ensued.

There seems to have been some kind of climax in February 1800. His journal records tantalisingly:

Tuesday February the 4th. From the above date until Saturday Febry the 15th, many things happened which I could wish to forget. I certainly feel myself hurt, and justly, but in defending myself, I took the exact method of putting weapons into the hands of my Adversaries;

and for the remainder of the month his laconic entries are in red ink, as a result of some kind of undertaking – perhaps a symbolic warning to himself.

If anything was to survive of Cooke's talent, he had to get away from Dublin. Fortunately, at last, and perhaps in the nick of time, the opportunity arose.

On the 14th of this month, I received a letter from Mr Lewis of Covent Garden Theatre, acquainting me there would be an opening for me next winter, if I wished it. I answered it, and told him I did wish it. On the 24th I received another letter, desiring me to send my terms, which I did the same evening, and such terms as I think will be acceded to ... He made me an offer seven years ago, which I did not chuse to accept.

He later told Dunlap that the offer then rejected was the same that he now accepted. It was for three years at six, seven and eight pounds per week.[29]

The agreement with Harris was finally settled in June, at a time when Kemble was making another of his star visits to Dublin. This time they acted together, Cooke playing the Ghost to Kemble's Hamlet, Austin to his Count of Narbonne, the Bastard to his Lear; and doubtless he watched Kemble's Shylock and Richard and the rest, to see what he was up against. It was a fascinating situation. At last Cooke had achieved what all along he had wanted – a leading position in a London theatre; and it was Kemble, the leading actor at Drury Lane, who would be his chief competitor. Was the rivalry open, as yet, or covert? Perhaps nothing was said. But Dunlap has an anecdote told him later by a member of the Dublin company who claimed to be present when it happened, that may be apocryphal, but seems characteristic in spirit. If it did happen, it must have been on June 7, when Cooke played Austin and Kemble the Count of Narbonne.

While Mr Cooke was waiting at the side scene for his cue to go on, Kemble came up, and reproached him thus:
"Mr Cooke, you distressed me exceedingly in my last scene – I could

scarcely get on. You did not give me the cue more than once – you were
very imperfect."

"Sir, I was perfect."

"Excuse me, Sir, you were not."

"By —— I was, Sir!"

"You were not, Sir!"

"I'll tell you what, I'll not have your faults fathered upon me. And
damn me, black Jack, if I don't make you tremble in your pumps one of
these days, yet!"[30]

Kemble was followed by Incledon, soon to be Cooke's colleague at Covent Garden, who then went on tour with the company to Cork. He left at
the end of August; Cooke stayed on till the end of September. And it was in
Cork on Tuesday September 30 that he gave his last performance as a
member of Jones' company – his first and only performance in that city of
Richard III, the role he was to open with in Covent Garden a month
later.[31]

The common reaction expected in a situation of this kind would be
exhilaration. At last Cooke was standing on the threshold of a notable
career, in a position to poise himself on one of the pinnacles of his profession. Doubtless he did feel that on occasions; but it seems more likely that
his dominant emotion was one of fear – fear lest he could not live up to the
opportunity. W. S. Clark has an account from Croker, an acquaintance of
F. E. Jones, of Cooke's departure from Cork that, if it be true, would
strongly suggest this. According to it, after curtain fall on the final night
Cooke disappeared, and only after days of searching was he finally discovered dead drunk in "the Bulk", a cobbler's tenement near the
playhouse. All his money had gone, so his fellows in the company had to
gather together enough money for his passage to England, and deposit
cash and actor in the hands of a packet master, who finally saw to his em-
barkation on October 13.[32]

The ingredients of the story are so standard, of course, that it could be
merely rumour's embellishment of the kind of end-of-run party that would
be not unnatural in the circumstances. But Dunlap confirms his departure
from Cork on 13th October, a fortnight after his last recorded performance.[33] It could be psychologically congruous – the challenge, the fear of
inadequacy, the running away in the usual manner. If it were so, the omens
for success in the new venture were not happy ones.

Chapter IX

The Vintage Year. Covent Garden
1800-1801

Cooke landed at Pill, near Bristol, on Wednesday October 15. Late on the evening of Sunday October 26 he reached London; on Wednesday the 29th he attended his first rehearsal at Covent Garden; and on Friday evening 31 October, 1800, he made his first appearance there, leading the company as Richard III.[1]

Behind that bald recital of fact lies a world of strain and tension. He had to establish himself again in London, to which he had been a stranger for some years; he had to meet for the first time his new manager, Thomas Harris, and more particularly the deputy manager, W. T. ("Gentleman") Lewis, who had immediate control of the acting company; he had to become a working associate of that company itself, one or two of whom would greet him as old friends, but others with wariness, some with suspicion, and one or two, doubtless, with outright hostility; but most of all, as a new leading member of the company he had to face and to conquer the metropolitan audience, an audience many of whom prided themselves on being knowledgeable and sophisticated, familiar with the classical repertory, and connoisseurs of leading actors' varied approaches to it.

It was a formidable challenge, and from the London newspapers we are able to see how he faced it. From the bare programme announcements of the provincial papers, with their scarcity of comment or assessment, suddenly we are plunged into a metropolitan world in which each of the daily and weekly prints felt it necessary to keep up with new theatrical events, and was prepared to devote half a column, or more, to the subject; the problem henceforth becomes not one of collection of material, but selection from the mass that is available. The *Morning Post*, the *Morning Chronicle*, *The Times*, the *Sun*, the *Courier*, Bell's *Weekly Messenger*, William Cobbett's *The Porcupine*, not to mention periodicals like *The Monthly Mirror*, all have their theatrical correspondents, and all record and assess the novelties, as they appear. Much of this comment must have been subjective, of course – the greater part of theatrical journalism usually is; but out of a perusal of it in bulk, a consensus emerges. A handful of extracts must serve as representatives of the general comment of the time.

The man they saw on that October evening appeared

> to be between forty and fifty years of age. His figure is stout and of a proper height. His features are thoughtful, bold and marking, and calculated to give the expression of scorn, envy, hatred, brutal ferocity and overbearing pride with unrivalled force and effect. His voice, though the modulations of it are not always pleasing, is extremely articulate and powerful; equal, when exerted, to any pitch or variety of passion; and, in a subdued key, his very *whisper* may be distinctly heard throughout the house.[2]

The *Morning Post* described him as follows:

> In person he is tall, and his countenance is of the Roman cast, strongly marked. His utterance is very distinct, but occasionally harsh and grating to the ear; this effect was most perceivable in the declamatory scenes. When it was not necessary to raise his voice, which he sometimes did much too high, it was pleasing, and not destitute of modulation.

It found that while in some respects he upheld the reputation that had preceded him, in others there was some disappointment. His acting was unequal – in the heroic side of Richard "he displayed uncommon force and energy", he depicted successfully "the violent passions in all the full extent of their fury", and admirably "the deep plausible and subtle hypocrisy of the tyrant"; but in scenes which require "nice discrimination, varied expression, delicacy, and a knowledge of human nature" he was less successful.[3]

The *Morning Chronicle* was a little puzzled.

> We do not know what time might not accomplish, by familiarizing an audience to his manner; but his first essay was certainly not prepossessing. His voice is uncommonly harsh, and at times unmusical. It seems even in some of the notes to be cracked; but it is full of strength and articulate. He has the art, too, of sliding into a falsetto, which has pathos and impression. In several instances he used this talent with felicity, and marked the transitions with which this character is so pregnant, with good effect; but that fine art of modulation which gives harmony to declamation, and without which no candidate for so high a department of the drama can be justified in his claims, Mr. COOKE wants. The ear is incessantly offended by harsh violences, which a correct

judgment could not commit, and which are not atoned for by occasional beauties. It is possible that in characters which demand less exertion – where the voice is more level – and in which he might make more use of his lower, and less of his upper tones, he may be a valuable acquisition to the Theatre. He is certainly no common Ranter. He discriminates accurately and the volume of his voice makes his whisper audible. He does not appear to be a very young man, but he is a good figure, and his deportment is easy.[4]

The *Times* had fewer reservations. What impressed it was the originality of Cooke's conception of the character, which it found

masterly and impressive. There did not occur from the beginning to the end a single instance of imitation. He evidently acted from his own feelings, and there was not a scene in which he was not rewarded by the plaudits of the audience. Mr. COOKE is second to Mr. KEMBLE only in the happy faculty of nice discrimination. Many of his readings evinced great critical knowledge, and in the most difficult passages he felt so strongly the elements of the character, as to appear completely free from every other consideration. His features are remarkable for great powers of expression.[5]

It was this originality, based on observation of real life, that also impressed the *Sun*, in a review which, with its evocation of his master, must have pleased Cooke.

Mr. COOKE possesses the rare merit of evidently founding his acting upon an observation of real life, and a full consideration of the character he is to represent. He therefore comes forward with an original air, and with all the force of truth and nature. His acting certainly bears a strong resemblance to that of GARRICK, but it appears to resemble GARRICK, only because he draws from the same source. We do not, however, venture to place Mr. COOKE on the same form with the great Actor we have mentioned, though, in many points their mode of acting is similar. Mr. COOKE possesses a good-toned voice, and one of extensive compass. His tones are dictated by his feelings; they are neither above nor below what passion suggests. At times we thought that the biting irony in the character of Richard was conveyed in a manner that seemed to be somewhat too jocose and familiar for Tragedy. It is certain, however, that with all his sternness and cruelty, *Richard* is drawn with strong traces of humour, and therefore the text will justify Mr. COOKE, though he might perhaps give that humour with too familiar an appearance of easy levity. The subtlety was well expressed, and throughout properly sustained. Mr. COOKE's face is capable of great expression and variety, and his eye is bold and intelligent. On the whole, his performance was by no means of the common order, and though we saw passages that did not entirely harmonize with our feelings, yet we will not pretend to say that they deserve critical censure, or that we may not hereafter like, what at present may seem more distinguished by its novelty than precision.

Among other great merits in this Actor, it should be observed that he never loses sight of the character, or the situation of the other Performers who are engaged in the scene with him. Every look and every gesture co-operates towards the main effect. In his soliloquies, also he appears to be delivering the natural workings of the mind, and not to be speaking an address to the Audience, which is the common error of most modern Actors. He was received with very great applause, and that applause obviously came from those parts of the Theatre where most taste and judgment might be supposed to reside.[6]

It refused to be drawn into a comparison between Cooke and Kemble:

while they both possess distinguished merits, their style of acting is essentially different. Indeed it may be said that KEMBLE, HENDERSON, and COOKE are the only *intellectual Performers* that we have seen since the days of GARRICK, and we cannot but feel much surprize that such an able Actor as Mr. COOKE should not long ago have made his way to a London Theatre.[7]

With the benefit of a little more time for reflection, since it was not appearing on the morning after that first performance, the *Monthly Mirror* summed up most accurately the general consensus; there were peculiarities that might take a little getting used to, but the overall impact transcended them. Cooke

seems to possess an active and capacious intellect, with a profound knowledge of the *science* of ACTING. He has read and thought for himself. He appears to have borrowed neither from contemporary nor deceased excellence. He sometimes passes over what have been usually conceived to be *great points* in the character; and he exalts other passages into importance which former *Richards* have not thought significant enough for particular notice. His object seems to have been to form a grand, characteristic, and consistent *whole* – and that whole is the result of deep thinking, and well-directed study, judiciously adapted to his individual powers of action; – for Mr. Cooke not only *thinks* originally, but he looks, speaks, and walks unlike any other man we ever say. *"He is himself alone"* : – he is, therefore, in some degree a *mannerist*; but his *settled habits* are not injurious to the characters he has hitherto played, or is likely to play, in Covent-Garden: and his talents are so uncommonly brilliant, that though we cannot be altogether blind to his defects, they are forgotten almost as soon as noticed. Admiration supersedes objection; and such are the insinuating effects of his acting, that the peculiarities, which rather offend at first, grow more pleasing by degrees, and, before the close of his performance, have lost nearly all their weight in the scale of criticism.[8]

Whatever reservations individual writers might have, they all agreed that the audience had heard of his reputation in Dublin, and attended excited and expectant; and that for the bulk of them that expectation was not disappointed. "We have seldom witnessed so flattering a reception". "The audience was fashionable and numerous and there has not been for many years any first appearance so generously applauded."[9] Cooke himself knew and felt the warmth with which they responded.

> Never was a reception more flattering; nor ever did I receive more encouraging, indulgent, and warm approbation than on that night, both through the play and at the conclusion. Mr. Kemble did me the honour of making one of the audience.[10]

Not, perhaps, altogether reassuringly for Kemble. For according to another contemporary,

> The critics of the pit, shouting "Bravo!" until they were hoarse, called out to Mr. Kemble, who was placidly surveying the performance from a private box, and whom, until they had got a new idol, they had extolled above Henderson, "What do you think of that, Kemble?"[11]

What, indeed?

II

The theatre Cooke had now joined was the rebuilt and enlarged one of 1792, successor to that made famous by Rich, Beard, Colman, Henderson and Macklin. Thomas Harris had now been principal proprietor for more than a quarter of a century; though the stormy days of his battle with Colman were long over, he had just had another dispute with eight of the leading members of his company, including Munden, Pope, Fawcett and

Holman, over what they conceived to be the dictatorial powers management held over the players as a consequence of the theatrical monopoly.
The trouble had come to a head over the raising of the house charge on
benefit nights from £140 to £160, and the stoppage of salary in cases of
sickness; but behind it lay the knowledge that because of the monopoly, actors at the top of their profession had nowhere else to go, other than Drury
Lane or Covent Garden, and could therefore effectively be black-listed if
they did not submit to managerial decisions. The dissidents had taken their
case to the arbitration of the Lord Chamberlain, whose decisions had supported the management throughout. It is fair to say that in many cases
Harris used his despotic powers with benevolence, and though he might
have got rid of the "rebellious eight", as they came to be called, did not do
so (with the exception of Holman, apparently the leader of the group);
though perhaps that was as much due to an acute sense of self-interest as to
generosity – Munden and Fawcett were too valuable commercially to
lose.[12]

Nevertheless, there must have been a good deal of lingering unease and
dissatisfaction within the company as a result of these recent events, and
Lewis, as Deputy or Acting Manager, must have needed all the resources of
his whimsical personality to keep the atmosphere in the Green Room
reasonably happy. Lewis, too, had been connected with Covent Garden for
over twenty-five years, and his reputation as an actor in elegant comedy
was undimmed by increasing years, "an old man, whom nobody can discover to be old, sporting on the stage with all the vivacity of youth", as
Leigh Hunt wrote of him at about this time.[13] That he had been Acting
Manager for some eighteen years says a good deal for his conscientiousness
and ability, and he seems to have been well-liked by the company. Whether
it was a reflection of his own interests or not, the company at this time
seems to have been stronger in comedy than tragedy – Munden and John
Fawcett and Thomas Knight were superb low comedians in any context – and there were some very good character actors like Charles Murray
and John Emery, Simmons and Farley, Claremont and Betterton and Waddy. Cooke's old friend Incledon headed the singers of the company; the
doyenne of the ladies was Isabella Mattocks, youngest daughter of Lewis
Hallam, whom Cooke had known nearly twenty years before at Liverpool
and Manchester, when her husband was in management there. She, too,
was no tragedienne; pert chamber-maids were her speciality, and she was
playing them until her retirement in 1808 in her mid-sixties; as Betty Hint
in *The Man of the World* she was to play with Cooke many times in the next
few years. Mrs. Powell took the "heavy" female parts; the leading young
actresses this season were Harriet Litchfield and Maria Ann Pope, who as
Miss Campion had been Cooke's nineteen-year-old Lady Macbeth during

his first visit to Dublin six years before; Mrs. Litchfield was to be his Lady in London. There were reserves like Miss Chapman, Miss Leserve, Miss Murray, and Mrs. Henry Johnston; it was her husband, once known as the "Scotch Roscius", and Alexander Pope who were the other leading players in tragedy; and if Leigh Hunt is to be trusted they gave Cooke little to worry about in the way of competition; Pope had a good voice, but nothing else to match; Johnston was too full of self-importance, and had not lived up to his early promise.

It was a company the core of which had remained constant for some years; of known stature in comedy but with room for a firm lead in tragedy to be able to compete with Sheridan's house down the road, where the Kemble family were in reigning possession. It was precisely for this purpose that Harris and Lewis had taken their gamble with Cooke. Through the theatrical grape-vine they knew of his quality; they must also have known of the risks they were taking. Doubtless they had faith in their ability to "manage" him.

From a professional point of view they managed him superbly. From the contemporary accounts already quoted, it is clear that on the first night he had not yet fully adjusted himself to the size and accoustics of the new theatre. They gave him a second performance in the same role the following week, and then, ten days after his opening, they brought in *The Merchant of Venice* with Cooke as Shylock. By now the news was getting round and audiences were pouring in to take the measure of this new actor; they still found his voice unusual, but the power and originality of his reading was unmistakeable. The correspondent of *The Porcupine* was not one for hysterical over-valuation; all the more powerful, therefore, was his commendation. Cooke

came as near to SHAKESPEARE as any of his predecessors, if we except MACKLIN, to whose manner he bears the strongest resemblance. His acting was uncommonly striking, his knowledge of the author complete, but his declamation jars upon the ear, as he is accustomed to give a whole line on one unvaried harsh note; his good sense will not blush to take a friendly hint, which is so well meant. In every scene there was much, very much, to commend; in the great scene with Tubal, every thing. The audience seemed electrified by his excellence in it.[14]

The evocation of the memory of the great Macklin in the theatre where he had worked so long was clearly intentional; it had originally been planned to follow the play with Macklin's farce of *Love-à-la-Mode*, in which Cooke, like Macklin, would play Sir Archy MacSarcasm; because of the illness of Johnstone, who was to play Sir Callaghan O'Brallaghan, it had to be postponed on the first night, but at the second performance on November 13 the two were brought together, and Cooke gave the first of many virtuoso performances in the two contrasting roles, Shylock and Sir Archy. And as with Macklin, so with Cooke – his Shylock was to remain, along with Richard III, one of his most sought after performances.

By Monday November 17 many people had to be turned away from the third performance of Richard III; from then till Easter every Monday was to be Richard III day. On November 26 Their Majesties came to see what it was all about, and Cooke played Shylock for them; at last he could use the phrase that became so familiar later – "I that have played before Kings ..." Two days later London saw him as Iago for the first time, to the Othello of Pope and the Desdemona of Mrs Pope; both the *Morning Chronical* and *The Porcupine* gave it a close look, and approved – the latter found it even better than his Richard and Shylock.[15]

The *Morning Post* in its retrospective review also noted another characteristic of Cooke that was revealed clearly in this role (as it had been in the Trial scene of *The Merchant of Venice*) – his total involvement, even when he had no lines to speak; though it also felt again that he sometimes took this too far.

> Mr. Cooke's *Pantomime* (as it may be called), his action while others on the scene with him are speaking, is often of a higher excellence than even his most powerful passages.
>
> In the whole scene before the senate, where *Iago* has apparently nothing to do, Mr. Cooke effected a great deal; yet not without some extravagance now and then. Of this last kind was his mockery of the *Moor*, while he is pleading his cause; and afterwards, when *Desdemona* is present; which seemed to say – *I anticipate your downfall, Sir*; in too open a manner for Iago's character and designs.

Summing up a long analysis of detail, the *Post* felt in general that the character was particularly adapted to Cooke's qualities as an actor, and though it was unequal, his performance contained "higher and longer flights of genius than any other part".[16]

On 5 December Macbeth brought the first more generally dissatisfied press. There were good moments and scenes that were commented on, but somehow the performance did not cohere. The *Post* wondered if he was trying too hard to be different.[17] *The Porcupine* was the most outspoken on the following morning

> Mr. Cooke, who performed the part of the regicide, was not so successful, either in conception or execution, as in the former parts of

1. George Frederick Cooke, the Actor. As Richard III (artist and date unknown). (*National Theatre.*)

I wish the bastards dead

Act 4 Scene 2 Richard 3rd

MR COOKE

in the character of Richard the 3rd

Engraved by A Cardon from a Miniature by J T Barber

Published June 4 1805 by John P. Thompson, G^t Newport Street. Printseller to His Majesty & the Duke of York &c &c

2. Cooke as Richard III, from a miniature by J. T. Barber, 1805. (*Theatre Museum*.)

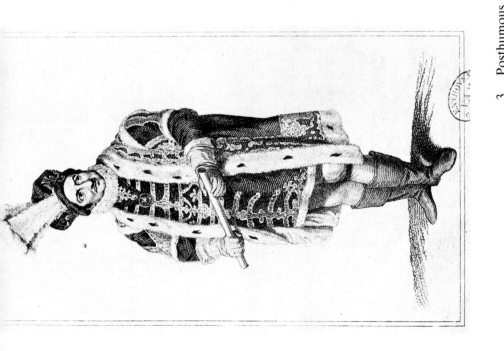

3. Posthumous portraits of Cooke as Richard III.

Left — England (De Wilde, 1813) (*Theatre Museum*).

Right — USA (Leslie, 1813) (*Collection of the author*).

THEATRE ROYAL; COVENT GARDEN,

This prefent FRIDAY, October 31, 1800,

Will be prefented the TRAGEDY of

King Richard the Third.

With New and Appropriate Dreffes, Scenery, and Decorations.

King Richard by Mr COOKE,
(From the Theatre Royal, Dublin, being his Firft appearance on this ftage)
King Henry by Mr MURRAY,
Buckingham by Mr WHITFIELD,
Stanley by Mr DAVENPORT
Treffel by Mr. BETTERTON,
Prince Edward, Mrs Findlay, Duke of York, Mafter Standen
Lieutenant by Mr WADDY,
Catefby, Mr Claremont, Ratcliffe, Mr Klanert,
Lord Mayor, Mr Thompfon, Oxford, Mr Atkins,
Terrel, Mr Abbot, Norfolk, Mr Seaton,
And Richmond by Mr POPE,
Lady Anne by Mrs LITCHFIELD,
Duchefs of York by Mifs Leferve,
And The Queen by Mifs CHAPMAN.

To which will be added (in 2 acts) the Comic Opera of

The MAID of the MILL.

Sir Harry Sycamore by Mr. MUNDEN,
Lord Aimworth by Mr. HILL,
Ralph by Mr. KNIGHT,
Farmer Giles by Mr TOWNSEND,
Fairfield, Mr. DAVENPORT, Mervin, Mr. CLAREMONT,
Fanny by Mifs SIMS,
Lady Sycamore by Mrs. DAVENPORT,
Theodofia, Mrs. FOLLETT,
And Patty by Mrs. ATKINS.

No Money to be Returned.
DOORS to be Opened at HALF paft FIVE, and begin at HALF paft SIX o'Clock.
Places for the Boxes to be taken of Mr. BRANDON at the Box-Office in Hart-ftreet.

Tomorrow, will be produced a New Comedy called
LIFE.
With New Scenes, Dreffes & Decorations. The Principal Characters by Meff. Lewis,
Munden, Fawcett, Murray, Emery, Farley, Mifs Chapman, Mrs St. Ledger, Mifs Cox and
Mifs Murray. The Prologue to be Spoken by Mr. Whitfield—the Epilogue by Mr. Munden.
To which will be added the Comic Opera of ROSINA.
Two New Mufical After-Pieces are in Preparation.

Printed by E. MACLEISH, 2, Bow-ftreet, Coven.-Garden.

4.   Cooke's debut at Covent Garden as Richard III. (*British Library.*)

5. Cooke as Sir Pertinax MacSycophant (De Wilde, drawn 1806, engraved 1808). (*Collection of the author*.) This portrait also exists identified as "Sir Archy MacSarcasm".

MERCHANT OF VENICE.

Act IV.   Scene I.

Mᴿ COOKE as SHYLOCK.

Baſs. Why dost thou whet thy knife so earnestly?

Shy. To cut the forfeiture from that bankrupt there

London Pub. as the Act directs, by I.Roach,Russell Court, Drury Lane, February 9ᵗʰ 1804.

6a. Cooke as Iago (J. Corbett, engraved W. Ridley, 1800). (Collection of the author.)

6b. (Right). Shylock (J. Archer, 1804). (Theatre Museum.)

7a. Falstaff in *King Henry IV i* (engraved J. Alais, 1802). (*Theatre Museum.*)

7b. Macbeth (De Loutherbourg, engraved Parker, 1803). (*Theatre Museum.*)

8. George Frederick Cooke, the man. Left — England (Ridley, 1807). Right — USA (H. R. Cook, from a miniature by Dunlap, c. 1813). (*Collection of the Author.*)

Richard, Iago and *Shylock*. Some of his new readings were more than injudicious, they were absurd; rendering many passages entirely unintelligible; his action is never very graceful, and his heavings of agitation are not only too frequent but out of nature. With a mind like his, there must be many beauties in the performance of *Macbeth*; but unless he re-studies the part he will lose as much in it as he has gained by his preceding ones.[18]

Whether he re-studied it at all as *Porcupine* suggested we do not know. Certainly not immediately. There was not time, even if he had wished to do so, for another part was to be brought in to the repertory before Christmas – Kitely in Ben Jonson's *Every Man in his Humour*. This was perhaps more of a team effort than the earlier plays, and Fawcett's Bobadil, Munden's Brainworm, Knight's Master Stephen and Miss Chapman's Mrs. Kitely were all well spoken of. It was Cooke's first London appearance in a comedy, and the *Times* thought that with the exception of Iago, it was the best thing he had done. The *Chronicle* was more acidulated in its comment; perhaps the *Post* strikes the balance between the two extremes. It was the inequality of his Macbeth that it had criticised; Kitely

was perfectly free from this objection, the whole being so uniform in ability as to render it almost impossible to quote any one scene in preference to another ... In *Richard, Shylock*, &c, there is a variety of passions, in some of which an actor may be calculated to shine more than others; but *Kitely* is not of this description. He is a husband within whose breast jealousy has lodged itself. It is there a fixed, firm, and steady passion. Mr. COOKE therefore, treading upon even ground, was even in his performance, and the audience was equally uniform in their approbation.[19]

With two exceptions, Cooke's repertory for the season was now complete. On 27 January 1801 he was to play The Stranger for his benefit, and after Easter he was to introduce Sir Giles Overreach for Lewis' benefit. In all, during the season he gave 67 performances, of which 23 were of Richard, 10 each of Shylock, Iago and Kitely, 7 of Macbeth, 5 of Sir Giles, and 2 of The Stranger. He coupled Sir Archy with Shylock on five occasions. With the exception of The Stranger and the addition of Stukely, Sir Pertinax M'Sycophant, and Falstaff, these were to remain his great roles; and it was on them that his reputation was based.

Cooke's Benefit in January was a remarkable occasion. It produced "One of the most crowded houses ever witnessed"[20] in the Theatre, and takings of £960 for Cooke himself, "besides which Mr. Harris presented him with the customary charges of the house" wrote the prompter on the theatre's file copy of the playbill – another £160. Clearly Harris could afford it – later that year we find him buying additional land adjoining his house at Uxbridge out of the season's profits; he had the delicacy to name part of it Cooke's Field.[21] Artistically the choice of play was a mistake. The Stranger was a role which fitted Kemble – defects as well as qualities – like a glove. Doubtless Cooke's choice was a challenge, and as such it may have helped to swell the audience; but it was a challenge Cooke could not make good. He had been ill during the week before, and had not fully shaken off the effects. Bell's Weekly Messenger wrote:

> Notwithstanding the disadvantages resulting to his voice, and powers from his late illness, which he did not appear to have entirely surmounted, he succeeded in giving a very impressive delineation of the misanthrope. Many of his passages boasted beauties which could only be produced by genius and judgment; but had he thrown into his representation more of that deep-rooted melancholy and sullen temper which Kotzebue certainly has depicted, the general colouring would have been more highly finished.

It was in just that deep-rooted melancholy that Kemble excelled, and Cooke knew it. The play was given one more performance and then quietly dropped from the repertory, while a week later at the other house Kemble played it in his best style. Cooke never played it again in London; in this role, at least, he gave Kemble best.[22]

Even so, it had been a season of not inconsiderable triumph. Financially Harris' gamble had paid off handsomely. "No season was ever so profitable. COOKE has certainly drawn a mint of money" reported the Morning Post on 19 June, the morning after the theatre closed for the summer. Artistically he had made a remarkable impact. That his limitations were chronicled too is no denial of that; so were Kemble's; and it was accepted without question that Kemble was Cooke's only rival – to that extent, at least, he had achieved what he wanted to do.

Moreover, he seems to have kept himself well under control during what must have been a gruelling and nerve-racking season. One performance of Richard had to be postponed on March 2 "on account of Mr Cooke's accidental lameness" is written on the playbill, but there is no hint of anything unprofessional about this; other players' illnesses are noted in the same way, and if he had been drunk the writer would have said so – he certainly did in later seasons.

The news of the success of his first night in October had reached Chester quickly, and from there, on November 3, one who by now knew him very well, wrote him a letter.

Dear Sir,

Although I never doubted your success, let me congratulate you on your first appearance at Covent Garden Theatre. As I told you in a former letter, you have it in your power to please. You have done so. The public are your friends; – look to them *alone*; for while you merit their patronage you will ever experience it. Be not, therefore, persuaded into company; that is, tavern company: for there are those, who will, under the mask of friendship, endeavour to obtain your society in such places, or at their houses, knowing the easiness of your temper, (excuse my bluntness, it can only be for your future comfort) to betray you into excess, to undo you with the town. I cannot point out those I allude to – your own judgment must be your tutor – only be aware of what I say.

When you are not too much occupied, I shall receive a line from you with pleasure, corroborating your favour with the most disinterested audience in the kingdom. Success continue to attend you, is the sincere wish of,

Dear Sir,
Yours most truly,
T. A. WARD   (23)

Cooke kept that letter till the day he died.

III

As the news of Cooke's London success spread, invitations for visiting engagements during the summer began to come in from circuit managers all over the country, both from areas where he was known and had worked in his provincial days, and elsewhere. He gave his last performance of the London season as Richard III on Monday 15 June; early on the following morning he set out on the first of the summer tours in which for the next decade he was to exploit his reputation and satisfy provincial curiosity.

It was a punishing schedule on which he embarked. In the space of thirteen weeks he gave at least sixty performances with five different companies, and in six different theatres, three of which he had never played in before. In between he travelled up through the midlands to Scotland, from east to west coasts, back down the west to Manchester and Liverpool, and then north east again across the Pennines to Newcastle-on-Tyne, with only travelling time between engagements. Nor was he just ringing the changes

on a handful of parts; we can document more than fifty of his performances from newspaper or playbill sources, and in them he played no less
than 21 different roles. Richard had pride of place with eleven performances; Sir Archy next with seven, followed by Shylock and Macbeth with
five each. Sir Giles Overreach had four, Hamlet, Iago and Jaques and The
Stranger three each, with Othello, Stukely and Petruchio receiving two.
There were then nine single performances, most of them major roles like
Octavian, Kitely and Sir Pertinax. Throughout he performed almost six
times a week, on what must have been minimal rehearsal. For a young man
in the prime of his physical and mental condition it would have been a
great strain; for a man in middle age, who had never treated his body with
any great respect, and who was just ending an exhausting London season,
it was, looked at objectively, an impossible assignment. But then Cooke
doubtless never looked at it objectively. When sober, he could never say
no; he was wanted, courted, perhaps cajoled; he would go. Doubtless the
enthusiastic applause of his audiences buoyed him up; and the knowledge
that he was now going as a great visiting star to places where previously he
had been simply a working member of the local company, must have been
an excitement and a stimulus. Nevertheless, to any dispassionate observer
contemplating the undertaking, it must have been an open question as to
whether he could possibly reach the end without a breakdown of some
kind.

He left London on the morning of 16 June; on the evening of the 17th
he was giving his first performance as Richard at the Theatre Royal, Birmingham, with M'Cready's summer company there. Sarah Siddons had
just left so Cooke's stature, by association, was high. But Sarah was wiser in
the ways of touring, and had more experience of its strains than Cooke; she
had limited herself to six performances in a fortnight; he was to give nine
in ten working days.

It was his first visit to Birmingham; the theatre, rebuilt after a fire nine
years before, was new to him. The company was a mixed one. There were a
handful of faces from London, some of whom, like Mrs. St. Ledger from
Covent Garden, must have been familiar to him; Miss Decamp from Drury
Lane was there, playing especially in the farces, and Mrs. Second in musical
pieces, though they all supported him in some of his performances, Mrs.
St. Ledger as Emilia, Lady Anne, and Lady Macbeth; Mrs. Second as
Jessica, Miss De Camp as Portia. The other leading lady was young Miss
Marriott, making her first appearance in Birmingham and playing Mrs.
Haller and The Queen to his Richard. Of the nine performances Cooke
gave, three were of Richard, one each of the Stranger, Shylock, Othello
(not Iago – Harley played that), Sir Giles and Macbeth; and there was one
anthology evening which they called *The School of Shakespeare* in which he

appeared in excerpts from Hamlet, Shylock, Wolsey, and the Falstaff of *The Merry Wives of Windsor*. *Aris' Birmingham Gazette* of 22 June welcomed him in fulsome fashion and commended especially his Richard and Shylock; on Monday 29 June he played Richard again for his own benefit and took £130, a not unreasonable sum. That was his last performance for M'Cready; a week later he had reached Edinburgh and was opening there in Shylock.[24]

The Theatre Royal, Edinburgh, in Shakespeare Square at the east end of what is now Princes Street, was just under thirty years old, and had recently had a change of management. For the last six years Stephen Kemble had worked it in conjunction with his other theatres in Newcastle, Sunderland, Durham and Berwick. Now he had given up the Edinburgh end of his circuit, and Francis Aickin and John Jackson had taken over (Jackson for the second time), running a winter season, and a special summer one commencing in the local Race Week. For the local correspondents who sent long reports to the *Monthly Mirror* the standard of this summer company seems not to have been very high.[25] Woods, a "correct good actor" according to Cooke's recollection,[26] and Rock, a low comedian, were the principal survivors from the winter company, with Miss Biggs from Drury Lane leading the ladies, and Talbot as the other principal visitor. During the two and a half weeks of his stay, Cooke played Richard three times, Shylock, Sir Archy and Sir Giles twice; and Penruddock, the Stranger, Iago and Othello. (Over the last two there is a conflict of evidence – Cooke's own recollection was that he and Woods exchanged roles; but according to the announcements, Woods played Iago to Cooke's Othello on July 13, but on July 9 when Cooke played Iago, Talbot was the Othello.) Miss Biggs supported him gallantly as Portia, Desdemona, Emily Tempest and Mrs. Haller; for her Benefit he played Jaques to her Rosalind, and Petruchio to her Catherine, while, for Talbot's Benefit on the last night of the concentrated season, they played Hamlet and Ophelia, with Rock as Polonius, Talbot as Horatio, and Mrs. Woods as the Queen.

For his own benefit on July 20 he paid his audience the delicate compliment of playing Macbeth, coupled with Sir Archy MacSarcasm, and they responded, according to the *Mirror's* second correspondent, with receipts of about £130. The first correspondent gives us an interesting sample of Scottish audience reactions to Cooke on their first taste of his quality.

His Iago, Sir Giles Overreach, and Sir Archy MacSarcasm, have been particularly admired. We, of course, regard ourselves as better judges of the latter, than any other audience; and it excited so much admiration, that we regretted not a little that we were not indulged likewise with his performance of Sir Pertinax MacSycophant.

For this particular writer, however, Cooke's finest achievement on this occasion was his Othello.

> His sarcastic manner is admirably suited to Othello's ironical treatment of Desdemona in presence of the ambassadors from Venice, and he is equally successful in all the scenes where the workings of his mind are displayed in his conduct to Desdemona. The great scene with Iago called forth all his powers, and he only failed in the violent bursts of despair, which, on account of the harshness of his voice, did not produce all the effect that could be wished.

The other correspondent wrote more fully about his Richard, pro and con, and praised highly his Sir Giles Overreach – "it was well conceived, and the great scene was finely represented". He did not see Cooke's Iago or Othello; but

> I cannot, however, avoid mentioning, in terms of the highest praise, his Sir Archy MacSarcasm, which he performed for his benefit. In dialect, and in manner, it was the most forcible and characteristic representation of Macklin's Scotch baronet I ever saw, or could conceive.[27]

Clearly, in the area where he could expect to find his audience most difficult to satisfy, Cooke had disarmed criticism.

The company gave its last performance in Edinburgh on Wednesday 22 July; on the Friday it opened in Glasgow in the Dunlop Street theatre, again with Cooke's Shylock. The company and repertory was basically the same as in Edinburgh, which may have eased the load a little, but there are indications that by now the strain was beginning to tell. In Edinburgh Cooke had performed on 14 evenings in 17 days, including 12 different roles; in Glasgow he was to give 11 performances in 13 days.[28] At some time during the Glasgow fortnight he seems to have had the first symptoms of a chest haemorrhage, which was to have disastrous repercussions later.[29] He managed, however, to finish his undertaking there, on 5 August, and almost immediately must have been on the road to join Aickin's main company at Liverpool, for he opened there in Richard III on Monday August 10 to a bumper house of no less than £240. On the following days he played Shylock and Macbeth, at which point it looks as though his overstrained body and nerves rebelled again. He was announced to play the Stranger on the Thursday, and a playbill for that performance survives in the British Museum collection; but Johnson, in Volume III of his manuscript collection of *Liverpool Theatrical Material 1772–1945*, records the performance on that night as Bannister in *A Bold*

Stroke for a Wife and *The Prize*.[30] Unfortunately Johnson gives no indication of his sources, and it has not proved possible to confirm it, but it seems likely that Bannister, who was also a guest with the company, substituted for him that night; and it may well be that Cooke was also unable to play the following night for old Mattocks' Benefit, when he was down for Leon in *Rule a Wife and Have a Wife*, since the playbill which announces him as Kitely for the following Monday, for Bannister's benefit, adds –

> The public are respectfully informed that Mr. COOKE, though not entirely recovered from his Indisposition, to prevent any disappointment will have the honour of appearing before them this Evening.[31]

Whether the haemorrhage was troubling him again or whether at this point he rebelled against the strain he had imposed on himself and walked off the treadmill, we have no means of telling; it may well, and understandably, have been a combination of both.

So far as we know he completed the engagement in the second week – Earl Osmund in *The Castle Spectre* for Murray's Benefit; Jaques, and Richard III on Friday the 21st for his own Benefit; before leaving for Manchester where he was due to open on the following Monday. That his engagement in Liverpool caused great local excitement there can be little doubt. On the day of his first appearance the local newspaper was informing its readers that a model of him as Richard III, carried out in rice-paste by G. Bullock, was to be put in the Lord Street Museum alongside those of Kemble and Mrs. Siddons; that must have given Cooke a warm glow of satisfaction.[32] But in retrospect he cannot have looked back on this part of the tour with any great pleasure; whether he took the road for Manchester with a sigh of relief, or with the ominous shadow of more hard work ahead of him, at least he was going back to friends, a theatre with which he was familiar, and a welcoming audience.

There had, of course, been changes in Manchester since he was last there in 1797. Ward was still the senior manager, and Mrs. Ward was holding on doggedly to her ration of leading parts; but Banks had retired, and been succeeded by Cooke's old acquaintance of Dublin days, Thomas Bellamy. With him was little Mrs. Bellamy, Grist's daughter, and Cooke's old friend of long standing, her father, Thomas Grist, aging now, but still holding his own in the company. There were two other visitors, Mr. and Mrs. Pope, Cooke's colleagues for the last season at Covent Garden; the rest of the company consisted partly of members of the winter company, partly, it would seem, of auxiliaries who happened to be available. The Manchester correspondent of the *Monthly Mirror* reported:

At length, his "brows crown'd with victorious wreaths," came our long
expected favourite Cooke, to revisit his Manchester friends: though now
a "bird of passage", the loud and general plaudits which greeted him on
his entrance, appeared so many congratulations on his success in a *hap-
pier clime*.[33]

The warmth of his reception may have acted as a tonic; certainly there
was no relaxation of the pressure – eleven consecutive nights he played,
with only Sunday for rest. Richard, Iago, Shylock and Sir Archy ("most
excellent"), Stukely ("never was duplicity more strongly marked by the
voice; never was it more faithfully depicted in the countenance, than by this
able performer. We are not merely regarding with admiration a change of
features, but with astonishment are exploring the inmost recesses of the
heart"). He played Harmony and Petruchio, also – Kitely had been intended, but had to be withdrawn because of the weaknesses of the company; Octavian; and in the second week Hamlet, and Sir Pertinax, which
drew a very crowded house. For the Popes' benefit he played Mercutio to
their Romeo and Juliet, and Alberto in *The Child of Nature*; the following
night he repeated Iago and Sir Archy "to an over-flowing house", and on
the last night of the season, Friday 4 September, for his own Benefit played
Macbeth (Pope as Macduff, Mrs. Pope as Lady Macbeth, Bellamy as
Hecate) and recited Collins' *Ode on the Passions*, an old favourite in
Manchester, for which they rewarded him with a house of £110.[34] It had
been a tough but exhilarating fortnight. A brief holiday and then a quiet
return to London to prepare for the beginning of the new season could
have ended it admirably. Instead, unfortunately, he set off immediately
north-east over the Pennines for a six nights-plus-Benefit engagement at
Newcastle-on-Tyne for Stephen Kemble.

There are many occasions on which one cannot help feeling in exaspera-
tion that Cooke was his own worst enemy; of them all, perhaps this is the
most acute. It was an engagement that in all sanity he should never have
taken on. He had had an almost impossibly strenuous summer, during the
latter part of which he had been, not surprisingly, fighting illness; he had
had splendid financial reward, and had no need of additional money. The
engagement he was taking on was for a man he did not much care about;
and it was not even with his main company, but with an *ad hoc* one
assembled for the purpose. Cooke himself admits

We had a motley group: Mr. K.'s company was at Scarborough, so with
himself, one lady, and one gentleman, the remainder were a small un-
disciplined set in the neighbourhood, engaged for the time.[35]

It was normal practice for Drury Lane to open on 16 September after the expiry of the Haymarket licence on the 15th, and for Covent Garden to follow on the 17th;[36] so Cooke had at this stage no reason positively to believe that he would be required on the opening night; on the other hand, he was their leading man, and might assume that he would be expected to open the season. Nevertheless, he might have argued that if he finished as planned at Newcastle on the evening of September 14, a hurried journey on the mail – if everything went right – could get him into London by the evening of the 17th if necessary. But was it reasonable to expect that everything would go according to plan in such a split-second schedule? And could he rely on his long-suffering body not to let him down? Why on earth did he agree to go?

The only possible explanation is a combination of what Ward in the letter already quoted called the "easiness of his temper" – his inability to say no – and a desire to show Kemble, and Newcastle, both of whom he had last left in the spring of 1791 in some disarray, what he had achieved since then. It is understandable, perhaps; but in the event it was to prove disastrous.

For what he did not, and as it turned out could not, know, was that the political rivalry between the two theatres in London had erupted again. Covent Garden, departing from precedent, had announced its opening for the 14th, three days earlier than usual; not to be out-done Drury Lane had retorted by proposing to open on the 12th, and to open with Kemble as Richard III, a role which he had been re-studying during the recess. This was an open challenge, for Harris and Lewis had also announced Cooke as Richard III on the opening night, and Lewis wrote to him at the Theatre Royal Manchester informing him of this, and hoping to have the satisfaction of seeing him in perfect health at rehearsal on the previous Saturday, that is, September 12. The letter was dated from Covent Garden on September 5, and marked "if gone, to be forwarded". On that day, or the next, Cooke must have left for Newcastle; the letter did eventually reach him, for it was in the papers left to Dunlap, but since it had to be forwarded to Newcastle by way of Manchester it would be very surprising indeed if it reached Cooke in time for him to extricate himself from an impossible situation.[37]

Dunlap, typically, over-simplifies the position, and roundly condemns Cooke for irresponsibility and degrading behaviour. Certainly it was foolish and thoughtless – but scarcely more than that. He had simply been making the most optimistic assumptions throughout to enable him to do what he wanted to do; as indeed was Lewis, if he thought that a week was sufficient for a letter to reach Cooke if he had left Manchester; it was the sort of administrative muddle that is not unknown in theatrical – and other – affairs. It was the results that in the end turned out to be so damaging.

At Covent Garden they waited anxiously over the week-end for Cooke's arrival. By Monday afternoon it was clear that an emergency was on, and

> At 4 o'clock a bill was issued stating that as Mr. Cooke had not arrived in town it was apprehended some accident had occurred and the piece would be changed to *Lover's Vows* . . .[38]

This information did not reach many of the audience, who had come to see how Cooke would compare with Kemble's performance of a few days before. It was only when the curtain went up and Miss Chapman appeared as Agatha Fribourg that many of them realised that something was wrong, and a considerable disturbance followed. Murray came forward and tried to repeat the explanation of the emergency bill; he was shouted down at first, but in the end applauded, and the play began again. Still there were hisses and argument; once more the play was stopped, and first Murray and then Lewis himself came on to try to pacify the objectors. Lewis strongly denied some suggestions that Cooke was in town. To a more knowledgeable member of the Pit who asked why Cooke was announced to play that night in Newcastle, Lewis denied all knowledge. They knew, he said, that Cooke's engagement would end there on Friday night last, "and that he had full time to be here to do his duty."[39] Eventually Lewis gave a money-back guarantee to any who wanted it, and in due course the substitute programme was allowed to proceed.

But the disturbance in the theatre was by no means the most sinister by-product of the situation. Reports and rumours as to the reasons for Cooke's defection began to circulate, and some of them were what might be expected from anyone who had had experience of him in his provincial days, so that the *Morning Post*, in its balanced and judicial summing-up of the situation as its then stood, felt it had to defend him. Having recorded the history of the changes of customary opening dates it went on:

> Now, whether Mr. Cooke was duly apprised of this change, we cannot pretend to say, or whether he made any engagement at any other Theatre in ignorance of it. If he, by the custom of the theatre, or express covenant, had a right to dispose of his time until the 17th, he had in no respect violated his duty to Covent-garden. Into this point, however, it would be premature to enter at present. We do not wish to give a turn to the public mind, but to keep it cool and open for a fair trial. To the reports, then, that either idleness or intemperance prevented the attendance of Mr. Cooke, we must give a positive contradiction. Mr. Cooke is

at Newcastle, neither abusing his time nor his talents, but increasing his popularity by a faithful discharge of his professional duties.[40]

And in confirmation of the fact it went on to quote the advertisement from Saturday's *Newcastle Chronicle*, received in London on the Monday, announcing Cooke to perform that night, his last, for his own benefit, in *The Gamester* and *Love à la Mode*.

But back in Newcastle matters were not straighforward either. Cooke seems to have got through Stukely satisfactorily on the Monday evening, but afterwards while reciting Collins' *Ode on the Passions*, he was suddenly taken ill and left the stage. After some delay and explanations between Stephen Kemble and the audience, the farce was changed to *The Village Lawyer*, and the performance completed without the leading actor; who four days later issued a statement to the press.

To the Ladies and Gentlemen of Newcastle and its Environs.
MR. COOKE feels infinite Regret that the accidental Recurrence of a Bleeding from his Breast (which attacked him at Glasgow) should have prevented him from fulfilling the whole of his Duty on Monday; but more particularly so, when he reflects that it prevented him from personally thanking them for their Kindness and Support, – which, both now and on former Occasions, have left such an impression on his Mind, that neither Time nor Circumstances can ever efface.
    Percy-street Sept 18th.   [41]

But before that appeared, the London press had already carried two more important statements that had been sent post-haste from Newcastle and were received at Covent-garden on September 18. The first was from a local physician.

SIR,
    From great fatigue and exertion, Mr. Cooke has ruptured a Blood Vessel in his Chest, which renders it unsafe for him to travel. He is at present under my care, and I hope, in a short time, to be enabled to permit him to proceed to town.
        I am Sir,
            Your obedient Servant,
            E. KENTISH M.D.
Newcastle Sept 15, 1801.

On the same day another letter was written to Thomas Harris.

SIR,

I trouble you with this at the request of Mr. George Cooke, who is at present so much indisposed as to render him incapable of writing to you. He had been very poorly for several days past, but yesterday evening was attacked with such excruciating pains in his breast, that the Doctor took a large quantity of blood from him; and he hopes in a few days he may be able to travel, if he has no relapse. He received a letter from Mr. Lewis, dated the 5th inst. but it being directed to Manchester, did not reach here until too late. The distress of his mind, on your account, is beyond anything we can say. The Faculty, as well as his Friends, will do everything in their power for his speedy recovery, in order that he may soon be with you.

I am, Sir,
You most obedient humble servant,
GEORGE DUNN.   (42)

The playbill for September 21 carried an additional apology from the proprietors for Monday's disappointment, and an assurance that

Ladies and Gentlemen who have Places for his next Appearance, will have due Notice of the Day, as soon as his Recovery shall enable them to fix it.

And there, for the time being, the matter rested.

It was to rest for nearly a month, for Cooke did not hurry his return to London. Having had his breakdown, he did what he ought to have done earlier, and so perhaps avoided it – he took a holiday. By his own account he was fit to travel after about a week, and on September 21 he left Newcastle for Matlock in Derbyshire, where he arrived the following day, there to remain for three weeks.(43) He tells us nothing of his stay there, but at the end of it he made a leisurely and pleasantly social journey to London by way of Leicester and St. Albans; by October 15 he was back at his apartments in Bolton street, Piccadilly, ready to face Harris – and the Covent Garden audience.

Though, sadly, he had already had experience of this kind of situation in the provinces, he had never yet had to face a London audience in similar circumstances; and there is little doubt from the contemporary accounts that the more boisterous element in the audience thought the actor was fair game when this happened. Both the *Morning Post* and the *Morning Chronicle* agree substantially in their morning-after accounts of what happened when Cooke reappeared on October 19, as Richard III. The play "came forth with more than usual attraction" reported the former.

Mr. Cooke was to make his first appearance this season, and the public expected an account of the cause of his long absence, and their late disappointment. Much more amusement than the bills promised was consequently expected. During all the previous time the galleries were unusually turbulent. Loud clamour and strange noises prevailed. Indeed everything portended that Mr. Cooke would meet a rude and boisterous reception. – At length he presented himself just before the commencement of the piece, and all his bows and obeisances were received with a furious miscellany of groans, hisses, shouts and plaudits. The opposition continued a good while, but not so long as its first burst might have induced us to suppose. – Mr. Cooke made no effort to speak until it had completely died away. He then made the following apology:– "Ladies and Gentlemen – with the most painful concern I feel myself under the necessity of apologising here for the first time since I had the honour of appearing before you." – Here Mr. Cooke was interrupted with a loud cry of "Off, Off," from the Galleries, mixed with plaudits from the boxes. Every part of the house seemed to take an interest in the business – all was tumult and confusion. Silence being restored, Mr. Cooke proceeded – "When I left London, I had no permission to be absent on the opening of the theatre; but I had many reasons to think I would not immediately be wanted. The letter which Mr. Harris sent to me, did not reach Manchester until after I had left it; and when I did receive it, with no possible exertions could I have been here in time." Here another interruption took place, but not so great as the former. Mr. Cooke continued:– "The events since you well know; I can only say, that I am sincerely sorry for what has happened: and, though I may fail of success, it shall be my most earnest endeavour to deserve it."

This address was followed with loud shouts of *bravo, bravo*; and Mr. Cooke retired amidst loud and unqualified applauses (*sic*).

He had won over his London audience, as he had done his Manchester crowds in the past. But there is an additional sentence in the report that gives some indication of the strain it cost him.

He appeared, when he came forward, extremely agitated; he delivered the first sentence in a tremulous tone, and it was not until the concluding line that his voice recovered its firmness.[44]

With the audience now completely on his side, he went on to give one of the most spirited of his performances of Richard, surviving even the contretemps of a fall in the tent scene, when one of his spurs accidentally caught up in a covering, and tripped him. It was a triumph both of acting ability and personality.

Yet, like so much of Cooke's life, it was an ambivalent situation. He must have revelled in the relief and affection of that ultimate warm reception. But it also removed a sanction. So far his new audience might have been a spur to keep himself under control. He had got at last where he wanted to be, and the incentive to stay there was stronger than anything before in his artistic life. But now he had found that in London, too, he could, if necessary, ingratiate himself with an audience he had offended. From now on it would be easier to risk a second, or third time, and for more dubious reasons. This was the real tragedy of the Newcastle affair. Perhaps it was already too late, and if it had not happened in this way, some other like occasion would have presented itself. Nevertheless, to the observer patiently following the triumphs and follies of Cooke's career, there comes at this time the very real sense of a turning point having been reached. Nemesis does not appear immediately. But like the action of a Greek tragedy she is remorseless, and her arrival henceforth is inevitable.

Chapter X

The Challenge to Kemble – 1801-1803

I

Not that this appeared to anyone at the time. On the surface all was well. The Battle of the Richards provoked much argument and discussion among the theatrical amateurs; for the remainder of the year, as in the previous season, Monday night was Richard night at Covent Garden, and on some of those evenings, including Cooke's first, Kemble played the same role at the other house. But as time went by, Kemble seems to have accepted that, in this part, at least, Cooke had the superior drawing power, and quietly resigned it to him, as Cooke had had to do in reverse with The Stranger.

His other successful roles of the previous season were all brought back, Shylock and Sir Archy, Sir Giles, Iago, Kitely – even Macbeth, which had been more equivocally received; and from time to time new ones were brought forward. On November 27 it was Stukely in *The Gamester*, with little Mrs. Litchfield as Mrs. Beverley, and at least one observer felt he had rarely seen "a more finished portrait of this unprincipled monster".[1] But when on the 2nd January he played Jaques in *As You Like It* with Miss Murray as Rosalind, he split the critics. The *Morning Post* felt he played it

in a new and expressive manner, with such eccentricity and many strokes of original beauty. He was greatly applauded.

But the *Chronicle* felt he was misguided in setting himself up against Kemble in this, one of the latter's most admired roles. Cooke's powers were not suited to the part; instead of being mild and benevolent, though melancholy and sad, he

appeared one of the sturdiest of the Duke's attendants, and in the highest spirits; to pursue the stag with the greatest keenness and to feed upon it with the greatest voracity. *Jaques* sometimes displays a degree of gaiety, but there is a tenderness in it, and his smiles are those of a man filled with dismal reflections. In COOKE this was broad humour and rustic merriment. Instead of the pensive philosophic *Jaques*, we seemed to ourselves to behold a ploughman returning from the alehouse.

And though the writer found some things to praise he ended by drawing a moral –

He has great powers as an actor, and if he uses them judiciously he will remain at the top of his profession. A struggle to shine in a walk for which nature never intended him, can only end in his own disgrace and the triumph of his enemies.[2]

Audiences were too conditioned by Kemble's romantic view of the character for a frontal attack to succeed.

Two days later Covent Garden revived, for the first time for fifteen years, Young's tragedy *The Revenge*, with Cooke as Zanga. "Cooke seems determined to pursue Kemble through the entire range of his characters" said the *Morning Post*, and both it and the *Chronicle* were lukewarm – though the latter, at least, imputed most of the blame to the weaknesses of the play itself rather than the actor.[3] With this diagnosis Cooke himself would doubtless have agreed, for he was under no delusions about the play. About four years earlier he had assessed it shrewdly in some of his memoranda, and liked it no more than the *Morning Chronicle*.[4] He and Henry Siddons played well, but not well enough. *The Revenge* dropped back into oblivion, and four days later they tackled *King Lear*.

With three new productions within a week, it must have been under-rehearsed; the *Morning Chronicle* also suggested that he had been pressed into it against his will. Whether or not this was true, he was again tackling a major role in which Kemble had already established his view of the part. Kemble exploited the pathos of the feeble old man: Cooke played for the authority and power of the man who had been – and still was – a king; and so his performance, as we shall see in more detail later, was found to be too vigorous and lacking in tenderness. As had happened with Jaques, he was playing to an audience conditioned by Kemble, and Kemble had been in London many more years than he. The *Post* in the end made no bones about it all.

Few of the beautiful passages with which the piece abounds received that exquisite colouring and embellishment with which Mr. Kemble in the same character calls down such plaudits in the other House. Mr. Cooke having so evidently placed himself in the way of comparison, this allusion cannot be deemed invidious. – This new essay should, however, make him slow to venture beyond his depth, and justified our apprehension that he does not possess an elasticity of mind, a pliancy of powers, to enable him to pursue his rival through all the variety of his characters with the same success that he encounters him on Bosworth Field.[5]

Game – and set – to Kemble.

A week later Cooke was creating the character of Orsino in M. G. Lewis' new piece of theatrical fustian *Alfonso, King of Castile*, and he was to play it nine times during the rest of January and February. He was no longer exclusively a classical actor. There were other subtle changes in status; in the previous season he had only been allowed to play in management Benefits – now he could, and did, play for his colleagues, sometimes using his popular roles, at other times introducing new ones. For Fawcett, for instance, he played Sir Edward Mortimer in *The Iron Chest*; for Mrs. Lichfield Bajazet in *Tamerlane*. But it was for Lewis that he made the first of his many appearances as Sir Pertinax MacSycophant in Macklin's *The Man of the World* on April 10th, and helped to pull in a benefit of £549.15.0. If he had let down Lewis in September, he was making handsome amends now. (Brandon, the Box-Keeper, did even better when Cooke played Macbeth for him; but one suspects that the box-keeper's better organisation and publicity may have made the comparison not strictly fair.) His own benefit was less of a phenomenon this season, though at £409.13.6. still in the middle bracket, and Harris again gave him the fees of the house, and raised his salary to 14 guineas a week, extending his contract for a further three years. Partly, this was an obvious expression of confidence; perhaps also it implied the hope that Cooke would not feel so pressed to go whoring into the provinces after filthy lucre in the coming summer. For his own benefit he played Falstaff for the first time in London, and this was much more liked. But he was not the same kind of sensation that he had been during his first season. Partly this was because it was now the musical pieces that were more in fashion; it was Braham and Mrs. Billington, and Anna Storace who drew the crowds, and the large benefits, and the publicity for their successes and their squabbles. It was sixteen years since Signora Storace had been Mozart's first Susanna in *Figaro* in Vienna; she had become more mannered, and her voice had lost some of its flexibility. But she knew her value and how to exploit it, still; as did the other two singers. When Cooke played before Their Majesties at a Command performance this season he played Sir Archy – *after* Mrs. Billington had starred as Rosetta in *Love in a Village* Did he feel that his status was slipping?[6]

In the contest with Kemble, Richard, Iago and Shylock had more than held their own, and Kitely, Stukely and Sir Giles had succeeded; but the Stranger, Jaques, Zanga and Lear had been critically received. Certainly the failure of *Lear* must have been a great disappointment to him; and though *The Man of the World* had been a popular success later, it had not attracted the kind of press coverage under which *Lear* had sunk. Did he feel let down because his second benefit was not as good as his first? Or could he not bear the thought of Monk Lewis succeeding where Shakespeare had not been given an adequate hearing? Or was it a combination of all three? Whatever may have been the motivating factors, the crisis came for the first time in London on 11 May 1802. Billed to appear once more as Orsino for the Johnstones' Benefit, the file playbill records laconically:

> Cooke attempted to perform but was too inebriated to proceed beyond a few speeches. The remainder of the part was read by Mr. Claremont.

For the next fortnight his performances had to be postponed because of his "severe indisposition". What had happened before in Manchester was now beginning to happen in London. His sense of responsibility was losing out to his need for escape.

And yet, as so often with George Cooke, the facts reveal a paradox. He returned to the theatre on May 24 as Sir Pertinax, and in the first fortnight of June played leading roles steadily through the Benefits. On Thursday the 10th he played for Brunton and Blanchard; and then immediately on the Friday he must have taken the road to Bath; for there, on Saturday June 12, he played Richard to a crowded and enthusiastic house for the Benefit of the Bath and Bristol Theatrical Fund. The performance over, again he must have begun to travel back immediately on the Sunday, for back in Covent Garden on the Monday he was playing Sir Pertinax once more, for Glassington, the prompter. For this strenuous Bath visit, involving 220 miles of travelling in three or four days, he had volunteered his services, and he would take no fee.[7] There was no lack of public spirit and sense of responsibility here.

Perhaps he felt he owed a special debt to Bath and Bristol. In December 1801, when he was not needed for a time in London, he had made a fleeting but concentrated visit to the west, performing from Thusday 17 December to Wednesday 23, Richard III, Iago, Shylock and Sir Archy. He was splendidly received in Bath on the Thursday and Bristol on the Friday. But after playing Iago in Bath on the Saturday he was taken ill and confined to bed on Sunday and Monday, so that a crowded house in Bristol on the Monday evening, with every box taken in expectation of seeing his Iago, had to be disappointed, and his commitments in London after his Bath performances on the 22nd and 23rd, prevented him giving a substitute night.[8] But he had already discharged that debt, for in April 1802 he had once more been given leave of absence and made a hurried visit to the west again to play Shylock and Sir Archy in Bath on the 5th, and Bristol on the 6th. The playbill in Bristol made a special point of his mortification that illness had prevented that previous performance, and his anxiety to take the earliest opportunity of expressing his gratitude.[9]

The greater likelihood was probably that he had enjoyed his reception in Bath and Bristol. Here was a quality audience comparable to that in London, that gave itself to him for what he was, not for how he compared with Kemble. This, perhaps (subconsciously, maybe), was the fundamental drive that spurred him on to those punishing provincial tours that to the end of his career he never abandoned. Even when his London reputation was in decline, in the provincial ponds he was a very big fish indeed.

Certainly, as soon as his London commitments were over on June 17 (a week before the final end of the season) he was preparing to depart, and on the 20th he set off once more for Manchester, for another touring summer.

It was a less punishing schedule this time – he had learnt something from the experience of the previous year. It involved only 48 performances as opposed to some 63; and about 850 miles of travelling as against 1,100 or more in 1801. Moreover he confined himself to a dozen roles this time – Richard, Sir Pertinax, Sir Archy, Shylock, Kitely, Falstaff, Macbeth and Iago being the mainstay of the tour; in Manchester he added Octavian twice (once for his benefit); for his Benefit in Birmingham, he played Hamlet; and in Bath and Bristol he added Orsino and Bajazet. With three of the four companies (Plymouth was the exception), he had worked either in the previous summer or more recently; this, too, must have eased the strain a little.

The first six weeks were concentrated enough: he was at Manchester, again under Ward and Bellamy, for 11 performances from 21 June to 2 July; the company then moved to Chester for the Fair week from 5 to 10 July and he gave 6 performances there; on the 11th he left Chester, travelled all night, arriving in Birmingham for breakfast on the 12th, and afterwards being so ill that his first appearance that night had to be postponed for 24 hours. During the next fortnight he gave 9 performances there; but then gave himself ten or eleven days for a reasonably leisurely progress down to Plymouth, visiting Shakespeare's birthplace at Stratford, Blenheim Palace, Oxford, Stonehenge, Salisbury and Exeter Cathedrals among other places en route. The bulk of August he seems to have spent in Devon, giving 12 performances at Plymouth and Plymouth Dock; on the 28th he travelled from Plymouth by way of Exeter and Taunton to Bristol, establishing himself there at 36, Queen Square, where until September 13 he played 7 nights, and a further 3 in Bath. On the 14th he left for London, and on the evening of the 15th was giving his first performance of the season as Richard. This time he was keeping himself well under control – there had to be no repetition of last year's affair.[10]

Perhaps it was with this in mind that throughout the whole of September he kept a regular journal, which Dunlap reprinted apparently in full.[11] It is a fascinating and revealing fragment – Cooke living a normal and apparently quite relaxed existence, carrying out his professional duties without fuss or bother, and in between taking an intelligent traveller's interest in his neighbourhood, mixing a little with local society, visiting local occasions of entertainment. We see him searching the carriers' inns for his trunk from Plymouth, ordering horses well in advance, paying his bills; rehearsing and playing in the two theatres, marking his copy of *Alfonso* from the theatre's prompt-book, reflecting on audiences and performances, sometimes on fellow-performers. He goes to St. James' Fair in Bristol with a lady and a child, and buys the young one a fairing; invited to dine in Bath with Walmsley, the local painter, he notes a gala that evening in Sydney Gardens and buys tickets for it, so that after dinner he can take his host and fellow guests; there, along with many others, they watch wonderingly as two people go up in a balloon, to descend eventually no-one quite knows where.

He finds the late night journeys back to Bristol from Bath after the theatre tiring, as who would not; but as two of them are on Saturday nights he can breakfast in bed the next morning at leisure. On one Sunday he visits the cathedral and finds the Dean's sermon true but trite; he is more moved to visit the grave of the actor William Powell, who had died in 1769; he finds in the *New Bristol Guide* a copy of the playbill for the opening of the King Street theatre in 1766, and reflects sadly that of all the names mentioned not one is now living. He walks about Bristol, along the quays, in the village of Clifton, where he marvels at the gorge and the vessels moving up the river at high tide, yet so far below. He buys books to read – finds Colman's *Broad Grins* at five shillings "very dear indeed" – even more so after he has read it. He plays Orsino in *Alfonso* and feels that he has never played it better, though the day before at rehearsal he had forgotten every word. But what rubbish it all is:

This gentleman's [M. G. Lewis] imagination seems entirely taken up with murders, ghosts, old castles, and ancient Spanish ballads. There is certainly some good writing in Alfonso, but both fable and construction are miserably bad. It abounds with so many improbabilities, and even impossibilities, that to point them out would be an endless task. It is a sanguinary tale, for the four principal characters die violent deaths. One lady poisons another, and is stabbed by her lover, who, after mortally wounding his father in battle *by mistake*, stabs himself, and leaves a half-dead king behind to mourn the catastrophe. . . . It struggled through nine nights to tolerable audiences, partly procured through the interest of the author, and went to rest for the remainder of the season. I hope for ever, at least as long as I remain in the theatre.[12]

With that judgment who could quarrel?

Thumbing through a three-volume novel leads him to the reflection that a licenser is as necessary for a circulating library as for the theatre, since young girls often procure, sometimes in secret,

> books of so evil a tendency, that not only their time is shamefully wasted, but their morals and manners tainted and warped for the remainder of their lives. I am firmly of opinion many females owe the loss of reputation to the insinuating, seductive, and pernicious publications too often found in those dangerous seminaries.[13]

And after his fourth performance within a week of Sir Pertinax MacSycophant, he reflects on the play and its author; since it was a play with which he was so uniquely identified, the thoughts are worth quotation in full.

> The comedy of *The Man of the World*, as I was informed by Mr. Austin, of Chester, was produced in Dublin so long since as the year 1759 or 60, in which Mr. A. played Lord Lumbercourt. It then bore the title of *The True-born Scotchman*. At what time it was licensed and produced in London, under its present name, I know not, as I have not read Mr. Macklin's life. It, at that time, underwent various alterations. The fable is simple and well-conducted, the characters, though highly coloured, naturally drawn, and the language nervous and correct. So fastidious was the author in imitation of ancient comedy, that he has not allowed a single change of scene in the whole play. A library from beginning to end: the same scene through his *Love-à-la-Mode*. He seems to entertain a strong prejudice against the Scotch in general, yet he appears to make some atonement by pourtraying the knight's family as very different in sentiment from himself. The Scotch are certainly very national, but whether more than the English, Welsh, or Irish, I will not presume to say. They frequently carry their point, whether of good or evil tendency, by a steady perseverance in adapting their behaviour to the exigence of the moment. When this comedy was printed by subscription, (together with his farce) there were again some alterations introduced, but, not being in the licensed manuscript, they are not usually spoken. One

speech of Egerton's in particular, is a just and glowing picture of the atrocious and flagitious enormities too often practiced at elections by all ranks of people. The province of comedy is to expose and censure, as well as to ridicule. It cannot shew mankind as they are, without exhibiting their vices and deformities. The easiest method of appreciating the just merits of this comedy is to compare it with those of the present time![14]

It is all so intelligent, urbane, and civilised; a world away from the antics of the tavern or Mistress Byrn's, or the actor of Orsino who was "too inebriated to proceed beyond a few speeches". If only he could have maintained that balance.

Cooke ended the tour playing Richard III at Bristol on Stepember 13, with the Corsican General Paoli in the audience; he settled with the theatre Treasurer, supped, and then sat with Taylor and Walter Smith of the company until his chaise came to the door at two in the morning. He travelled east overnight, breakfasted in Marlborough and bought three Wiltshire cheeses to take back to town with him, ending the day at the Crown in Slough; from there he was roused at 4 a.m. to leave for Hounslow and London, where he breakfasted at 8 in Albemarle Street. That evening at Covent Garden he was applauded as Richard for the 36th time in London.[15]

II

The new season had actually opened on Monday the 13th, but while Cooke was in Bristol, Harris had visited him in the Green Room, and Cooke had taken the precaution of confirming that he would not be needed on the opening night this year.[16] When he appeared again on the 15th, there was clearly no falling off of interest in his Richard – the house was as full as ever (nearly £400), the Pit and Galleries overflowing at Full Price. And Cooke was in splendid form. The *Morning Post* the following day confirmed the evidence of his journal.

> Cooke played in his best stile and was most warmly applauded; his health appears to have benefited by his trip to the country; his hoarseness is gone, and his voice is clear.[17]

The journal continued to record the routine of his life for the rest of the month. He read the newspapers, paid his bills, visited his wine-merchant; went to Astley's Amphitheatre and was bored rather than amused, and to the Pit at Drury Lane to support the first appearance there of his old colleague from Dublin and Bath, Cherry; he read *Robinson Crusoe*, and from Grosvenor Square saw Mons. Guarnerin, who he had watched in Sydney Gardens at Bath, make another balloon ascent, and the first descent by parachute. But there were also symptoms of indisposition, and he was not satisfied with either the rehearsals or his performance of Falstaff on September 22. And on September 18, with Mr. Harris' compliments, he was desired to prepare for Hamlet on Monday the 27. He read and marked his part; he had two rehearsals at the theatre; and then on the appointed day, to a packed and excited house (the box office took £524.10.0) he tackled the last of the major Shakespearian roles in which London had not yet seen him.

With so much anticipation in advance, it was bound to be either an overwhelming theatrical occasion, or if not, it would be a major disappointment. Unhappily it proved to be the latter. The *Morning Chronicle* review was the most forthright.

> It is painful for us to state, that those who were disappointed in gaining admission have no reason to think themselves unfortunate. Are there any who would find pleasure in seeing a great man's laurels wither on his brow? It is much to be lamented that Mr. COOKE chose, or was compelled to make, this experiment . . . His well-earned fame may be able to stand the shock; but had this been his first appearance in London, it is our serious opinion that he would not have been tolerated a second time, and that his vast talents in other departments of the drama must have remained forever in obscurity.[18]

The *Post* was less direct, but took substantially the same view; its analysis shows very clearly why. It is a reasoned judgment, not a hatchet piece. From his experience of Cooke the writer had expected him to fall short of Kemble in the passages of deep feeling, grief and terror, but that this would be counterbalanced by his superior excellence in the "mad irregular scenes", the "flighty and incoherent passages", the sneer and the satire. But in the event Cooke failed in these, too; and the final assessment could only be that "he supported the character respectably", but not more so than many other actors in the country could have done.[19] It was a harsh review, but it gives the impression of being a fair one. That Cooke was upset by it and others is evident; he thought that some of the attacks were premeditated, and that they attacked him

> in a manner that would have been deemed impossible to have happened to anyone who had ever received the slightest approbation from an audience – a London one I mean.

And years later he could still feel:

> I do not doubt but I had faults in abundance; but had I acted as well as I had seen it acted by Garrick, my reception *in that character* would have been much the same.[20]

In a sense perhaps he was right, though not because of any cabal or conspiracy. As with Lear, his audiences were so conditioned by the Kemble reading that this was the norm from which he could only deviate if by doing so he was able to reveal new insights; and this he was not able to do. Many of his natural characteristics were liabilities in this context, as the review makes clear. He would have to exploit them wherever possible, and transcend them if he could. Clearly he could not. It is hard to escape the feeling that he was overawed by the occasion, or rather the attempt – for when he played it a second time on 4 October, the *Post* went again in the hope of better things, but found nothing materially different.[21] Dunlap may well be exaggerating when he suggests that it was a mistake to take on the part while Kemble was abroad, since the part was regarded as so much his property it would be felt dishonest to seize in his absence – "It was like taking possession of a man's house, while he was making a journey." Nevertheless, there is much to his other point that had Cooke been in a position to play the part in London 20 years before, at the age of 25, not 45,

> we might have seen in him a Hamlet, though essentially different, not inferior to Kemble's or to Garrick's.[22]

When he played it at about that time in Chester he was at the peak of his powers, as Munden felt. Now it was too late. Instead of setting up to rival Kemble indiscriminately he should have been exploiting what he could do better. Whether this was a failure of insight by Harris, or whether he was swayed by a desire on Cooke's part to emulate his rival in all the major roles, we cannot now know. Perhaps, indeed, every major actor feels he has to prove himself in Hamlet. So the failure cut deep. The journal was broken off suddenly. The new-found balance had, as so often, been short-lived.

Richard and Sir Pertinax and Sir Archy continued to draw. The Falstaff of *The Merry Wives of Windsor* was brought in, but while not a failure, was not generally popular. Again a *Morning Post* review suggests how the very qualities that could lend force to Richard and Sir Giles could be a liability in comedy where geniality and relaxation were needed.

Cooke's feature are too keen, and his voice too formal and ranting for this character. He had not the careless, easy manner of him who loves only his bottle, and his pleasures. Suspicion now and then scowls in his face, and almost makes one believe that he is not to be bit. His air is sometimes even tragical, and gives him the appearance of a stern commander about to engage the foe. – He however, in some parts, keeps up to his character, as in the scene, where (after hiding himself) he plumps out upon *Mrs. Page*. There his hurry, confusion, and fright, all seem natural. But he is even greater, when he is finally detected by *Ford*. Then he appears truly chop-fallen.[23]

Just before Christmas Addison's *Cato* was revived, but though the critics had little fault to find with Cooke's central performance, the play itself was not to their or the audiences' taste, and it mustered two nights only. With the new year he found himself playing in Lewis' *Alfonso* again, though a command performance of Sir Pertinax must have been a considerable consolation. But on 31 January the theatre playbill records him as "taken ill – Murray played Iago", and that illness, one suspects, was alcoholic – for he must have known by then that *Hamlet* was about to be revived early in February, and he was not to play it; moreover to add insult to injury, it was to be played by one who was little more than an amateur, Captain Henry Caulfield late of the Guards; and in the event was to reach five performances, three more than his own.[24]

This he must have seen as a public humiliation – though never, of course, would he openly admit it. Sir Pertinax was the only success to which he could cling for self-respect – he had not even played Richard since the end of November. By the beginning of March he found himself creating the role of Peregrine Rochdale in Colman's new comedy *John Bull*; while it was not a play that he despised like *Alfonso*, the part was not one in which he had to do much more than speak the dialogue straightforwardly, and be the stereotype of the honest, manly, good-hearted Englishman.[25]

However the play was enormously popular, and throughout March he played it to overflowing houses, until it came to the 20th performance, when he rebelled and once again Murray had to stand in for him. He was back in the cast two days later; but four days after, on April 20, he had to face another humiliation. On that night he played Sir Pertinax and Comus for his own Benefit to what the playbill annotator called "a very indifferent house". Since it took just over £220 it must have been less than half-full, and with no remission of house charges from Harris this year, it was a blow both to his pocket as well as his self-esteem. Cooke really was going through a very bad patch, and he was not now the man to battle with circumstances without recourse to alcohol. When nine days later he played Sir

Philip Blandford in *Speed the Plough* for his old friend Munden's Benefit, the house overflowed and took £619.8.o. Reflecting on the difference between their receptions could only for Cooke induce either self-pity or self-recrimination, or both; and in either case he would run for escape to the brandy bottle. When on May 4 he was expected to play in another of Lewis' confections, *The Harper's Daughter* (a version of Schiller's *Die Räuber*) for the Johnstons' Benefit, he again rebelled and refused to play, and Henry Siddons had to read in the part. He was away for over a fortnight.[26]

Yet in the end, resilient as ever, he did return on May 20 to play King John to Mrs. Litchfield's Constance for her Benefit; and as well as voicing the play's noble and patriotic sentiments (in Valpy's version), to make his apologies to the audience, if he could. And indeed he could. The *Morning Chronicle* was there.

> We are happy to mention that Mr. Cooke has resumed his theatrical duties. When he entered in the royal robes of *King John*, there was some hissing. – Upon this he came forward, and, seemingly without premeditation addressed the audience in a very neat speech. He said he could not affect to be ignorant of the cause of this disapprobation. He had lately failed to sustain a part in a new play (*The Harper's Daughter*) which it was announced he had undertaken. He solemnly declared that this was through no fault of his. For twenty four hours he was confined to bed by a violent disorder. There were many things in the part which he admired, and he never was more anxious to come forward. What ever acts of imprudence he might have committed, or might yet commit, in this instance he felt that his conduct was unimpeachable. The applause he had received in that house had made the deepest impression upon his mind, and it should be his study to shew himself not undeserving of the public favour. This address was extremely well received, and we doubt not will be considered by everyone as a satisfactory explanation. Mr. Cooke never acted better. The house was crowded in every corner.

The prodigal was home again. But the playbill annotator was more laconic and less impressed. He wrote:

> Cooke apologised to the public for his absence on H. Johnston's Benefit which he solemnly assured them was caused by *real* illness.[27]

Perhaps there was one other matter exercising Cooke's mind at this time and casting a shadow on the future. The April number of the *Monthly Mirror* had made public the fact that Kemble, at present travelling on the continent, had bought a sixth share of the proprietorship of Covent Garden for over £20,000. What precisely this was going to mean in the coming season, only time would show, but it was not difficult to guess. The further three years of Cooke's contract might turn out to be security or humiliation.

One other incident before the season ended was to cast a very long shadow. Dunlap makes a long and complicated story of it, but the essence can be briefly told. The young American actor, Thomas Cooper, over on a visit, was playing at Drury Lane, and some time in May made Cooke's acquaintance. When during the course of their meeting Cooke learned that Cooper had been offered a Benefit on June 10, which, as a stranger, he thought not worth taking, Cooke offered to play for him, provided Harris would give permission. In the end, Harris did give permission, and so after he had finished at Covent Garden, Cooke played for the only time at Drury Lane, Iago to Cooper's Othello. Doubtless Cooke thought comparatively little of this at the time; his concern was much more for their Desdemona of that evening, Mrs. Pope, whom he had first met as a colleague years before in Dublin, when she was Miss Campion, and whose path had crossed his several times since. On that evening she was taken ill on the stage, and Cooke had to help her off. A few days later she died.[28]

That *memento mori* was much more likely to occupy his thoughts as he left once again for Manchester and the start of his summer tour. But in fact in years to come Cooper was to have an influence on him far more momentous than at this time could ever be guessed.

Meantime his friends in the north-west were waiting. His three weeks in Manchester from 13 June to 1 July involved him in 12 performances, and produced the most original playbill excuse so far for the abandoned 13th. The public were respectfully informed that

> *through the Indisposition of Mr. Cooke* (Owing to a Recent DEATH in his Family) He is Ordered by his Physician not to attempt Performing THIS EVENING, *As it might be attended with serious consequences to him.* Fri. JUNE 24th 1803.

The usual week at Chester for the races followed from 4–15 July.[29] Thereafter, an earlier invitation to York having been dropped – presumably because of Tate Wilkinson's death that summer – he wandered round the Midlands. At Cheltenham he got more benefit from the air and the waters than the theatre; he went to Worcester, and at Ludlow joined up briefly with the Henry Siddonses, who were on a longer engagement there;[30] and then finally he toured the Wrench and Robertson circuit, visiting his old haunts at Derby, Chesterfield and Nottingham,[31] playing four nights at each. It can hardly have been either as enjoyable or as profitable as the previous summer. Like his third season in London, symptoms of decline were evident.

He finished at Nottingham on September 8. The new Season at Covent Garden opened on September 12. Whether Cooke was back by then does not appear. Nor did he, until September 21. But in any case things were to be different this season, and from now on. Gentleman Lewis had retired from management and there was a new Acting Manager. His name was John Philip Kemble.

Chapter XI

Decline – 1803-1808

To follow Cooke strictly chronologically through the next seven years would prove at times tedious and repetitive. The basic pattern of his life was set; if we chronicle the departures from routine, it should be remembered that for a large part of the time the routine was there. There were to be hardly any new major Shakespearian roles; there were a handful of additions from the eighteenth century repertory, and a few new creations, none of which could extend or enhance his reputation. Each season he gave on average about sixty performances at Covent Garden; each season he defaulted at some time in some way, either by not performing as announced, or arriving in such a state that his performance had to be abandoned. Each summer he went on a provincial tour; from time to time during the winter seasons he was released also for a week or two to take engagements in places like Bristol and Bath, or the Yorkshire towns, or Manchester; and usually in the autumn he went down from London to Brighton to give some performances. He also gave occasional performances elsewhere, often at benefit performances for former colleagues working in some part of the provincial theatre network.

That with Kemble in charge there would be changes at Covent Garden was obvious to everyone. What he really wanted to do, according to Boaden, his friend and biographer, was to make it

the palace of Shakespeare; all that he had done, at the other theatre, towards a more perfect representation of his plays, was to be now therefore transferred to one devoted to a different scale of expense at a less ambitious principle of management.

But Kemble was, of course, a minority shareholder. While he held a sixth of the equity, Thomas Harris held a half, and hence had the last word if it came to an argument. And Harris' preference was for highly profitable novelties, not too expensive to put on; while Kemble could expect to have

149

his passion for Shakespeare indulged, he would have to keep it within financial bounds. "Still, as may be supposed", recorded Boaden,

> considerable alarm was felt, by the old friends of the concern, at the coming in of a gentleman so inflexible in his taste; and the performers of the company had no few apprehensions that the future business of the stage might be more troublesome than the past had been, from the great zeal and critical accuracy of the new manager.[1]

That Kemble's zeal and critical accuracy would take him in directions different from those of Cooke goes without saying. That Cooke could hardly be expected to relish a situation in which his chief rival had over-night become his administrative superior is equally obvious. Apart from any personal relationships, what would happen to the allocation of parts?

Kemble was, of course, aware of the apprehension, and he began by trying to establish a cordial relationship with his new colleagues. He invited all the leading men to dinner at his house in Great Russell Street, and the occasion went well. Boaden, who was there, noted that Cooke attended, as it seemed to him, "with very sincere pleasure", and

> Before dinner was served up, I fell into conversation with Cooke in the library, and if I had not acquired too decisive evidences of his indiscretion to doubt the charges against him, from anything done or said by him on that day, I should never have suspected his firmness, but have left him thoroughly a convert to his well-informed mind and gentlemanly manners.

H. Johnston, who had left Covent Garden and gone over to Drury Lane, was one of the party, and at some point entertained them all by imagining the sudden indisposition of Harlequin in the Christmas pantomime, and gave imitations of various members of the company trying to substitute for him.

> No man in the room more enjoyed the Harlequin of Mr. Cooke, than he did himself.[2]

After that cordial beginning, they seem to have come to an amicable agreement each to play from time to time, second rate parts to the other, and in the early stages of their relationship, Kemble played Richmond to Cooke's Richard III, and Antonio to his Shylock, while Cooke played Angelo to Kemble's Duke in *Measure for Measure*, Macduff to his Macbeth, and Hubert to his King John. But as time went on it was noticed in the company that somehow or other Kemble's were generally very good second rates, while Cooke's very nearly receded to third rates;[3] this naturally rankled with Cooke, and he began to misbehave. Gradually they appeared together less; in later years it was also felt that the supporting roles were under-cast in Cooke's plays, the best supporting players being kept for Kemble.[4]

But in fairness to Kemble it has to be admitted that Cooke could be extremely difficult. His contract had another three years to go; he felt that he was too valuable to be dismissed, so from time to time he cocked a snook at audience, Acting Manager, and Proprietors alike. As early as the 17th of October, when down to play for the first time as Pizarro to Kemble's Rolla and Mrs. Siddons' Elvira, he arrived at the theatre drunk.

> Upon his entrance it was soon apparent that he knew nothing that he *did*, and the audience could understand nothing that he *said*. He fell back over-powered, before the conclusion of the first act, and, in the opinion of the spectators, was dead drunk. Mr. Kemble came on and assured the house that 'Mr. Cooke was *really* unwell, and unable to proceed', of which, in truth, there could not be the smallest doubt;[5]

and Henry Siddons had to read the part for the rest of the evening. Three days later (and on 12 other occasions during the season) Cooke played it, so far as we know, perfectly soberly; the trouble was that nobody could be sure when a crisis would occur. The following year, when down to play the Ghost for the first time in London to Kemble's Hamlet,

> The Ghost was drunk and found so much difficulty in expressing his "mission" and in keeping himself above ground that the Pit "rose at him" indignantly, to which he replied with a motion of defiance whereupon a row ensued which for some time interrupted the progress of the Tragedy.[6]

For a man who was building a temple to Shakespeare, this was brawling in church with a vengeance, and one can sympathise. It might happen only twice a year, but the damage was done. Cooke might arrive late, or not turn up at all. On 17 April 1805 he was missing for Peregrine; on October 29 he defaulted as Macduff and was missing for a month. On 20 May 1806 he was unable to finish Dumont at Mrs. Litchfield's farewell Benefit (though their relationship survived – two years later he went down to Gravesend to play for her Benefit there) and on 16 April 1807 he was drunk as Sir Pertinax.[7] Harris seems to have accepted the situation philosophically. On one occasion he was heard to say:

If Cooke don't get drunk oftener than once a month, the odd lapse will do no harm; for when he is *not* inebriated, the audience will not only give him credit for his excellent acting, but they will applaud him for a negative virtue: "Only see," they'll cry, "how very *sober* he is!" a sort of commendation which a really praiseworthy actor would never aspire to be entitled to.[8]

Kemble did not have that kind of relaxed detachment.

Michael Kelly was writing the music for Dimond's piece *Adrian and Orrila*, which was due to have its first performance on Saturday 15 November 1806. That morning Cooke, who was to play the Prince of Altenburg in it, arrived at rehearsal so drunk he could scarcely stand. Both Dimond and Kelly wanted to withdraw the play; Kemble insisted it should be done, whatever the risk. Harris was sent for to decide.

In the interim, Kelly records, Cooke was pouring out a volley of abuse against Kemble, calling him, "Black Jack" &c. all which Kemble bore with Christian patience, and without any reply. At length Mr. Harris, with his faithful ally on all emergencies, the late James Brandon, the box book-keeper, on seeing Cooke's situation, decided that the play should not be performed on that night; but that Kemble should make an apology to the audience, on the plea of Cooke's sudden indisposition; which Kemble refused to do. . . .

Harris declared he would have the play changed. Kemble, on the contrary, was as peremptory to have it performed; and vowed, that if it were changed, under the pretence of Cooke's indisposition, he would go forward to the audience, and inform them of the true cause of their disappointment.

Harris said, " Mr. Kemble, don't talk to me in this manner. I am chief proprietor here, and will have whatever orders I give, obeyed."

I shall always remember Kemble's countenance, when, with the greatest calmness, he replied:-

"Sir, – you are a proprietor – so am I. I borrowed a sum of money to come into this property. How am I to repay those who lent me that money, if you, from ill-placed lenity towards an individual, who is repeatedly from intoxication disappointing the public, choose to risk the dilapidation of the Theatre, and thereby cause my ruin? By Heavens, I swear, the play shall be acted."

Words were getting to a very high pitch, when Brandon coaxed Cooke into his house, put him to bed, and applied napkins, steeped in cold water, to his head, in the hopes of sobering him. He slept from twelve till five o'clock, when he took some very strong coffee, which brought him to his senses, and he consented to play the part; and considering all circumstances, I was struck with astonishment to see how finely he acted it.[9]

He played it another ten times that season.

It is easy to understand and sympathise with Kemble's predicament; it is equally easy to see how Kemble's rigidity and humourlessness would irritate and provoke a man like Cooke. They were unfortunately like oil and water, and their association could never prosper.

Yet Kelly, immediately after recording that incident, notes a delightful evening that he and Mrs. Crouch spent with Cooke when the latter was acting in Brighton on one occasion, and how impressed they were by his affability, intelligence and good nature; and recalls that on one evening in the Green-room of the rebuilt Covent Garden, during the O.P. riots, when attacks were being made on Kemble both as a Manager and an Actor, he asked Cooke if he agreed with the assertions being made that Kemble was an indifferent actor.

No, Sir, he replied; I think him a very great one; and those who say the contrary are envious men, and not worthy, as actors, to wipe his shoes.[10]

Whatever he might dislike about the man, or disagree with his interpretations or attitudes, Cooke when sober was fair minded and able to be objective. It was an objectivity that stayed firmly this side of idolatry, however. There is a tantalising reference in one of his journals that Dunlap reprints to his reading the morning papers, and noting in the *Post* a paragraph of what he calls "theatrical blasphemy". No more. But a glance at the newspaper of the appropriate date reveals the following sentence in a review of Kemble's recent performance as Prospero:

Unimpassioned as the character of *Prospero* is, yet so much interest is thrown into it by the talents of Mr. KEMBLE, that the *Tempest* will owe its celebrity to *his*, rather than to SHAKESPEARE's magic.[11]

Indeed, yes, one sees Cooke's point.

But though Cooke still had value to the company, his antics inevitably led to a decline in his status as the years went by. In Kemble's first season, apart from Kemble himself and Lewis, Cooke with his 14 guineas was the highest paid member of the company, Munden, Fawcett and Charles Kemble coming next with £14 (£5-8 being the average). By 1806-7 Cooke was still on £14, but Munden, Fawcett and Charles Kemble had gone up to £17, Miss Smith was getting £19, and Incledon had joined Lewis at £20.[12] His Benefit in 1804 brought in only £215.18.0. – slightly less than the previous season; and in the two following years he did not take Benefits. In 1807 he tried again, reviving his Lear for the first time, and this brought in a house of £370, a considerable improvement – though compared with Munden's £603 of the same year, and others in the £500 range it must still have been a disappointment to him. But he had no cause for complaint. If he treated his audience in a cavalier fashion, he could hardly expect their patronage. They were still prepared to risk his non-appearance on a normal night, for the sake of his performance in one of his major roles; but on a Benefit night they were not prepared to encourage him in unprofessional behaviour.[13]

The performances which continued to draw audiences throughout his ten years at Covent Garden remained the same as those in which he had his initial success (the figures in parenthesis indicate the total number of performances he gave during the decade) – Sir Pertinax MacSycophant (89), Richard III (77), Sir Archy MacSarcasm (48), Iago (44), Shylock (42), Falstaff (34) and Kitely (31). Stukely, too, (20) was a fairly regular choice; Sir Giles Overreach (13) turns up in most seasons, but only in one or two performances – it seems to have been connoisseurs' enjoyment rather than a popular success.[14]

Hamlet, The Stranger, Jaques, Zanga, Cato, he never played again after Kemble's arrival; Macbeth and Lear he had to abandon to his rival (except for the 1806–7 season, when he was allowed to give two performances of each, with Mrs. Siddons playing Lady Macbeth and Miss Smith Cordelia).[15] In that same season he played Prospero once, and for two seasons he played a few evenings as Iachimo. Glenalvon in *Douglas*, Pierre in *Venice Preserved* appear from time to time over the years. But his basic classical repertory was very much a restricted one.

He was not often called upon in the new plays – to his relief, doubtless, for his journals indicate the low opinion he had of current playwriting. In 1804–5 he gave 20 performances as Lord Avondale in Morton's *The School of Reform*, and 17 as Lavensforth in Mrs. Inchbald's *To Marry or Not to Marry*. The only other new role he played for any length of time was the Prince of Altenburg, which we have already noted.

From time to time there were breaks in the theatrical routine other than those Cooke provoked himself. In the 1804–5 season London succumbed to an attack of theatrical hysteria over the visit of the eleven-year-old W. H. Betty – at Covent Garden billed as "The Boy Wonder", at Drury Lane as "The Young Roscius", and the theatres were crammed to the doors for his performances. At Covent Garden Kemble and Mrs. Siddons prudently avoided performing while the theatrical comet flared, but Cooke found himself supporting him, and played Glenalvon to his Douglas eight times, a duty he can hardly have relished. In that same season there was a violent uproar in the theatre one evening when a disagreement between Braham, the singer, and Kemble, erupted in public.   Both addressed the audience, and cheers and counter-cheers held up the performance till after 8.30, after which Braham left the company and the dispute continued in the newspapers. In June 1807 Brandon's Benefit was sadly truncated when Kemble himself did not play as announced in *Jane Shore*, his substitute was unsatisfactory, Miss Smith had hysterics, and the bulk of the third and fourth acts had to be omitted; and there were disturbances from the audience side of the curtain from time to time.[16] These, in which Cooke was in no way concerned, should be borne in mind when trying to put his own escapades into perspective.

His private life during these London years was as paradoxical as his professional activities. We find him spending evenings of intellectual argument with Godwin and Holcroft, relaxing at the Sans Pareil and Astley's Olympic Pavilion, spending a pleasant day in Chelsea with the Davenport family, or a quiet day at home reading; sitting for his portrait to de Wilde and Drummond, walking in St. James' Park, watching Lord Nelson's funeral. We also find him interrupting a stranger's conversation in a tavern, calling him a damned liar, being knocked down for his pains, and then trying to challenge him to a duel. It is the mixture we have by now come to expect.[17]

Each summer when his duties were over in London he took to the road again for anything up to three months, and his progresses are reflected in the provincial playbills and newspapers, and occasional reports in the *Monthly Mirror* and elsewhere. In 1804 he spent a profitable fortnight in Birmingham, under M'Cready, supported in his usual roles by Mrs. Litchfield and Miss Smith; and then went on to Northern Ireland for a week in Londonderry and three weeks in Belfast under Atkins. In 1805 he again started off in late June and early July with five popular nights for M'Cready in Birmingham, then went on to Ward and Bellamy in Manchester for a fortnight, returning to Birmingham for another seven performances in late August and early September. According to his own recollection he also played in Stroud and Lichfield that summer, possibly between Manchester and the return to Birmingham.[18]

In the summer of 1806 he was a worried man. In late March and April he had had leave of absence to go down to Bath (the recently opened Theatre Royal in Beauford Square) and Bristol, and there he had had a splendid reception. He played for thirteen nights – Richard, Sir Pertinax, Macbeth, Shylock, Sir Archy and Sir Giles – and the theatres were crowded and the audiences delighted, as the pages of the local newspapers make abundantly clear. He had contracted for £20 a night (the fee Mrs. Siddons received for her performances in Covent Garden) but the managers were so delighted with the response that they gave him £300. But after his final performance in Bath on 17 April, something went wrong. He was due back at Covent Garden on Monday the 21st, where a bill had gone out announcing him as Stukely with Mrs. Siddons. But he did not return. Among the Harvard papers there is a tantalising fragment of a memorandum – "Remember Sunday the 20th April 1806, at Bath"; and Cooke recalled later that he had delayed nine days at Marlborough on the return journey, so that when he did arrive back at the beginning of May he had missed the allocation of Benefit nights; once again, a theatrical triumph had ended in a shambles.[19]

He could hardly have timed it worse, for his contract with Harris was due to end this season. On 4 June, he sat down to contemplate the future, both immediate and long term. He wrote a series of questions and answers, three of which are especially significant.

... 2. How to avoid contracting further debt in my present residence, and the speediest means of leaving it?

By leaving it, at the latest on Thursday morning, the 12th and leaving all my property, but what is absolutely necessary, as security for my debt.

... 6. How to come to some explanation and future determination respecting Covent-garden?

By writing to Mr. Harris, on, or before the day of my departure, being very plain and explicit, and abiding by his determination.

7. How to lay down a plan for the future, as far as foresight can enable me to judge?

By returning to Covent-garden next season, if eligible & possible; if not, from the time I commence in Ireland, to endeavour to form engagements at Edinburgh, Bath and Bristol, Manchester, &c. and for one year from next September, & prior to the expiration of it, to apply for a situation at Drury-lane. Industry and Prudence must be the basis of my conduct.[20]

To be unable to pay his lodgings bill after just earning £300! And for Cooke of all people to be planning a life of industry and prudence for the future! There must have been laughter in the Elysian Fields.

In the event, he left Aldersgate Street on June 11th with Rock, a fellow member of the Covent Garden company, who was a leading actor in the summer with Manager Jackson at Glasgow and Edinburgh, and soon to become his partner in management. They had an eventful journey of missed connections and catchings up by postchaise and gig, but eventually reached Glasgow, where Cooke played for a fortnight at the new Queen Street theatre,[21] before going on to Dublin for an engagement under Jones; notable dramatically for one unusual addition to his usual run of parts – Ventidius in Dryden's *All for Love*, to the Mark Antony of Holman, whose benefit it was. As, so far as we know, he had never played it before, one wonders what kind of a performance he produced; in his younger days he had the reputation of being a correct and quick study, but at the age of fifty he might expect to find learning a little more slow. His season ended on 6 August. By the 18th he was opening in Liverpool as Richard III; he was to remain there until 11 September before returning to London.[22] Projected engagements in Sheffield and Birmingham seem to have disappeared en route.

In Liverpool Cooke gave thirteen performances in three weeks, plus an additional performance of his own, which is worth recording, because in the sequel it reveals so clearly the attitude of his provincial audiences to him. On 28 August he played Richard for the second time with an alcohol content high enough to interfere considerably with the quality of his performance. Of what happened then we have no direct contemporary account, but it may well have been the occasion that gave rise to the story so frequently told about him in Liverpool in later years. Mrs. Mathews' version of it was that the audience began to object audibly, which in turn roused Cooke's wrath, and

stepping forward to the stage lamps, with his powerful brow contracted with disdain, he addressed his reprovers in the following pithy sentence:–

"What! do you hiss me? – hiss George Frederick Cooke? – you contemptible money–getters! you shall never again have the *honour* of hissing me! Farewell! *I* banish *you*!" And concentrating into one vast heap all the malice of his offended feelings, he added, after a pause of intense meaning, "*There is not a brick in your dirty town but what is cemented by the blood of a negro!*"

He then left the stage.

It is clear from the *Liverpool Chronicle's* account of what followed on 1 September that something of this sort must have happened.

The theatre was thronged on Monday evening, to witness the *fracas* which was expected to succeed the appearance of Cooke, after the *symptoms* of a *falling sickness* which he had shewn the preceding night of his appearance in Richard. After some bustle, Cooke came forward, apparently with considerable agitation, but cheered by incessant peals of applause, he soon displayed his usual self-possession ... he addressed the house nearly in the words we shall give: His manner was singularly impressive, and the feeling he exhibited throughout the whole of what he said, proved that there was more of the *man* than the *actor* in it.

"*Ladies and Gentlemen*"

"When last I had the honour to appear before you, I undertook a part which I did at the time consider myself fully equal to: It was your pleasure to think differently, and to that decision I bowed (*loud applause*). The explanation I then attempted to give was not such as I wished; and I now declare, by my most sacred oath, that the meaning it conveyed was directly the reverse of what I intended. (loud and reiterated applause.) To insult an audience whose chearing approbation I had so often felt with grateful pride, was as distant from my intention, as it could possibly be from my interest or duty; and I again assure you, that the sentiment which I most unhappily conveyed, was the very reverse of what I felt. (*thunders of applause, and a cry of enough! enough!*) With the Managers of this Theatre I have an engagement to fulfil, and if I be permitted to go through with it, it shall be my utmost care, as often as I appear before you, to undo even what may be regarded as the appearance of having given just cause of offence." (*three distinct peals of applause*)

Mr. Cooke afterwards performed with unequalled excellence, the part of *Sir Archy MacSarcasm* in Macklin's fine little comedy of *Love à la Mode*. We never saw him so animated, so easy, or so studious to please. His success was complete, and we hope from the feeling which he evidently discovered, that he will not abuse so distinguished a proof of indulgence and partiality. With the habits of his private life we have nothing to do, so far as they do not interfere with his public engagements; but what he undertakes to do, he should not voluntarily disqualify himself from performing ...

With all Cooke's imperfections he is a great man, and we would rather forgive him than lose him. ....[23]

It is difficult to know which to admire the most – Cooke's practised skill in extricating himself from an awkward situation or the magnanimity with which it was greeted; but clearly respect for his audience was no longer any kind of inhibiting factor to him, when the bottle began to circulate, and the next such occasion could only be a matter of when, not if.

After the *Adrian and Orrila* affair on his return to London, he steadied up for a while; Harris must have renewed his contract, though under what terms does not appear, and he spent a quiet and hardworking winter, the best in London for several seasons. In March he payed a fleeting visit to Shatford's playhouse in Salisbury[24] and at the end of the season prepared for another extended tour in the northwest and Scotland. Here things began to go wrong again.

For the last week of their season in Manchester, Ward and Young (Charles Mayne Young had bought Bellamy's share in the management in 1805) announced Cooke as Richard, Sir Pertinax, Shylock, Sir Archy and Iago, and produced playbills for the first two performances on 16 and 17 June. Cooke never arrived, and they had to announce the closure of the theatre a week early.[25] Cooke's own records say that he began his summer at Glasgow, which indeed he did. What he does not say is that he arrived late, for Jackson and Rock had announced him as Richard for Monday 29 June, but he did not in fact play it until 10 July, when they announced that he had been attacked by a severe illness, but was now recovered and arrived.[26] From then on things seemed to go normally, first in Glasgow and then Edinburgh; he played the usual roles, with Miss Smith as his leading lady for this engagement − she was his Portia and Lady Macbeth, he played Glenalvon to her Lady Randolph − and he stayed with Rock, presumably so that the manager could keep an eye on him. He ended in Edinburgh on Tuesday, 4 August, though the company still played on till the end of the week. Then he took an engagement that took him for six nights back to Berwick-on-Tweed, where he had lived as a boy; he was going back in very different circumstances, and one suspects that his prime motive was sentimental, for he admits that he only received £90 of the £180 he had originally contracted for.[27] He finished there on August 17; four days later in Liverpool the managers were announcing that he would open on August 24 as Richard. A week should have been plenty of time to cross the Pennines, but in the event a special broadsheet had to be printed:

Theatre Royal. Half past 4 o'clock
The Managers most respectfully acquaint the public, that having a few days since received a letter informing them that Mr. COOKE was on his Journey to Liveerpool, they announced his first appearance for this evening; but in consequence of his non-arrival (the cause of which is unknown to them) Mr. GRANT has, with great readiness, to prevent further disappointment, kindly undertaken to perform the part . . .[28]

The cause is unknown to us, too. He disappeared completely until October, when the *Monthly Mirror* was reporting him to be "in durance vile" in Kendal.

II

In fact, it proved to be Appleby, and he was to be held there until the end of December 1807. What seems to have happened was this. When Cooke did not turn up in Manchester, Ward and Young had to end their season prematurely and must have suffered a financial loss. Moreover it appears that they had made an advance payment to Cooke. They therefore sued and obtained judgment for the return of this. Presumably the legal officers charged with serving the demand on him, located him somewhere in the route across the Pennines as he was making his way to Liverpool, and when he could not pay, held him in Appleby until he could arrange for the money to be made available. There he remained for nearly three months, until at the end of December he obtained his release and went north again to Edinburgh and Glasgow to join Rock's company, where he spent the first two months of 1808, presumably working off money advanced to him by Rock to enable him to pay his debt.[29]

The Appleby period is an important and revealing one, for to help pass the time during a period of enforced solitude, he kept not only his fullest journal so far, but also employed some of his time in writing up from memory the Chronicle of his life up to that time, which served Dunlap as the major source for his account of Cooke's early years, and from which we have quoted from time to time. It provides us with some valuable information; but it is important to note that, like the journal, it is selective. What Cooke does not wish to recall he omits; and since he is writing largely without access to documentary material, his dates are not always precise or accurate when compared with external evidence. We have taken account of this earlier in these pages.

Having said that, it must also be admitted that a good deal of it is tedious – excerpts or abstracts of what he has been reading not always particularly interesting or illuminating, but written down simply, one suspects, to pass the time and keep his mind occupied with some kind of activity. Dunlap rightly omitted this element from the long extracts which he reprinted from the journal; these begin on November 28, for the commencement of the journal was missing, "it beginning abruptly with a reference to No. 2, which No. 2 is not to be found" says Dunlap. In fact it has survived – perhaps through the accident of not being taken to America with the rest of the papers Cooke had with him in 1810.[30]

It follows the same pattern as the later journal, beginning with a sequence of anecdotes from his reading, sometimes without comment, sometimes with his own reflections. Reading about Mme. de Maintenon sets him thinking.

I much doubt whether the world is right in what they call being in love.

Pure love as I have heard and perhaps read is Friendship, and what we generally call love, Desire. Indeed I have heard it called a coarser name.

Reading David Hume's thoughts on tragedy, and the way in which writers magnify all the experience they describe in order to excite the attention of the reader, leads him to some stringent comments on the editors of the London newspapers. The anecdote of Dr. Johnson's inattentiveness during a violin recital and a friend's comment on how difficult was the piece – "Difficult sir, do you call it?" replied the Doctor. "I only know that I wish it was impossible." – reveals that Cooke, too, lacked an ear for music.

I am proud to be of the doctor's opinion. I would as soon be obliged to turn my eyes from an elegant couple while moving in a minuet to behold a man or a monkey vaulting upon a tight-rope, as to have my ears so tortured.

Reading some of Lord Chesterfield's essays makes him think of

the late Mr. Boswell, who in his Life of Johnson fatigued his readers with a large quarto when a moderate octavo or middle-sized twelve would have answered the purpose much better. However among the chaff there is some wheat ... Although I do not agree entirely with Dr. Johnson that Lord Chesterfield's writings inculcate the morals of a whore and the manners of a dancing master, yet his whole aim and tendency is to recommend and strongly persuade the practice of insincerity and discrimination. A man who would endeavour to form himself exactly upon Lord Chesterfield's precepts would be highly disagreeable to any and every company he chanced to mingle with.

He remembers F. E. Jones and some of the Dublin players, especially Philip Lamash ("in a certain department of comedy I never saw him exceeded by any actor I remember"); he unpacks his trunk and airs and washes some of his costumes. He waits for his writing desk to arrive; when it does it has been badly damaged in transit. He waits anxiously for replies to his letters – the weather is wild and the mail delayed – and recalls the letters he has never answered through procrastination, until it was too late to answer them at all. He reflects acidly on Appleby and the limited resources of local society.

I have had it hinted to me that I might receive the visits of some gentlemen if I were so inclined, but this I declined. Doubtless there are many worthy men round about, but the *gentlemen* of a place like this are generally comprised in the parson or parsons, the apothecary, and the attorney, a supervisor of the excise, if one is resident, and should a justice of the peace be added, the circle is deemed great. The general conversation of these gentlemen may be classed thus – the clergyman is either political or an adept in rural sports or both. Every sentence he utters belongs to one or the other. Not a word of divinity, and therein perhaps he is right. Should the church be at all mentioned, it is only to dwell upon its privileges and authority. The apothecary gives you what little chat he may have heard in his round, and the scandal of the whole county. The attorney, if the bent of his discourse be rightly taken, understands the whole science of the law, tells how such a cause was lost, and how it might have been gained, mentions with an air of superiority the eminent counsel he is acquainted with, whom he has *seen* at the assizes, and to some of whom perhaps he has presented a brief. What the Supervisor says, who is also a man of consequence, is complimentary to those present, and so truly orthodox is he in his opinion of the constitution of his country, no doubt justly asserting the king can do no wrong, he places his *ministers* in the same irresponsible situation. The justice, if he attends to anything but his glass and his pipe talks of Acts of Parliament and statutes at large, and county or turnpike meetings where he thought himself a great man. These and anecdotes of the Quarter Sessions, and toasting the county and Borough members, at least one *half* of them, fill up his share of the conversation. "And thus he plays his part". To all these the stranger must be little more than a listener, each of the party endeavouring to exalt himself in his opinion, and if he has an opportunity of speaking, it must be merely to answer a number of questions, most of which proceed either from curiosity or ill-breeding.

The memory of many tedious evenings spent in provincial society must be distilled in that paragraph.

But all the time he was fighting illness, worry about his situation which he would not write about except in the most indirect and guarded terms, and reflections on himself.

These seasons of indolence and idleness which occur all too often in the lives of those that do not attend to order and act upon a plan are most dangerous moments. A mind unhappy in its situation and clinging to every object which can occupy or amuse it is then apt to throw itself into the arms of every vice and folly . . . About 5 drank tea. The weather continues tempestuous. The time for the mail arriving from London here is before noon. It arrived between 5 and 6 this evening. Between tea and supper, which was about 9, the evening passed dull and stupid, thoughts unsteady, confused, and perplexed. Add to this indisposition. I rescued a short space of time before supper by reading the story of LeFevre, but could not bring my mind to anything else. Mine host beguiled a few moments by a little commonplace chit-chat. He recommended medical advice, but I hope to do without it. A short portion of the fleeting moments spent in writing. I was surprized on Thursday morning early by the sound of a drum and learnt from mine host it is an old man who during part of the winter torments parchment a little before six in the morning to awaken those who begin their daily occupations at that hour. Any circumstance, however trivial, serves for an anecdote from a place like this.[31]

That was one of the darker hours, of which there were not a few during those ten weeks. By early December even the movements of a fly became an obsession. He watched it on Friday, again on Saturday, and by Sunday –

Found the poor fly again (I am almost sure it is the same) struggling in a basin of water. I extricated the benumbed insect.

And his nights were wakeful and disturbed.

I remember hearing a reverend gentleman of Newcastle, whose death I recorded last Thursday, say, that when a person, on being asked what he was thinking of, replied nothing, he was thinking of a multitude of things, but not any thing distinctly. I have often experienced the remark to be just, and last night was an additional proof of it. I tried to fix my thoughts but in vain. The body would feel a distaste, sometimes approaching to disgust, at being long supplied with the same kind of food, and nothing but the craving of hunger would enable it to endure it. The mind is much in the same state when forced to recur over and over again to the same mental repast, particularly if scantily supplied. If I remember right, Colley Cibber said he could employ his thoughts satisfactorily for six hours; but were those six hours to be repeated for six days successively, to the most acute and distinct thinker (unless upon some particular or important object) instead of a relaxation or amusement, I think it would rather be a painful endurance.[32]

By 19th December his endurance was being stretched to its limit.

A clear, pleasant, frosty day. Indisposed all the morning, with a disagreeable sensation in my head, and a sickly affection at my stomach.

The mind partakes of the body's uneasiness. Dined between one and two: appetite small. For these ten weeks past, I have neither tasted pork, ham, bacon, poultry, fish eggs, puddings or game, one partridge excepted. Except my provisions being fresh, I have lived as if at sea. The bread, coals, and candles, are not good, and the wine I have drank – I wish it had been better. Tea between five and six. But that the weather was pleasant, this day would have been one of the most wearisome, tedious and heavy I have passed for some time. There were not any letters that demanded an answer, and as for any other writing, my mind was entirely out of tune. Books I had not . . .[33]

But deliverance was on the way. After the following day, the journal breaks off abruptly, presumably because of the arrival of the mail from Glasgow. Agreement had been reached with Rock, and he was able to extricate himself. Ten days later he was in Glasgow acting Richard III. A new journal recorded "My reception favourable, as usual."[34] He was back in his own world.

Chapter XII

Disenchantment – 1808-1810

He was in Glasgow for four weeks, playing 12 nights and a Benefit, for which he took £182. Towards the end of the month the company moved to Edinburgh, and there he repeated his Glasgow roles, adding one or two more, so that during the five and a half weeks there he gave 20 performances, plus a charity Benefit for the City Workhouse, and his own night which brought him £205. His roles were the usual ones, though for his Benefits he played comedy rather than one of his heavier parts – Lord Townly in Glasgow, and Joseph Surface in Edinburgh. In Edinburgh also he produced *Every Man in his Humour* which was apparently unknown both to the city and the company. He marked up the prompt book, and the play had five rehearsals; but when it did appear it proved a disappointment. "I believe I never acted it worse," he wrote. "The greater part of it was *caviare* to the actors as well as the audience."

His brief journal for this period reveals him being more receptive to Edinburgh society than to that of Appleby. He dined out regularly, and even went to a concert at Corri's rooms, where he listened to young Master Gattie from London playing a violin concerto. One of the regular guests at these social evenings in the particular circle in which he was moving was a Miss Lambe, and their acquaintance ripened.

Perhaps the oddest element of these two short seasons was that a leading member of the company was the young Charles Mayne Young – who was also one of the partners in management whom Cooke had let down so badly in Manchester six months before. What their relation was at this time we cannot help wondering; but there is no evidence either way. All that we can say is that publicly they worked together – in *Othello* and *Douglas*, for instance. Whether they were on speaking terms privately we can only guess.[1]

Uncomfortable engagement or not, it served its purpose. It enabled Cooke to extricate himself from the law, and make his way back to London to make his peace with Thomas Harris and John Kemble, if he could. At four in the afternoon of Friday March 4 he left Edinburgh in the mail coach; on the following Tuesday evening he was in Leicester Square, and two days later

> On Thursday the 10th I made my re-appearance at the Theatre-Royal Covent-garden, in Sir Pertinax, to the greatest money-house, one excepted, ever known in the theatre. Never was a performer received in a more gratifying or flattering manner.[2]

He had made his peace – in the way that pleased Harris most.

The independent evidence confirms Cooke's own record. "Such a house has not been seen since the *little hour* of *Little Betty*" said the *Monthly Mirror*, and the *Chronicle* and the *Post* agreed both about his reception and his performance. . . . "Never did he acquit himself with greater ability or more happy effect, than on this occasion," wrote the latter. . . . "COOKE was, in the *sober* and proper sense, perfectly himself; and when so, the stage at present certainly furnishes no parallel to him."[3]

Harris' commercial judgment had indeed been shrewd, felt the *Mirror*, quoting a story (whether fact or rumour we cannot now know) that Sheridan had, while Cooke was in detention, offered Harris a premium to allow him to extricate Cooke and get him to play a certain number of nights at Drury Lane; a request which Harris had prudently refused, knowing that Cooke's absence would increase his drawing power when he did eventually return. And as Cooke appeared once more in all his favourite characters, the box office was indeed crowded and the audiences overflowed. Again, it was probably not good for Cooke – he was realising what he could get away with. Munden recalled a performance of Richard at this time in which Cooke was not answering his helm very effectively, but the audience was unaware; they,

> far from assigning the true cause, discovered, in each lapse of memory, a studied pause; and in every stagger, a new point.[4]

But, on the whole he behaved himself reasonably well. His Benefit was a disappointment, though why on earth he chose to take it playing Catarach in Colman's *Bonduca*, a play nobody knew or cared about, passes comprehension. For Charles Kemble's Benefit he played Kent to John Philip's Lear, for the first time, and gave three more performances before the end of the season. And in June, when the veteran Mrs. Mattocks took her last benefit as Flora in *The Wonder*, and bade farewell to the stage, Cooke supported her, playing for the first time in London, Don Felix, the jealous lover, a part which years before he had watched Garrick perform. The memory must have been in his mind, for he also spoke Garrick's

Shakespeare Ode that evening. When Mrs. Mattocks had first appeared at Covent Garden in 1761, Garrick had still fifteen more years left of his reign at the other house; and she was in the cast of *Midas* when Cooke in his teens had paid his first visit to Covent Garden in 1771. Their paths had crossed many times since then, both in the provinces and London, and her going was the end of a chapter for him, as well as for the theatre.[5]

With June came the preparations for another summer tour. He began down in the west country again, where he had a successful season for Dimond in Bath and Bristol from 11–25 June; then on to Manchester, where M'Cready was now in management at the new Theatre Royal in Fountain street, opened the previous year after the end of the Ward–Young regime at the old theatre. After a fortnight in Manchester M'Cready took him on to Newcastle, which theatre he had also taken over from Stephen Kemble. There, after a triumphant opening on the 18th, Cooke was "taken violently ill" the following morning, and was out of circulation for a week, attended by two local doctors. The local paper attributed his illness to over-exertion; by now we may be less sanguine about that.[6]. However, when recovered, he extended his season for a week, then went down to York for four nights with Tate Wilkinson's son, and then back north to Edinburgh for the last week of August. He was expected in Liverpool on 12 September, but a similarly worded notice to that of the previous year had to be published in the end – he never arrived.[7]

He did not appear again in London until the beginning of October, and September remains an obstinate blank. The reason was that he was again getting married. One of the ladies he had met socially in Edinburgh earlier in the year, as we have noted, was a Miss Lambe; the acquaintance must have been resumed and have ripened in August, for on 21 September 1808, in St. Andrew's Church, Edinburgh, he was married to Miss Sarah Harvey Lambe, and when he returned to London she went with him – the latest of the line of Mrs. Cookes.[8] We know almost nothing of her, except that the marriage lasted for all practical purposes a little less than nine months. We cannot attempt to assess the motives behind the affair, though from Cooke's point of view it may be significant that, like the marriage to Alicia Daniels, it followed close upon a major crisis in his life; perhaps again he was hoping that a wife would help him to keep himself in order. But the dice were loaded against them. After a winter in London he took her home to Newark in February, and she never returned. That he was heavily in debt still in various quarters (including to Harris) seems fairly certain; and unless she had money of her own they must soon have found the flaws in the old saying that two can live as cheaply as one. In January her mother sent them a basket containing a leg of mutton and two fowls; in his journal Cooke refers to it grandiloquently as "carrying coals to Newcastle," but it may have been welcome all the same, for the same notes show him working over his accounts, and record sleepless nights and harrassed feelings.

It was a difficult winter professionally, too. By the time the Cookes arrived in London, disaster had already struck the Covent Garden company. Kemble had opened the season on 12 September with *Macbeth*; after the performance of *Pizarro* on the 19th, Brandon, the Box Book-keeper, made his usual tour round the theatre to see that all was well, and then went to bed. By 4 a.m. the theatre was burning fiercely, and by daylight the whole building, scenery and costumes and the priceless contents of its library and manuscript collections had disappeared in smoke and flame.[9]

The management reorganised quickly when they had got over the shock, and while plans for rebuilding were set in hand, the company moved over to the Haymarket, first to the cavernous acoustics of the Opera House at the King's Theatre, where they re-opened on the 26th, and subsequently in early December to the kindlier play house atmosphere of the Theatre Royal. It was at the King's Theatre that Cooke made his first appearance that season as Sir Pertinax on October 13.[10] There, and at the Theatre Royal, he went through his usual round of parts; taking time off in late November and early December for another popular visit to Bath and Bristol, where to his usual half-dozen roles he added King Lear. Doubtless he needed the money, though a great deal of his provincial gains must have been swallowed up in living and travelling expenses, and Cooke was no great economiser in these matters.[11]

Back in London he had an accidental fall on Christmas Day – genuine enough, though it may have been alcoholically provoked – that bruised him badly and confined him to his room for a fortnight. As a result he started another journal on January 1 – and it lasted almost to the end of the month – about average for him, now. Towards the end of February he left London again, with Harris' permission, this time with Mrs. Cooke bound for Newark, where they arrived on the 23rd. The following day he left alone, for Doncaster, and went on to Hull and York, where he played a short season for Wilkinson, then returned to London, again alone. Whether Mrs. Cooke had gone back to her parents for a holiday, from which she did not return, or whether they had agreed to separate, we do not know; but the fact that he spent some time in April making an inventory of household furniture, and refusing to sign a draft deed, may suggest the latter.[12] His one consolation during this difficult period seems to have been his copy of the 1685 folio Shakespeare, in which he was reading a great deal.

For his own Benefit that season on May 1 he played Sir Giles and, for the first time in London, John Cockle, the sturdy, rough, but good-hearted miller in *The King and the Miller of Mansfield*; for the Charles Kembles he played Don Felix once again. Over the last weekend in May he paid a flying visit to Maxfield's company in Chichester and Portsmouth, where he played Shylock and Sir Archy; giving in Chichester the performance of Shylock that sixty five years later Lord William Pitt Lennox was to recreate so vividly in his *Memoirs*. Elevated by a good dinner at the Dolphin, Cooke in the fourth act managed almost to sever his thumb on the knife he was whetting for Antonio, and the play had to be held up while he received medical treatment. As the doctor involved was the Lennox family physician, the boy was later taken to see Cooke in the Manager's box over the prompt-side stage door, which was being used as the star dressing room, and the meeting with the actor made an impression on the young boy that he was never to forget.[13]

This was in effect the beginning of his summer tour. By June 3 he had actually arrived in Liverpool, and Lewis and Knight, the managers, triumphantly issued a notice to that effect. Perhaps his previous absences had whetted appetites in Liverpool as well as London; at any rate, business was so splendid that at the end of the three weeks in addition to his fee and benefit, the managers presented him with a pair of silver cups. One hopes that the *double-entendre* was intended.[14]

Taking no chances, M'Cready collected Cooke personally in Liverpool and took him on to Manchester for his brief season there; there, too, Rock picked him up to convey him safely to Edinburgh. Though still a highly marketable commodity, the managers were realising that Cooke would have to be supervised like the wayward creature he now was.

He played in Edinburgh from 3 July to 9 August, adding to his usual repertoire another of his Scottish characters, Colin McLeod in Cumberland's *The Fashionable Lover* (which he had already tried out both in Bath and Liverpool), and reviving, for the first time in Edinburgh for some thirty years, Addison's *Cato*. It was a success of esteem, not popularity; still, "The Principal part of the house was full". [15] Cooke was to have performed Sir Pertinax again on the 10th, but he was indisposed, and his engagement disintegrated; as indeed did the Edinburgh company. Henry Siddons took over the management of it, but for the next three years removed his operations to the Circus in Leith Walk, and the theatre in Shakespeare Square remained dark.

Recovered by the 15th, Cooke set off with one of the young lady members of the company for his first working visit to Perth. There, in a theatre in the Glovers' Hall, which he found tolerably fitted up, but dirty and inconvenient as well as small (£47 was "a great house"), he played five nights, finding the audiences not very lively, but enjoying the countryside and the situation.[16] After the engagement he set off to return to Liverpool, but another bad fall when he was only twenty miles away from Edinburgh caused him to change his plans once more, and return to the Scottish capital, where he passed the next fortnight until he had to return to London for the opening of the newly rebuilt Covent Garden.

That should have been a splendid occasion. In fact it saw the beginning of the longest period of rioting the London theatre has ever known, and it was not until the end of the year that the atmosphere began to return to normal, and the theatre could be said to be properly open. The O.P. Riots as they were called have been sufficiently written about, and only the barest outline is relevant here. With the rebuilding the management took the opportunity to up-grade certain parts of the house, converting part of the gallery into boxes, and raising the prices of boxes and pit. This the audience decided that it would not accept (there was much talk of the private fortunes Kemble and Mrs. Siddons had been building up, and the exorbitant fees to be paid to foreign artists like Mme. Catalani), and it determined that no performance should be allowed to be gone through peacefully until the prices had been reduced. Organised chaos then ensued. For a time the theatre was closed while an independent committee examined the accounts, and eventually pronounced the new prices fair and reasonable; this took only a little of the steam out of the protest – it was felt that the Committee had been misled. Though programmes were presented, often large parts of them could not be heard; and though the objectors often took pains to make it clear that they were not objecting to individual actors (Cooke among them) they would not have Kemble on the stage. Eventually reason and compromise prevailed; in mid-December the proprietors announced that the pit prices would be reduced from 4s. to 3s.6d., and that in the next season the number of boxes would be reduced; Kemble attended a dinner with the principal objectors, and at last he was able to appear in his new theatre.[17]

But for the company, struggling against a situation that was none of their making, those three months must have been miserable indeed. Cooke escaped when when he could. For four days in early October he played for M'Cready in Leicester; later that month he made a hurried visit to Birmingham, now being managed by the younger John Boles Watson ("Young Gag" as he calls him), and played three nights there – finding Leicester more pleasant and profitable than Birmingham. In early December he played two nights in Portsmouth, and found "the receipts great".[18]

Hardly had his professional circumstances returned to normal in London, however, than Cooke was putting on another of his own special performances. Down to play Horatius in *The Roman Father* on December 26,

On this night Cooke was completely intoxicated – he was incapable of speaking and was led off amidst tumultuous disapprobation,

recorded the annotator of the theatre playbills. Young apologised for him, and Egerton read the part. Two days later, when he had been announced for Shylock he did not arrive, and Egerton was announced as substitute. What followed almost put the clock back to the O.P. riots, and was vividly described in the next day's *Morning Post*.

The Play began, but not a syllable could be heard. The noises were not inferior to those which marked the opening of the Theatre. – "Send on COOKE" – and "Let KEMBLE or YOUNG take the character," resounded from all parts of the Theatre. The utmost confusion and up-roar prevailed during the first two scenes; at length, when that in which *Shylock* makes his first appearance was about to open, Mr. C. KEMBLE came forward. He assured the audience that the circumstance which gave them so much displeasure did not originate in any neglect on the part of the Theatre. Mr. COOKE, he said, was really ill. – (Cries of "No doubt; he often is," etc.). As early as twelve o'clock in the day the Prompter waited on him. He then complained of indisposition, but expressed a hope that he should be able to have the honour of appearing before them that evening. They did not know till it was very late that he could not, and, situated as they then were, they thought it would be more respectful to the Public to change one character in *The Merchant of Venice* than to substitute another play. Bills were immediately posted at every entrance of the Theatre to announce the change:– ("No such thing" was here vociferated.)

On this Mr. K. went to the side of the stage, and returned with one of the bills, which he exhibited. He was proceeding to express a hope that they would be satisfied with the arrangement, when a Gentleman called out – "Mr. KEMBLE, is it not convenient for your brother to perform the part?" – Mr. C. KEMBLE replied, that if it were not a character his brother had not performed for some years, he was certain nothing on earth would give him greater pleasure than to come forward in com-pliance with their wishes – (Here he was interrupted by cried of – "Let him come forward, then") – The noise now became so great that Mr. KEMBLE could no longer be heard, and he at length retired.

The audience sang God Save the King and called for music. Murray came back to report that Young was out of town and Kemble not at home. Taylor then proposed that Charles Kemble would read the part, but the audience would have none of it. Finally Taylor announced that Charles Kemble would attempt to *play* the part, and anybody who did not approve

could have his money back. Few went, and after more music while Charles
Kemble changed into costume, the play went on.

The *Morning Chronicle* remarked mildly enough in the circumstances,
that

It was understood that COOKE had declined to appear, fearing to
encounter a storm of popular indignation, which he apprehended in
consequence of the irregularity which prevented him from going
through the character of *Horatius* on Wednesday night. He would,
however, have acted a much wiser part if he had come forward at once,
and made an apology, instead of placing the audience, the proprietors,
and the actors, in one of the most awkward predicaments that ever occurred in a Theatre.[19]

Inevitably the apology had to be made sooner or later; on his re-
appearance as Richard on 8 January he faced the audience, apologised, and
was forgiven.[20] The *Chronicle* describes the scene and his speech fully; the
playbill annotator was more succinct and less gullible.

Before the play commenced [he wrote] Cooke came forward to apologise
for his late offences. When he came to "If you will restore me once more
to the favour I enjoyed, I promise", here he was interrupted by un-
animous applause and retired without completing a promise not likely
to be kept.

About this period of his life, Dunlap several times makes the point that
Cooke was the victim of an unfair campaign against him in the press, and
singles out especially the *Monthly Mirror*, as the chief villain.[21] He may have
gained this impression from Cooke himself, who could well have
developed a persecution feeling to enable him to maintain some of his self-
respect; but a reading through the newspapers and periodicals of the time
does not support the accusation. Certainly they recorded, sometimes with a
joke, his various peccadilloes, but where these occurred in public this was
fair matter for public comment, and Cooke had no-one to blame for it but
himself. When he was the good professional they never hesitated to say so.
As late as March 1808, for instance the *Mirror* was saying of his Shylock:

We discover more qualities in Mr. Cooke, for the just delineation of
his smooth, usurious villainy, and diabolical spirit of revenge, than con-
cur in any other actor now living. In the scene with *Antonio*, where *Shylock*
confesses his hatred to the merchant; in the third act with *Tubal*, where
the conflict of passion arises for his daughter lost, and the hopes of
revenge; and in the trial in the fourth, he was exceedingly great . . .

And over the Horatius affair it let him down very lightly.

> Mr. Cooke was to have performed *Shylock*, but he absented himself, and the consequence was that a most ungenerous feeling pervaded the house against him. We call it *ungenerous*, because Mr. Bull should look at home, and recollect how much he likes to spend a merry Christmas. On the 26th he got drunk and appeared, for which they abused him (and he who abuses a drunken man, abuses an absent man, which is very unfair); now he gets drunk and decently stays away, for which they also abuse him – What at this season of the year can the poor man do? We have seen Mr. Kemble on the stage as intoxicated as we ever saw Mr. Cooke, but it was certainly not when he had to play a part. . . . Everything is good or bad by comparison, and by this test Mr. Cooke has behaved very well. His cups displeased the audience before, and being in them again, he would not trust himself to return.[22]

The satire is affectionate, not savage.

The truth is that Cooke was disenchanted with London, and increasingly disenchanted with himself. And the result was a vicious circle. Because he was not given the respect in London which he felt he deserved he treated his audiences with disrespect; but his increasing unreliability and undependability as a result made it more and more unlikely that he would be given the opportunities to reinstate himself; or that he would be able to take them, even were they given. So, as usual, he ran away.

Whenever he could he disappeared into the provinces, where he could still maintain his greatness; Manchester in late February and March, Warwick in late March and early April – and he was still playing there when he had been billed as Falstaff in London on April 5, so some substitute must have been made then.[23] In his only new part (Henry VIII in Kemble's revival of the play) he was miscast, and had a poor press. He had usually played Wolsey before; to be supporting Kemble in that role must have seemed to him another example of the unfairness of the world.[24] Twice in June he was drunk again, and last minute substitutions had to be made. When he gave his last performance in London as Shylock on 22 June for the Benefit of Mrs. Clarke, the young actress from Manchester whose first performance in London earlier in the season he had introduced by speaking an occasional prologue, no-one knew it was going to be his last performance at Covent Garden, but it must have been clear to his intimates that he was working up for another of his breakdowns.[25]

When he left for his summer campaign to Liverpool, Harris asked Munden, who was also going there, to keep an eye on him, and Munden agreed.[26] But Munden himself was suffering painfully from gout, and was something of a broken reed. Cooke arrived in Liverpool on July 23 as arranged, but too late for the performance of *The Man of the World* which had been announced, and then changed; so his engagement began the following day. From then until August 14, when he took his benefit, bills for a sequence of his familiar parts have survived, and there is no evidence that he did not perform them. Afterwards he went with Stanton to his company in Preston, and there played two nights – Richard and Sir Pertinax. These were the last performances we know of that he was to give in England.[27] For while in Liverpool he had met once again Thomas Cooper, now actor-manager in New York, who had just arrived on a visit in search of talent for the American circuit.

Dunlap devotes two chapters to a long and sometimes detailed account of how Cooper eventually got Cooke to America, an account which he had from Cooper himself.[28] Apart from the fact that he antedates Cooke's arrival in Liverpool by a fortnight, his story ties in with dates and facts we have from other sources. But the tale is coloured both by Cooper's attempt to defend himself against the charge, being widely made in Liverpool and London, that he had induced Cooke to depart by deceit and subterfuge, getting him drunk and aboard ship before he knew what he was doing; and by the good raconteur's technique of emphasis and embroidery to make the story effective. Shorn as far as possible of these elements, and the reconstructed dialogue that went with them, what happened seems to have been approximately this.

On his arrival in Liverpool from North America and Ireland, Cooper saw that Cooke, whom he had met some years before in London, as we have seen, was down to play Richard III, so he attended the performance, and afterwards went round to see him. Cooke did not at first remember him, but Cooper introduced himself, mentioned that he was now in management and in search of talent for the North American circuit, and asked Cooke if he could recommend any performers he might approach. Cooke suggested that Miss Norton might be amenable, and they then discussed financial prospects and the state of drama in America. Before they parted Cooke tentatively suggested that he himself might be interested if the inducement were adequate; he had no engagement, and no great wish to stay in England – quite the contrary.

Cooper departed for London, to brood over the financial aspects, and to consult Dickinson, the Boston manager, who was also over on a visit. From there he wrote to Cooke on August 5 offering him an engagement at 25 guineas a week for ten months to play New York, Boston, Philadelphia and Baltimore, with a benefit at each, 25 cents a mile travelling expenses, and his Atlantic passage paid for. To Cooke in his present position these must have been tempting terms, but with typical reluctance to make an important decision, he put off replying to the letter. In mid-August Cooper looked him up again on his short engagement in Preston with Stanton, but Cooke was in high spirits, and nothing was said. After his two nights there Cooke seems to have decided to abandon his next engagements at Nottingham and Derby, where he was expected on the 20th, sent word to the manager that his health necessitated some sea air, and went off to Blackpool.[29] By September 10 he was back in Liverpool, watching backstage while Cooper gave his performance of Richard III, but still nothing formal seems to have been said, and Cooke disappeared on another drinking bout, which would postpone the need for making a decision. By 16 September the Liverpool deputy manager was reporting that Cooke had gone through £150 of the £300 that he had made by his July-August engagement. Word seems to have got back to London that all was not well, and on the 20th Harris wrote to Cooke to enquire about his return. By this time Cooke was ill and needing medical help, which he seems to have received, and he then moved into an inn behind the Liverpool theatre, preparatory to returning to London. On Sunday September 30 he wrote to Harris:

My dear Sir,
   This morning I received yours of the 20th. Part of my luggage has been in town, I hope, this month past. I have not appeared on any stage since the 7th. From the night I finished my engagement in this town, Tuesday the 14th August, I have only acted five nights. I have been under medical care the greatest part of the time since I returned here, and indeed it was for that purpose I came. Munden, who is recovering from a very severe attack of the gout, requested me to stay a day or two for him. I have done so, and yesterday I paid for both our places on Tuesday morning next, (Sunday coaches being all engaged, and not one going on Monday, the Mail excepted). On Wednesday evening we shall, I trust, reach the Golden Cross . . .[30]

Because within a week of writing that Cooke was on board ship crossing the Atlantic, the letter has been taken as evidence of deliberate duplicity. In fact there is no warrant for such a view. That he was reluctant to return to London is almost certainly true; that he was contemplating another new start in America, but hesitant about it (as he had been in Cork before his departure to London in 1800) and procrastinating about making a decision is equally likely; but he still had both his options open, and even if he did decide to accept Cooper's proposal this did not – so far as he knew at this stage – preclude a return to London to settle up his affairs before leaving. It was, as so often, the responsibility of making a decision from which he was

175

abdicating, until circumstances made the decision for him. As they were shortly to do.

Cooke was still hesitating on the morning of October 2, when he and Munden were due to catch the London coach. Munden, still suffering from gout, made his way with some difficulty to Cooke's lodging. He found him up, and dressed, but sitting at a table with a guttering candle and an empty brandy bottle. To Munden's reminder that they must be up and off for the coach, the only reply was a hiccup and a "You be damned". Knowing his man, Munden clearly felt he was too settled in with the bottle to travel that day, so he departed to take his own place on the coach. Though neither knew it at the time, it was a squalid final farewell between two men who had been friends and close colleagues in the theatre, both in the provinces and London, for over thirty-five years.[31]

Meanwhile Cooper, too, was hesitating to make a formal approach. He had come to the conclusion that any public announcement of an engagement with Cooke, either in Liverpool or London, would bring down such strong pressures on Cooke against it, that he would never have the firmness to leave. So he planned to try and catch Cooke somewhere on the road, persuade him to agree to his proposition, and get him away safely before it became public knowledge. He therefore carefully kept Cooke under observation, either personally, or by proxy. That morning he too visited Cooke, found him well set with his cronies, and felt there was no danger of his leaving that day; to his surprise, however, later in the afternoon word was brought to him that Cooke had departed for London in a post-chaise. So Cooper set off on horseback in pursuit.

He overtook him north of Prescot, and when Cooke stopped his chaise to give a lift to an old woman he saw tiredly trudging along the road, Cooper approached him and put the direct question – would he go to America?

Cooke then agreed. He would go to London first, settle some business there, play a farewell night, and then he would be happy to be free. Cooper, however, argued strongly that if he returned to London he would be persuaded to change his mind; the only solution was a clandestine departure. To this Cooke seems eventually to have agreed, if Cooper would settle his small debt in London.[32]

Then began the process of getting Cooke unobtrusively first to an inn in Prescot, then to the house of an acquaintance of Cooper, a Mr. Tawbuck, where he could be left for the night. From this point on the story acquires elements of farcical comedy (including one patent crib from *She Stoops to Conquer*) that can be read in Dunlap, but need not be taken very seriously. The decision, rightly or wrongly, had at last been taken. Cooper succeeded with the rest of his stratagem, though not without moments of high tension; and on October 4 Cooke sailed on the *Columbia* from Liverpool.

When the news eventually broke, both Cooke and Cooper were accused of cheating and deceit. Cooper wrote a long letter to the press justifying himself; the *Mirror* published both it and Cooke's letter to Harris, and commented:

> The writers are worthy of *any part* of *America*! Mr. Cooke was engaged to Mr. Harris, and owed him eight hundred pounds. All this Mr. Cooper knew as well as Mr. Cooke, and – and – but they are both transported, and let justice be satisfied.[33]

That fundamentally Cooke wanted to go, there can be little doubt. His conduct during the last months had made clear his unhappiness with his present situation in England. His status was slipping; problems abounded; yet another marriage had gone on the rocks. Escape was always Cooke's way in these circumstances, and he had taken a cavalier attitude to his obligations many times before. How cavalier he was on this occasion is difficult to assess. We do not know the nature of his engagement to Harris after 1806. He may no longer have been on regular salary. (Mrs. Siddons, for instance, never was. She was paid for each performance she gave.) In Cooke's case an arrangement of that kind would mean that he would not be paid if he did not turn up, and might well have been used as an inducement to regularity. If Cooke was on those sort of terms, he may well have persuaded himself that he was under no legal obligation to Harris – moral obligations he could soon talk himself out of over a drink or two; and if he thought Cooper would settle his outstanding financial obligations – Cooke was always glad to get rid of those, and he could easily convince himself they were trivial. How great they were, again we do not know. The *Mirror*'s figure may be an exaggeration; and Harris, knowing his Cooke, may well have felt it better tactics to pay him smaller fees than he could have commanded in the market and additionally be prepared to lend him money from time to time, thus holding him financially rather than legally; but having to be prepared to write off the debt if necessary. That he would resent Cooke's departure was natural; but it does not seem to have been a permanent resentment, for in March 1812 he was writing to Cooke in America inviting him to return to London.[34]

That Cooper was guilty of deliberate duplicity is clear, and his own account shows him quite ruthlessly exploiting Cooke's weaknesses for his own ends. He knew what a commercial attraction an actor of the calibre of Cooke would be on the American circuit. He had probably never hoped to acquire anyone of this stature, but since circumstances had put him in the way of it, he was not going to let go of the opportunity if he could help it.

Whether either of them realised the miscalculations they were making we cannot know. But if Cooke thought that at the age of 54 he could still successfully make a new start, and if Cooper thought that while exploiting Cooke's weakness in England he would not be bothered by it in America, both of them were deceiving themselves. What followed in the next two years was as predictable, now, as it was inevitable.

Chapter XIII

U.S.A. — 1810–1812

In a sense the two seasons in the United States are a kind of epilogue and an epitome. They contain in concentrated form those qualities of Cooke, both good and bad, with which we have now become so familiar. He had both his theatrical triumphs and his embarrassments; in society he behaved like a gentleman, and like a vulgar boor; he gave money generously to the needy, he wasted it reprehensibly in tavern drinking bouts. But also he was battling now not only with his conscience, but with his physique. The strain his way of life over the years had placed on his body was now beginning to tell. During most of the time he was a very sick man.

In the theatre he created no new characters during this period (in fact he played only 21 altogether); for the most part he was repeating regularly his half-dozen major roles – and this was what his audiences wanted, this was what they were paying to see. Richard and Sir Pertinax were the big attractions, and most frequently performed, with Shylock, Sir Archy, Falstaff and Iago a little way behind. With no competition from Kemble he was also able to do Lear and Macbeth, and these ousted Stukely and Kitely from their position in the English scale of taste, though the latter had three or four performances. Sir Giles, as always, he was able to do once or twice in most places, but no more; it was a connoisseurs' delight. The play was not well known in America and not greatly to the American taste; after its two performances in New York in his initial season he was never to play it there again, though Philadelphia and Boston were more receptive to it.[1] In general his reception in North America was more like that in the English provinces rather than the metropolis, for here he had no peer. America had never before had or seen an artist of this stature; it was duly impressed and hurried to see.

The excitement and the success of his opening performance in Richard in New York has already been described. He had arrived five days before, dried out and sober as a result of the long Atlantic voyage and a compulsory adherence to what he came to call "the water system", and he was

179

in his best form both theatrically and socially.[2] But as soon as he got into managerial or theatrical company, round went the bottle. In some cases it was no doubt a well-meaning demonstration of warm American hospitality to the distinguished visitor; in others it was the result of meeting once again old acquaintances from his provincial days in England who had emigrated much earlier, like Billy Francis, and reminiscences and absent friends were equally indulged; but there were also those young hangers-on to the theatrical scene who deliberately encouraged his drinking for their own thoughtless enjoyment of the antics he would get up to when his flash-point had been reached.[3] It is especially difficult to forgive them. But in either case, the result was the same. By his third performance on November 24, he was suffering from "hoarseness", and his voice was broken and out of control, one of his regular symptoms after over-indulgence. An unsuspecting audience gave him sympathy for his efforts in fighting what they thought to be genuine illness; but to those who knew him better, the signs were ominous.

Price, Cooper's fellow-manager, adopted Rock's and M'Cready's method, and persuaded Cooke to live with him; but to no avail. By 19 December, the day of his first New York benefit, he was chafing at the restraints of life in the Price household, and planning to move back into the Tontine Coffee House, where he had stayed on his first arrival. The play he chose was Addison's *Cato* (it is difficult to imagine why, since he had had so much bad luck with it from his Newcastle days onwards), a play neither very familiar nor popular with actors or audience. To make matters worse, he did not turn up to rehearsal, and though he did arrive in the evening, a packed audience saw him give a performance that was improvised and incoherent; he rallied for the afterpiece, and played Sir Archy in his best form, but the damage was done. For the first time he had alienated the sympathies of an American audience; and when two days later he played Shylock for a charity benefit, the house was more than half empty.[4] Nevertheless the engagement as a whole had been a splendid one for the managers. During Cooke's 17 nights they took a total of $21,578, an unprecedented sum; and Cooke's own account of his benefit in a letter to Incledon was that it exceeded four hundred guineas.[5] In the short term this doubtless made up for its artistic failure; its long term effects might cast a longer shadow.

Price took Cooke on to Boston for a fourteen night season there during January, which provided the same mixture of resounding theatrical success, and periodical social excess.

John Bernard, who was having his last season in management at Boston, had seen Cooke many years before at Chichester, during his boyhood. Now, with a lifetime's experience of judging actors, and considering the effect of Cooke's age and way of life on his capacity as an actor, Bernard did not expect to be very impressed.

> I had by this time seen Garrick, Henderson, Macklin, Reddish, Smith, Bensley, Palmer, and Kemble in one or other of Cooke's characters, and consequently not only had a high standard whereby to test him, but was in some degree prejudiced against the possibility of his competing successfully with such rivals. After this, when I say that however, in particular scenes and passages, some of the above performers had exceeded him, or however his own ability was inadequate to fill up with consistent force throughout the brilliant design he had formed, yet that as regards the general conception of his characters he certainly surpassed anything I had ever witnessed, it really amounts to ranking him, in his own peculiar speciality, above the level of even the greatest I have named. And when, perceiving what his conception was, I considered what his ability might have been, when unimpaired by age or bad habits, I could not but come to the conclusion that he must have been one of the most original and highly endowed tragedians the world has ever produced.[6]

A tribute of no mean order, and a witness to the impact of Cooke's Boston performances.

But when in February Cooke returned to New York after a bitter winter journey, the honeymoon was over. Because of the weather, these were traditionally bad months in the New York theatre; also, Cooke's novelty had worn off. Many of those who rushed to see his first performances must have gone out of curiosity, to see this new strange performing animal; having seen him once, he had been "done" – there was no need to turn out again on a bitter winter's night. And for others, that wayward benefit performance had done its disillusioning work. It matters little which motives were primarily at work; the end result was that from the packed and clamorous houses of three months before, Cooke began to play all his main characters again to houses half empty or less. As usual, he took it hard, and as usual, he sought his now time-honoured comfort. It was in that context that he left Price's house one bitter winter night, and had to be rescued by Dunlap from the poor widow's house in Reed Street, muttering Lear's storm-driven lines on the ingratitude of his daughters. (Though even there, as we have seen, with the perennial Cooke paradox, he was also giving charitable help to a poor widow financially much worse off than himself.)

He finally moved from Price's household back to the Tontine Coffee House; doubtless Mrs. Price was as glad to see the last of him, as he was of her and her husband. Price may have regretted the loss of opportunity to keep a managerial eye on his property; but that must have been counter-balanced by the thought that the property was now less valuable. To Cooke's further chagrin he now found himself teamed up with Master Payne, the American "Young Roscius", playing Glenalvon to his Young Norval, and Lear to his Edgar, to bolster up his own waning attraction. No wonder Cooke began to loathe New York. On March 11, advertised for Richard, as his last engagement before going to Philadelphia, he refused to perform; a messenger sent from the theatre to inquire if he was ill was given an uncompromising reply: "he was not sick, but he did not chuse to play, and he *would not play*;" and later in Philadelphia he was swearing he would never go back to New York again.[7]

The first Philadelphia engagement produces Dunlap's most intimate picture of Cooke, for he was with him during most of the time, having agreed to accompany him on behalf of Price, to look after the New York theatre's interests (Cooke was still under his year's contract to them, and was being sub-let, so to speak, to other managements).

At times they got on well together; at others they clearly infuriated each other. On the one hand there was Dunlap's strong puritan streak and his lack of a sense of humour, his penchant for reading Cook long moral lectures on the evil of his ways; on the other, Cooke's irresponsibility, his regular promises of reformation, and his appeals for support, which, when it came to the point, he treated with disdain or contumely. They could hardly be expected to understand each other; and yet, at times, they seem to have got on well and happily. Cooke at his best could be a charming and fascinating companion. Taken by Dunlap to his home in Perth-Astoy, New Jersey,

> never man appeared to greater advantage in the quiet of a domestic circle, than he did for the remainder of this day and evening. Attentive, polite, full of cheerfulness, and abounding with anecdotes, which he related with all the urbanity of the finished gentleman of the *veille cour* (*sic*); giving and asking for information, he seemed to forget the evils of the past, and anticipate for the future nothing but good.[8]

It is to hours such as these that we owe some of Cooke's genial and sometimes amusing recollections of his past colleagues across the Atlantic – Billy Lewis, who "was the model for making everyone do his duty by kindness and good treatment"; West Digges, who was easy enough on his own, but when managing for Daly became so disliked that it became a custom after his death for the actors who remembered him to visit his grave in the churchyard in Cork and "insult it" – in a manner that needs little imagination. There is a vivid vignette of George Colman writing *John Bull* act by act, as Harris advanced the money, which he then drank away, until Harris demanded the fifth act and refused any more money until he had it; whereupon Colman wrote it in an evening sitting, scattering the scraps of paper on the floor as he wrote, so that eventually Fawcett had to collect them and take them to the theatre in his pocket handkerchief, while Colman slept off another bottle. There is Harris getting the best of a commercial argument, as he must so often have done.

In London two nights a week were enough; at three I grumbled; four I would not do. I complained to Mr. Harris of playing four nights a week: I said, "it's too much, Sir." "Why, yes," said he, "it's almost as much as playing six nights in the country at a race-week." There he had me. "But consider, Sir, what I get at the race-week." "I do, and I consider that what you get there comes to you from here; if you had not played here, you would have got nothing there."[9]

There are glimpses of Kemble. About to play in *The Gamester*, Cooke remembered:

I hope we shall not do tonight as Kemble and I once did in this same play. We played a scene of the third act in the second. I was frightened out of my wits. "We're wrong" says I: "Go on", says he – and we went through it. When we came off, I exclaimed, "Do you know what we have done? We have played the scene of the third act." "I know it", says John, very coolly. "And what shall we do in the third act?" "Play the second." And so we did. But the best of the joke was, that the papers never found it out.[10]

Away from London, he was genial and relaxed about Kemble.

John deserves his good fortune, he's a noble fellow! He says, if his father had succeeded in making a priest of him, he should have become a cardinal. "Yes", says I, "a pope". John takes his bottle sometimes as well as other people; I have had some hard bouts with him. "Come, Cooke", says he, "we dont play tomorrow, let's get drunk:" and if he said so, he was sure to do it. Charles is the good fellow. He always used to keep himself steady, and in the morning he'd put John to bed and carry me home in a coach."[11]

How far recollections like these were really factual is difficult to judge. Dunlap himself recognised on a number of occasions Cooke's propensity now for romancing, and talking of things as he wanted them to be, rather than as they really were; he did a good deal of this in his boasting to the Americans about his supposed exploits during the War of Independence. He had obviously read some accounts of the battles, and his vivid imagination did the rest.[12]

He rather enjoyed teasing the Yankees, as he called them. When he rallied Dunlap about his proprietary interest in Shakespeare, and asked what part an American could have in the bard of Avon, Dunlap argued rather pompously that,

The younger brother, who leaves his paternal roof, though he does not inherit his father's estate, is heir to his father's fame as much as the elder.

And went on to claim shares in Shakespeare, Milton, Locke, Bacon, Newton, *et al.*

"And where do you draw the line", asked Cooke.
"Why, the year 1776 must be the chronological mark of separation, I believe. I have no claim upon Britain since then, though I owe her much."
"And you will owe her a great deal more before you are able to pay anything in return,"

was Cooke's reply. It was sharp, but good-natured enough and without bitterness.[13] There were other times when he was bitter. Like many visitors to the United States, before and since, he found it hard to take some aspects of men and manners, and on more than one occasion he proclaimed his intention to write a satirical pamphlet on his return home. He would never have found the energy to do it, of course, as even Dunlap realised; but some things rankled with him, and when his tongue was loosened, out they came, to the understandable offence of his company. In fairness to Cooke, he never, as we know, suffered fools gladly, and pompousness and hypocrisy were there to be punctured, so that the gentleman priding himself on his family history as belonging to some of the first settlers of Maryland may well have provided a provoking target. Cooke asked him if he had carefully preserved the family jewels. When asked what he mean, he replied "the chains and handcuffs".[14]

Some of the popular anecdotes were clearly deliberately provoked, and Cooke was led on by the company to see how far, in his cups, he would go; like the gentleman who told him that the President of the United States proposed to go from Washington to Baltimore to see him act.

"If he does, I'll be damned if I play before him. What, I? I! – George

Frederick Cooke! who have acted before the Majesty of Britain, play before your Yankee President! No! – I'll go forward to the audience and I'll say, Ladies and Gentlemen – "

Here he was interrupted playfully by Mr. W. who happened to be dressed in black;

"Oh, no, Mr. Cooke, that would not be right in this country; you should say, friends and fellow-citizens."

Cooke, surveying him contemptuously, cried, "Hold your tongue, you damned Methodist preacher," and then proceeded to rant at length about the "King of the Yankee Doodles", and to tell almost certainly fictitious tales of his own deeds of arms in the war against the rebels.[15]

He went sight-seeing with Dunlap; he sat for his portrait to Sully, and kept a lady and her little daughter fascinated and amused by his anecdotes; he attended the spring dinner of a society of gentlemen at the Fish House, behaved well, and enjoyed himself.[16] Theatrically the Philadelphia visit was as big a triumph as New York had been in the beginning; but after the crowds and the welcome and the applause in Chestnut Street came the celebration and the recrimination of the morning after.[17]

There was no repetition of the New York benefit fiasco in Philadelphia; Dunlap, to his credit, saw to that. He sat up conscientiously with Cooke the night before until the bar was closed, and then saw him grumbling into bed. Among other things that night he had to listen to Cooke's views on Cooper, and they were revealing. Cooper had at last arrived back in New York from his travels, and had upset Cooke by not writing to him. All the smouldering resentment over the way in which he had allowed himself to be smuggled out of England by Cooper broke out.

I came away, Sir, without preparation – without my stage-clothes – without my books – as if I was running away by stealth from my creditors – like a criminal flying from the laws of his country. Now Holman will come out after making every preparation; after making a bargain by which he will put that money into his own pocket, which I am putting into the pockets of men who treat me as if I was an idiot. They think I am a fool, and that I will receive as a generous gratuity from them, a part of what I enrich them with! Sir, I shall have lost money by coming here – and when I go back, how do I know in what manner I shall be received, or whether I shall be received at all! – To come away without seeing Mr. Harris! my best friend – the man who did everything for me! The man who pitted me *against them all*! His son, too, is my friend, notwithstanding that in his anger he published my letter, fixing the time that I was to play in London – No! No! by – I will never play in

New-York again! They have got their Cooper there to play for them! – He has treated me unlike a gentleman, Sir!

Moreover Cooke had been receiving anonymous letters, one of which had warned him of the consequences of his defaulting on the last night of his New York season.

I am to be hissed off for not acting the last night that I was advertised for – the writer signs himself my friend and countryman – he advises me not to submit to being hissed by an American audience – an American audience! – No, not by any audience! – They'll hiss me because I deserted them? – Didn't they desert me first? Didn't they leave me to play night after night to empty benches? – Blast them! – No! I'll never play for them again! He says that Cooper tells the people of New-York that I am engaged to him for three years. Am I? – I'll show him! I'll write such a pamphlet on my return to England – I'll not forget the American theatres and their managers! I, play with Cooper![18]

But of course he did play again with Cooper, and in New York. He had no choice. He was tied by a contract and the fact that he had crossed the Atlantic; by a decision that, typically, he had never really made himself, but had allowed to be made for him. And whether or not Dunlap's recollection of that conversation is verbally accurate, it reveals clearly enough the anxieties that racked Cooke when he was sober, and drove him to the oblivion of alcohol. Unreasonable they may have been, but they were very real to Cooke.

This was his mental illness; but all the time, now, he was struggling with physical illness – the dropsical symptoms, the pains in his chest that may have come from his deteriorating liver. He was ill before they left for Philadelphia, and the doctors bled him; while there he again had trouble with his respiration and had to be bled again; it happened once more before they left Philadelphia. He knew that his time was running out; he feared the approach of the long dark; but he knew also that there was nothing he could now do about it; the drafts that he had made on his constitution over the years would soon have to be paid off.[19]

Cooper came out to Philadelphia, and in some degree they were reconciled. Together they played Iago and Othello, Pierre and Jaffeir, Stukely and Beverley; and Cooper succeeded in taking him back to New York, in spite of the arrangements Cooke himself had been making to go on to Boston, having persuaded himself that his contract to Cooper had run out.

Back in New York they played a short season together, adding to their joint repertoire Richard and Richmond, Clytus and Alexander, Falstaff and

Hotspur, Horatio and Lothario; though as Horatio Cooke managed at one point to dry up completely.[20] A brief season in Baltimore followed, and a final return to New York, where he not only had a much better reception, but after giving more than 80 performances, he ended his contract to Cooper. He also got married.

The fifth Mrs. Cooke remains almost as shadowy a figure as all the others except Alicia Daniels. She was Mrs. Behn, widow (presumably) of a German Merchant, and daughter of James Bryden, master of the Tontine Coffee House, where Cooke had stayed. Bryden would appear to have been an immigrant Scot, and with that common background they seem to have got on well together. Of the motives behind the marriage, we know nothing. Almost certainly it was bigamous; for there is no indication that his marriage to Miss Lambe of Newark had been ended by death or divorce; but with her a whole Atlantic away, Cooke was hardly likely to worry much about that – now. Dunlap's only comment about the new Mrs. Cooke is that she "proved to him a faithful and affectionate nurse to the day of his death,"[21] and in that respect the marriage may have been one of convenience rather than passion; but she eased his last year for him, which may have been the prime object of the exercise.

For Cooke's physical condition could not now have encouraged any optimistic prognosis. He had symptoms of dropsy, spells of dizziness, difficulty in breathing, bilious attacks, and constant pain in his chest and abdomen. Behind his shoulder during those summer weeks stood a *memento mori* – Doige, an English actor, member of the New York company in Cooke's first season, was dying of dropsy, and Cooke visited him and gave money to see that he was adequately cared for during his passing. He must have felt the shadows closing in on himself.[22]

With Mrs. Cooke he had a kind of Indian Summer during July and August, making various excursions into different parts of New York State, travelling on a steam-boat for the first time, visiting Lake George, and Saratoga, and the field where General Burgoyne surrendered the remnants of his army in 1777.[23] As always when travelling he took a lively interest in his surroundings. One hopes that he enjoyed that last respite from the theatrical treadmill.

He began his second season in New York at the beginning of September. Freed from his exclusive contract to Cooper he was now acting for himself, and making his own engagements. That he made one for New York reflects his better reception in the summer, and he played 20 nights over a period of two months – though there were two ominous periods of a week and ten days when he was indisposed. He went on to Philadelphia for three weeks, back to New York for a short season, and then in January to a very good season in Boston. He seems, in rather typical Cooke fashion, to have engaged himself at the same time to go to Charleston, but Powell, the Boston manager, came in person to New York to collect him, and possession was all the points of the law. Again he was ill in Boston, but Powell insists that it was real illness, another of his severe bilious attacks, and that during the whole of his engagement "he never occasioned a postponement to my knowledge but once, and that was owing to real illness".[24] He returned to New York and played another five nights in March, and then illness laid him low again. For weeks at a time he was confined to his bed, and when eventually in June he took on a three night engagement, it was only with great difficulty that he got through the first evening as Sir Pertinax, on June 22. He played no more in New York.[25]

Meanwhile he was planning to return to England, and at one point told Dunlap that he had booked his passage from Boston in a few days;[26] but nothing ever came of it, and one suspects that he was whistling in the dark to keep up his courage. That he was wanted back in Covent Garden there is no doubt. Both Thomas Harris and his son Henry had written to him inviting him to return; Dunlap had the younger Harris' letter.

Covent Garden Theatre,
March 28th, 1812

MY DEAR SIR

My father has written a letter to you, inviting a return to your old quarters at Covent-garden, where you would receive the most cordial welcome.

For fear his letter should not come to hand, I write this, repeating his request; and I hope that on the receipt of it, you will take leave of the Yankees, and come over and take t'other touch at John Bull, who is as fond of you as ever, and would be most happy to see his favourite again

Believe me,
Yours very sincerely,
H. HARRIS   [27]

In spite of his perversities, they were missing him in London, they wanted him back. On 24 May 1812 he wrote accepting the invitation.[28] But it was now too late.

He rallied in July, and with his wife went off to join the Boston company at Providence, where he played nine nights to excellent houses and made a profit of over five hundred dollars. He was on his best behaviour, assiduous in attendance at rehearsals, to which he walked three-quarters of a mile each morning. He went through, for the last time, all his favourite characters, Shylock, Richard, Sir Pertinax, Macbeth, Sir Archy, Zanga, Lear and Falstaff. And for his last night, his own benefit, to a crowded house he

played for the last time the character that, though never as generally popular as the others, he always stuck to and played for his own satisfaction – Sir Giles Overreach. It was his last performance.[29]

After the engagement the Cookes visited Boston once more, for a few
days, and then returned to New York, where they had apartments at the
Mechanics' Hall. There once again he had to take to his bed; and apart
from one occasion when he struggled up to dine with his old acquaintance
Holman and his daughter, newly arrived from England for an engagement
on the American circuit, he never again left it. He was attended by three
physicians, who did what they could to alleviate his condition; and his own
last exertions had ensured that he was not in poverty or want; but there was
nothing, now, that medical skill could do. On the morning of 26
September 1812, he died. He was 56.[30]

The doctors carried out a post-mortem examination and found, as they
expected, that during the last months his liver had almost ceased to func-
tion. The following day, with an impressive collection of mourners, that included the Governor of New York, the Mayor and Secretary of State, and
representatives of the professions, the services, science, literature and the
stage, Cooke's body was buried in the Stranger's Vault of St. Paul's church.
There it lay until 1820, when Edmund Kean, who revered Cooke's
memory, visited New York and had the remains reinterred in the spot they
now occupy, and erected a memorial over them. At the same time it
appears that the opportunity was taken to abstract Cooke's skull and one of
his finger bones; the skull, after one or two macabre vicissitudes, now rests
in a medical museum in America; the finger bone was said to have been
taken back to England by Kean, and kept in his house as an object of
veneration to himself and his colleagues until Mrs. Kean threw it away.[31]
Even in death a cynical spirit of comedy could not resist sporting with
Cooke, as it had so often done in life.

Back in England the news, when it reached Covent Garden, was received
with sadness and regret. As usual, Cooke's absence had emphasised his
special qualities in the roles he had made peculiarly his own, and no-one
could adequately substitute for him. Charles Kemble had been a shadow of
Cooke as Iago; when John Philip resumed the mantle of Richard in
January 1811, his audience found the experience an embarrassment.[32] Not
till Edmund Kean arrived on the scene was Richard himself again; and Kean
had modelled much of his performance on Cooke. As for Sir Pertinax, no-
one then, or since, has been able to breathe into him the unique life that
Cooke conveyed. Others may have approached him as Shylock and Iago.
As Richard and Sir Pertinax he had stood alone, and those characters
remained in the memory of all who had witnessed them as his intangible
epitaph.

Chapter XIV

The Actor

Contemporary accounts from the London newspapers are the chief sources from which can be built up a portrait of Cooke the actor at work. In addition some fifteen prompt books associated with his performances have survived, and there is an anonymous account comparing Kemble and Cooke as Richard III which gives additional detail of his playing of that character.[1] Many of the prompt books – especially those dating from his last years in North America – are tantalisingly uninformative. They represent basically the stock productions into which Cooke fitted, and by then he was not going to spend much time writing up performances with which he was so familiar. The Harvard copy of *Richard III* is fortunately an exception. It was written up while he was at Covent Garden (he dates it "Hampstead, Friday night, March 22 1805"), and taken in conjunction with the anonymous *Remarks* it helps to fill out our knowledge of one of his leading roles.

These themselves tell us something about his qualities. Richard III, Iago, Sir Giles Overreach, Kitely, Stukely, Sir Pertinax MacSycophant, Sir Archy MacSarcasm all involve – either from a tragic or comic viewpoint – hypocrisy, jealously, vengefulness, the darker passions of human nature, and they require broad playing rather than restraint. This Cooke was naturally suited to give.

Physically and vocally he lacked elegance. Of middle height, with shorter arms than normal, he moved angularly rather than gracefully. He was not handsome – all the portraits emphasis the too-prominent nose – but his features were under extremely flexible control, and his eyes could flash signals that even in the under-lit theatres of his day were unmistakable. His voice was harsh, limited in its tonal modulations, and easily subject to hoarseness. At the same time it was extremely powerful and flexible – again and again we find comments on his whisper that could penetrate right through the house. Power was its asset, lack of gentleness its limitation; he had no tones for the softer emotions, we are told.

There is much evidence of the thought and study that lay behind his performances. One such instance might almost anticipate Stanislavsky. In the New York *Othello* production of 1811 the prompter found himself, at Cooke's insistence, having to alter all the blocked-out movement for the opening of Act V Sc. 1, and he noted the reason.

> Mr. Cooke's idea is that Iago does not live in the Citadel, *and therefore sends Emilia off contrary side to his own home.*

Later, with Cooke safely out of the way, the prompter quietly changed the movement back . . .[2]

Contemporaries often found Cooke's readings original – sometimes perverse – but like the *Monthly Mirror* they accepted that they were intended, not accidental.[3] The *Richard III* prompt book gives many indications of this. The accepted text of the time was still basically Cibber's re-working of Shakespeare's original, but Cooke restored a number of passages which Cibber had omitted – "Now is the winter of our discontent . . ." in Act I Sc. 1, and other passages in IV 4 and V 6, for example. He worked over many of his speeches and carefully pointed the pauses and breathings, using dashes as notation for the length of time involved – one as the standard unit, four as the maximum. Richard's well-known soliloquy after Lady Anne's exit in II 1 of the Cibber version may be taken as an example of his method. (The dashes are all Cooke's pen and ink insertions.)

> Was ever woman, in this humour, woo'd? –
> Was ever woman, in this humour, won? – –
> I'll have her, but I will not keep her long. – –
> What! I, that kill'd her husband, and his father, I –
> To take her, in her heart's extremest hate,
> With curses in her mouth, tears in her eyes,
> The bleeding witness of my hatred by;
> Having heaven, her conscience, and these bare, against me,
> And I, no friends to back my suit withal,
> But the plain devil, and dissembling looks!
> And yet to win her! all the world to nothing! –
> Can she abase her beautious eyes on me,
> Whose all not equals Edward's moiety?
> On me, that halt, and am misshapen thus! –
> My dukedom to a widow's chastity,
> I do mistake my person, all this while; – –
> Upon my life! she finds, (although, I cannot,)
> Myself, to be a marvellous, proper man. – – –

> I'll have my chambers lined with looking glass;
> And entertain a score or two of tailors,
> To study fashions, to adorn my body. –
> Since I am crept in favour with myself,
> I will maintain it, with some little cost. – –
> But first, I'll turn St. Harry to his grave,
> And then return, lamenting, to my love. –
> Shine out, fair sun, till I salute my glass,
> That I may see my shadow, as I pass.   *Exit R*

There are other passages as carefully notated.

He gave detailed consideration to the stage business. Earlier in the same scene, for example, where during the funeral procession a guard tells Richard to stand back and let the coffin pass, and is answered

> Unmanner'd slave! stand thou, when I command,
> Advance thy halberd higher than my breast,
> Or, by St. Paul, I'll strike thee to my foot,
> An spurn upon thee, beggar, for thy boldness,

Cooke notes:

> The guard changes his spear at the word halberd, raises the point; at the word breast, places it erect.

All entrances, exits, and stage crosses are carefully located and keyed into the text.[4]

How did his audiences see the result? Compared with Kemble's performance in the same role, the anonymous writer of 1801 found Cooke much more natural. Kemble was stern and gloomy throughout; Cooke exploited the sardonic humour in the character, and through it underlined the hypocrisy. His levity was barbarous – "Horror gleams through it; and when he smiles, it is in malignant hypocrisy, and he seems to wound while he smiles." Cooke handled the soliloquies very differently from his rival.

> Kemble does not talk with himself but with the Pit . . . His soliloquies are harangues to the house.

Cooke, on the other hand, appeared to be arguing with himself, the spectator saw the thoughts rise to his face, and was listening to a man totally unconscious of being overheard.[5]

> Since the Heavens have shap'd my body so,
> Let Hell make crook'd my mind to answer it

etc, was for Kemble "horrid self-satisfaction". For Cooke it was "pitiable dejection". When Lady Anne appeared, Kemble's delivery of the lines –

> But see, my love appears – look where she shines,
> Darting pale lustre, like the silver moon,
> Through her dark veil of rainy sorrow . . .

had "all the trembling tenderness of studied passion", plus a stage effect from the use of his sword. For Cooke the whole speech demonstrated the witchery of a tongue that should wheedle with the devil – full of plausible smoothness.

In the scene with Buckingham and the citizens the writer recalled the interest Cooke "takes in Buckingham's information; his rising anxiety; his accompanying gestures; the rapidity with which he exclaims 'And did they so?' on Buckingham telling him that he urged the citizens to cry 'Long live King Richard'. His playing here is very fine and natural." At this point Kemble was merely stoical.[6]

In plotting the murder of the princes, Cooke was fighting his agitation over the dreadful deed. See Cooke

> try to smother his agitation, and then perceive his sense of dishonour overcome him, and he vainly essay to bring the disgraceful words to utterance. His colour change, his lip quiver, his eye speak![7]

In the final scene, where Richard was handed the scroll with the words

> "Jockey of Norfolk, be not too bold,
> For Dickon, thy master, is bought and sold"

Kemble read the words disdainfully, then struck it from him with his sword. That was that. Cooke read the first line curiously, the second quietly, thinking. Realising that it meant that he was betrayed, and the only expedient course was to pretend reliance on those who were left with him, slowly he threw aside the scroll, with the words

> A weak invention of the enemy.

A few moments later, after ordering the execution of Stanley's son, and being persuaded by Norfolk to delay the deed until after the battle – where

Kemble was fast and straightforward, Cooke made an awful pause. He swayed backward and forward in hurried contemplation of the situation. The house hung on his decision. His face was irresolute, his lip moved; he thought again. Only then did he speak. "Why – after be it then."[8] As with Kean, a few years later, it was the electrifying detail of such moments that told.

Cooke's exploitation of the sardonic humour and the hypocrisy of Richard was not to all tastes. For Charles Lamb it was not subtle enough. The hypocrisy was too glaring and visible, more shallow cunning than deeply concealed but carefully controlled manipulation; and the humour was the "coarse taunting humour and clumsy merriment of a low-minded assassin" rather than "the effect of buoyant spirits and an elastic mind, rejoicing in its own powers and the success of its machinations".[9]

On the other hand it was precisely the cool malignity, "silent in resentment, subtle in his designs," of Cooke's Iago that both the writers of the *Morning Chronicle* and the *Porcupine* singled out for approving comment. "We have had no such nice discrimination on the stage since the days of Henderson" thought the *Porcupine*, and for the *Chronicle* the performance would bear the closest examination from a discerning eye. It was the unity of the conception that impressed it – "look, gesture, and manner form so much of the excellence", and it noted the powerful effect of Cooke's final exit. "When taken away to punishment he casts a look of exultation at the wretched Othello, a look of exultation on the success of his schemes, with an expression and air diabolically good."[10]

Of Cooke's Shylock the writer in *The Monthly Mirror* wrote of his "deep, heart-rooted, diabolical malignity" and his "Caution, cunning, servility and moroseness," and went on:

In the *Trial Scene*, the "lodg'd Hate" of the impenetrable Israelite was observable throughout. And here, likewise, there were some striking novelties which surprised and delighted us: for instance, the abrupt reply to Portia's request that he would let her *tear the bond* – "When it is *paid* according to the tenour;" indicating a degree of apprehension lest she *should* tear it, and, at the same time, a malignant recognition of the penalty due:– the earnestness of his enquiry "Is it so nominated in the bond?" and his triumphant *chuckle*, when he returned it to Portia, "I cannot find it – 'tis not in the bond" – the division in this passage "I take this offer then; pay the bond – thrice": – and the eagerness with which he adds the last word, lest he should be excluded the benefit of the offer that had been made to him: – in fact, the whole of this scene was inimitable, and his last look and groan, on retiring from the court, expressed despair, hate, and disappointed malice.[11]

The *Morning Post* writer confirmed the extremely powerful effect of the trial scene, but had reservations about the manner in which Cooke went on living the part even when he had no lines to speak and was temporarily out of the scene. He had approved this characteristic in Iago[12] but here,

> Mr. Cooke sometimes used a *dumb acting* with *Tubal*, as if the latter were remonstrating with the *Jew* on the cruelty of his suit, and he were maintaining its fitness. This (beside there being no authority for it in the play) was an exception to the characteristic eagerness of *Shylock*, as to all that is passing in the Court, which Mr. Cooke gave (for the most part) so happily.[13]

Many of the commentators agree on Cooke's deficiency in presenting the quieter passions – Shylock's agony of sorrow over his daughter's behaviour, Lear's attitude to Cordelia, for example[14] – and this prevented him from giving a complete portrait of any individual. This "want of consistency" as the *Morning Post* writer called it in an article summing up Cooke's general qualities[15] was a limitation, but it did not exclude him from being judged at the highest level, since perfection would never be achievable, and his faults were counter-balanced by his virtues.

> It is this frequency of detached instances of great acting, that, in despite of gross faults, will justly maintain Mr. Cooke in high estimation; for the audience have scarce time to reflect on a palpable failure of this actor, before they are cheated out of their retrospect by some bold and successful essay of his genius.

For the same writer Cooke could sometimes misconceive an author's design, either in detached passages, or the whole scheme of the part, and sometimes resort to trickery to hold an audience's interest; but his counter-balancing merit lay in his passion – sometimes instinctive rather than reasoned.

> If we look at Mr. Cooke's excellencies or his faults, we see, in each and both, strong passions on foot, sometimes comprehending its object, and sometimes proceeding in total darkness, but always active and enterprising. This is his charm. After all, man has more of the animal than spiritual nature in him; and passion in the actor begets passion in the audience, even when the idea that gives it birth is erroneous.

Moreover, against any accusations of "coarsening" Richard or Macbeth could be set the rehabilitation of Falstaff (the Falstaff of *Henry IV*, it should be emphasised). The *Morning Chronicle* praised the subtlety of Cooke's approach:

In the hands of most actors *Sir John's* humour has been debased into clownishness and his wit has been lost by being exhibited in the garb of the coarsest vulgarity. *Sir John* is, however, no clown, and his familiarity is founded on interest, and does not flow either from vulgarity or ignorance . . . [Mr. Cooke showed] a masterly conception of the character, and in his hands it presents a performance of no inconsiderable interest. He showed that he understood the object and aim of *Sir John's* familiarity, as well as the real character of his humour. He drew a proper line of distinction between the acuteness which even in the coarsest part of his humour the witty Knight discovers, and the sorry jokes of his besotted companions. He evinces very correct judgment too in discriminating *Falstaff's* conduct in his interviews with the Prince, and in his treatment of *Bardolph* or his *Hostess*. In both cases he is familar, but in the one it is a familiarity which avoids giving offence, and seems to flow from affection; in the other it is the triumph of superiority, it is familiarity of a wit making himself merry at the expense of his inferiors. In studying the character in the closet, this distinction is obvious; but it is too often lost sight of on the stage.[16]

And looking back on Cooke's performance after his death, a writer in the *Bristol Gazette* confirmed this reaction.

Falstaff has suffered by the ignorance and buffoonery of mere players, helped on by popular misconception. *Mr. Cooke* had incomparably the best notion of his character; as *Mr. Stephen Kemble* has incomparably the worst; if indeed he had any notion at all beyond that of an excessive corpulency. *Mr. Cooke*, together with that genuine, warm humour which pervaded his *Sir Archy MacSarcasm*, combined a shrewd-witted consciousness of the very follies which he practised, and of the bragging and the cowardice which he affected: and he preserved a certain air of knightly dignity, natural to the man of rank and the courtier: and such as we should expect in the chosen companion of a Prince of Wales, amid all the habitual sensuality, the gross perversion of intellect, and the corruption of moral taste, which make up this admirable exemplification of prostituted talent. *Falstaff* has been too commonly turned loose upon the stage to make sport for the galleries: with the person of a bloated monster, that had no counterpart in humanity; with the vulgar antics of a common buffoon, and the drivelling fatuity of a lisping ideot. *Mr. Cooke* rescued him out of the hands of these *Bartholomew-mummers*, and we saw again the man of powerful sense and pregnant wit, debauched and unprincipled indeed; but glorying in the predominance of his fascinating powers over the fancy and affections of a discerning and accomplished Prince. To this end his vapouring and his lying, his bullying and his cowardice conduce: and this important point was carefully kept in view by *Mr. Cooke*.[17]

Leigh Hunt argued that Cooke, in the years when he knew him, was a better comedian than tragedian; certainly the part he played most frequently in his last decade was Sir Pertinax MacSycophant, and it was this that Hunt regarded as his most finished performance.[18] Again, the surviving prompt book of *The Man of the World*, though a late one,[19] shows something of the trouble he took, by cutting and shaping and small details of re-writing in the dialogue, to point his lines in the most effective way. A dullish line like

Why, are you mad, sir? You have certainly been bit by some mad whig or other

is made more forceful and effective by the addition of six words –

Why, are you mad, sir? Ye are stark, staring, raving mad.
Ye have certainly been bit by some mad whig or other[20]

and

What is it you shrug up your shoulders at, sir?

has another dimension added to it by the words –

and turn up your een to Heaven like a duck in thunder?

The central scene of that same act, in which Sir Pertinax describes to his son Egerton his progress achieved by "bowing" to all who might be useful to him, is extremely carefully worked over to get the rhythms and the emphases precisely right.[21]

And the trouble he took was reflected in the effect the performance had on his audience. For a writer calling himself RHADAMANTHUS in the *Bristol Gazette* –

THE Sir Pertinax MacSycophant of Mr. Cooke, we consider not only as his best character, but the *chef-d'oeuvre* of the English stage. In his delineation of *Richard* his genius often breaks forth and astonishes by its energy and splendour; but still there is something unreal, something artificial, which, as in painting, a skilful eye can easily distinguish from nature. But, in Sir Pertinax, all is reality; he seems organised for the character ... His description of his courtship to his first wife, and his turning up "o' the whites o' his e'en," was a portrait of hypocrisy which Beelzebub himself might have "eyed askaunce", with a leer of malignant pleasure. The virtues of "booing and pliability", as the shortest way to honour, in contra-distinction to virtue and talent, were impressed upon the mind of his son with the smile of a Jesuit, and the art of a Courtier ... His interview with Sidney, was one of the brightest beauties of this inimitable performance; the hollow profession of friendship, the crocodile tears, the ambiguous hints, in short, the *tout ensemble* was perfection itself and "beggars description".[22]

And Leigh Hunt felt that

you may see all the beauties and all the faults of Cooke in this single character; and this proves, perhaps, that it is his favourite one, since he feels inclined to indulge all his habits in its representation. The Scotch dialect which he so inimitably assumes is in vain undervalued by those who persuade themselves that he was born in Scotland. In the first place, to be merely born there is nothing to the purpose, for a man born upon the sea might as well be expected to talk like a dolphin. If he was educated by or with Scotch people, it is merely wonderful that he does not talk Scotch in his English characters, for he gives them none of those compressed vowels and liquefied consonants, none of that artlessness and undulation of tone so ludicrous in Sir Pertinax. It is this artlessness of tone that renders a hypocritical Scotchman or Welshman more humourous on the stage than any other hypocrite, and more successful, perhaps, in the world. Sir Pertinax, however, conceals an unavoidable ludicrousness, which might sometimes injure his cause, by apparently delighting in his dialect and by possessing much intentional humour. If Cooke bows, it is with a face that says "What a fool you are to be deceived with this fawning!" If he looks friendly, it is with a smile that says "I will make use of you, and you may go to the devil". A simple rustic might feel all his affections warmed at his countenance, and exclaim "What a pure-hearted old gentleman!" but a fine observer would descry under the glowing exterior nothing but professions without meaning, and a heart without warmth.

The sarcasm of Cooke is at all times most bitter, but in this character its acerbity is tempered with no respect either for its object or for himself. His tone is outrageously smooth and deep; and when it finds its softest level, its under monotony is so full of what is called hugging one's self, and is accompanied with such a dragged smile and viciousness of leer, that he seems as if he had lost his voice through the mere enjoyment of malice.[23]

This quality of appearing to enjoy his own villainy is remarked on by other observers, and in other contexts. In Edinburgh in 1813, Sir Walter Scott, after watching Kemble once more go through a sequence of his great parts, was driven to recall the now dead Cooke. Acknowledging Kemble's greatness, he nevertheless felt that his work was too studied and too contrived –

he shows too much of his machinery . . . sudden turns and natural bursts of passion are not his forte. I saw him play Sir Giles Overreach (the Richard III of middling life) last night; but he came not within a hundred miles of Cooke, whose terrible visage, and short, abrupt, and savage utterance, gave a reality almost to that extra-ordinary scene in which he boasts of his own successful villainy to a nobleman of worth and honour, of whose alliance he is ambitious. Cooke contrived somehow to impress upon the audience the idea of such a monster of enormity as had learned to pique himself even upon his own atrocious character.[24]

It was Cooke's own special hallmark, and the roles he re-created most vividly were those in which he could, either for comedy or tragedy, exploit this characteristic.

The two great disappointments of Cooke's last decade were his attempts at Lear and Hamlet. After the performance of Lear in January 1802, the *Chronicle* writer was disappointed and grieved, for he had expected Cooke to shine in the part. The *Post* was not surprised.

It is a character little suited to his talents. In the expression of strong and turbulent passions, he will always find his forte; but he wants gentleness and softness for melting and melancholy scenes.

Both writers were agreed on what was wrong – Cooke played against the element of pathos which they took to be central to the play.

He seemed to imagine that *Lear* was a man hale in body and vigorous in intellect, instead of a man in extreme old age, wrote the shocked *Chronicle*, and the *Post* agreed.

> His step was almost uniformly firm, and his whole deportment too vigorous for his years. The heart, therefore, could not feel that pity which the sight of a deserving object, physically unable to contend with unmerited hardships, never fails to produce. His enunciation, also, which was clear and strong, had none of the tremulousness of feeble old age, and his voice seldom succeeded in the modulation of tones sufficiently plaintive and delicate to express the agonies of a broken heart.

For the *Chronicle* this stemmed not so much from mistaken execution, but from an erroneous conception of the part.

> It is only the idea of Lear's helplessness that interests us in his fate. If a man in the perfect possession of all his faculties had behaved with such extreme absurdity, the parricidal cruelty of his daughters would only have made us detest *them*. Him we should have thought deserving of what he suffered. This misconception impaired the effect of the whole performance.

Some things he did well. The *Chronicle* writer felt

> He succeeded best in the early scenes. The *curse* he gave with very great effect, and his denunciations of unknown vengeance were admirable, when he renounced both *Regan* and *Goneril*, and preferred the raging elements to his unnatural offspring. His behaviour to *Cordelia* we cannot thus commend. It wanted tenderness ... There was a coarseness in his exultation upon his victory over the assassins, and the recovery of his crown. He appeared like a jolly old dog who boasts of the feats of his youth, and insinuates that his powers are not greatly impaired. Upon the whole, unless he shall acquire a considerable increase of discrimination, sensibility and delicacy of touch, we would not advise him to attempt the part a second time. We think the audience agreed with us in opinion. He drew down two or three rapturous bursts of applause, but upon the whole his reception was cold.[25]

Cooke might well have retorted that the jolly old dog was Nahum Tate's fault, not his or Shakespeare's, but he would have been beating the air. He was playing to an audience already conditioned by Kemble.

If the Kemble shadow darkened Cooke's Lear, it lay even more deeply over his Hamlet. By the time he came to play it in London in September

1802, critics and audiences knew a good deal about Cooke's qualities and limitations as an actor. They had also been accustomed for some years to Kemble's performances. From both they must have expected that some aspects of the character might be beyond Cooke, but that his limitations might be counterbalanced elsewhere by his special qualities. The *Morning Post* certainly did so.

> Those who are acquainted with Mr. Cooke's general style of acting, expected that in the mad irregular scenes which form so great a share of the business; that in those flighty and incoherent passages; that in the sneer and satire, and the art of *Hamlet*, Mr. Cooke would excel; while in the bursts of genuine grief and terror, he would fall far short of his rival Kemble.

In these latter, he clearly did.

> In the passages of deep feeling, of grief, surprise, and terror, he failed, as much as we expected. The harsh monotony of his voice, the total incapacity of his countenance, to raise a tender sympathy, debarred him of all chance of affecting the heart. He seemed conscious of the difficulties under which he laboured; he was collected, and governed himself, in the parts of the greatest passion and agitation, as if afraid, that by giving way to his feelings, he might the more strongly expose his natural defects. In the first scene with the *Ghost*, therefore, he by no means communicated to the audience that freezing terror which he describes. After the *Ghost* left him he communed with his attendants, in a deliberate, common conversation tone, not very consistent with the state of mind and body in which such a terrific sight should have left him. His description of man – "How noble in reason! – how infinite in faculties! – in form and moving how express and admirable! – in action how like an angel! – in apprehension how like a God!" &c. was also tame and unimpressive, not characterised by any beauty or even singularity. His reflections on how the player worked himself up into a fit of grief, what's – "Hecuba to him," &c. (*sic*) were of the same description, although this is an impassioned speech, in which *Hamlet* should be greatly agitated. The celebrated soliloquy of – "to be or not to be," was given without a mark that left anything on the memory to praise. These were the parts which we did not expect him to shine in, and we were not disappointed at his performance.

Unhappily, the compensating qualities did not emerge.

Mr. Cooke was as grave and sententious in the eccentricities of *Hamlet*, as in those parts to which solemnity was best suited. His sneers and satire upon *Rosencrantz* and *Guildenstern*, his mockery of *Polonius*, his reproaches of *Ophelia*, when he tells her to go to a nunnery, were not marked by any beauty, or distinguished by much applause, notwithstanding they are admirably calculated for an actor to display his discrimination, to blend those rapid touches of light and shade, to make those quick transitions which surprise and entrap applause, though not always merited. In the scene in which he tells *Ophelia* to go to a nunnery, in particular, he was unusually tame. It has always been played in a whirlwind of passion, and the satire on the female sex has been given with great point and variety, such as might be expected from a madman. We would not blame Mr. Cooke for not following the beaten path, if he had strewed his new course with some fresh flowers. As it was, we had not compensation for the breach of practice, and novelty was unaccompanied with pleasure.[26]

The writer found a handful of details to applaud, but he felt that Cooke's "greatness never continued for more than a sentence. He gave no one entire speech with good effect". It was a respectable performance, but not more so than many actors – in London or the country – could have given; and by Cooke's own standards, that was not good enough.

It was a harsh review, but other sources confirm it. The *Morning Chronicle* anxiously taxed its memory for something to commend.

Nothing at all presents itself. We can recollect no proofs of the polished education of a Prince; no symptoms of philosophic melancholy; no traits of filial piety; no expression of generous friendship; no throbs of smothered affection; no marks of suspicion; no ebullitions of resentment; no apparent desire for revenge; no conflict of doubt of being misled and obedience to the supernatural mandate. Mr. Cooke must have failed in expressing his notions ... To express the soft and tender passions Mr. Cooke is utterly unfit. Not only his voice and manner disqualify him, but even his smile. This is uniformly the same, and denotes a disposition to cajole and overreach, whatever be his internal emotions. His pathetic exclamation of "father!" to the ghost, raised a general laugh. We trust that he will keep henceforth within his own sphere.[27]

Though the more sympathetic *Morning Post* writer went again to see the second performance, he was not driven to change his mind; and Leigh Hunt called it a performance "of which one would willingly spare the recollection".[28] It was as much a failure as the performances in Chester in

1785 had been a success. Cooke never played it again.

One of the tantalising unknowns relating to Cooke's *Hamlet* prompt book is how far it might represent what was performed in Covent Garden in 1802. As Miss Byrne has pointed out[29] for the production in 1785 (and presumably for the performances Cooke gave in 1786, 1787, and 1788) it represents both Cooke as Hamlet and Austin's production into which he fitted; he used it also in 1790 for a single production in Sheffield, with the remnants of the same company; whether he used it with Banks and Ward in 1792 and 1793 we have no means of telling.

Even if at Covent Garden he was fitting into a quite different production, however, there is at least one piece of evidence to suggest that his conception of Hamlet had not changed over the seventeen years in between. We have seen the *Morning Post* chiding him for his tameness in the nunnery scene which "has always been played in a whirlwind of passion".[30] The prompt book makes clear that this flouting of contemporary fashion was deliberate, and emerged from Cooke's own view of the character. The scene runs as follows (with Cooke's action notes and additions keyed in to the text; the exit instructions are written in – presumably he left and then returned each time).

Hamlet ... Where's your father?

Ophelia At home, my lord.

Hamlet Let the doors be shut upon him, that he may play the fool nowhere but in his own house.
Goes hastily towards L.H.D. – stops and looks at Ophelia.
Farewell.
Exit L.H.D.

Ophelia Oh, help him, you sweet heavens!

Hamlet If thou dost marry, I'll give thee this plague for thy dowry. Be thou as chaste as ice, as pure as snow, thou shalt not escape calumny. Get thee to a nunnery; farewell:
Retires a little L.H. Stops, looks at Ophelia, goes and takes her hand before he proceeds with his speech.
or, if thou wilt needs marry, marry a fool; for wise men know well enough what monsters you make of them.
Throws her hand gently from him, & retires a little –
To a nunnery, go, and quickly too. Farewell. – *Farewell –
Farewell.*
Exit L.H.D.

Ophelia Heavenly powers restore him!

Hamlet I have heard of your painting, too, well enough. Heaven has given you one face, and you make yourselves another. You jig, you amble, and you lisp, and nick-name Heaven's creatures, and make your wantonness your ignorance. Go to; I'll no more on't; it hath made me mad. I say, we will have no more marriages. Those that are married already, all but one, shall live; the rest shall keep as they are. To a nunnery, go – go – go – go.

Exit Hamlet L.H.D.

And there is a further general note: *Ophelia must remember to give Hamlet a little time in this Scene.*[31] It is easy to understand audiences accustomed to Kemble's wild playing of the scene finding this more leisurely and gentle approach too different for acceptance.

This is not, of course, to say that Cooke was right and they were wrong. What an actor can give and an audience happily receive in a particular role is always relative – theatrical styles change (or are moulded) from generation to generation. The cards were stacked against Cooke, and it is hard not to believe that he knew it. Apart from three provincial performances in the summer of 1801 he had not played the part for ten years. He was 46 – hardly the age at which to find it easy to convince an audience that he was a young man – as the *Morning Post* said "neither his appearance or voice could, by any possibility, be brought to suit the youthful description and tender sorrows of the character". Admittedly Kemble was only a year younger, but he had been playing Hamlet in London since 1783, and though his predominantly gentle, graceful, lonely, philosophic Hamlet had puzzled audiences at first, he had had time to persuade them of its rightness; now it had become the norm against which any other reading had to be judged. Cooke's real problem was that he was twenty years too late.

So, to the audiences of his last decade, Cooke became not the great player of all the major roles, but the popular actor of a handful of parts – Richard III, Shylock, Iago, Sir Pertinax, Sir Archy, and Falstaff, with Macbeth, Kitely and Sir Giles Overreach in the background. They reveal both his powers and his limitations – coarse strength, the need for the broad effect and the sequence of brilliant theatrical moments, the absence of gentleness and refinement. And yet within these limitations his acting could be powerful, subtle, effective, to his contemporaries "natural". Thomas Robinson, writing in a letter to his brother Henry Crabb Robinson perhaps sums up the view, not so much of the critic, as of the man in the pit.

We were so lucky as to see him in Richard, his favourite character. Nature has assisted him greatly in the performance of this part – his features being strongly marked and his voice harsh. I felt at the time that he personated the ferocious tyrant better than Kemble could have done. There is besides a sort of humour in his manner of acting which appeared very appropriate, and which I think Kemble could not have given: and I think it likely the latter would have been surpassed in Shylock. Cooke's powers of expression are strong and coarse. I am persuaded that in dignified and refined character – in the philosophical hero – he would fall infinitely short of Kemble.[32]

It is, of course, impossible to say how far this excellence in a limited area only was due to Cooke's own personal characteristics, and how far to his long sojourn in the provinces and his late arrival to a London attuned to Kemble's style and approach. Though almost contemporary in age, Kemble had reached London seventeen years earlier than Cooke. If Cooke had been able to impose his view of Hamlet in 1785 on London audiences instead of those of Chester, might Kemble's reading have been the one to be rejected? This was the period when Munden felt that Cooke was at the very peak of his achievement; but for the next fifteen years, while Kemble was conditioning London to accept his view of Hamlet, Cooke was coarsening his concepts before a less discriminating provincial public. Yet the delay in metropolitan recognition was largely of his own making. His notorious unreliability was a self-manufactured ball and chain; even so, Harris would have engaged him seven years earlier than he did, had Cooke not chosen to refuse the offered terms.

Why did he do it? Was Cooke always to be his own worst enemy? Why did he let himself down so frequently and so tragically? Why was the potential of the actor so flawed by the weakness of the man? For many lesser mortals such questions need no asking. For Cooke, they bring us to the heart of the matter.

Chapter XV

The Man

And so finally we come up against the enigma of the man himself. The contradictions have all emerged in the foregoing pages. A man of undoubted intelligence, he read widely, as his journals show, and thought deeply and critically about what he read. He could be kind, thoughtful, benevolent – whether the helping hand was given to the pregnant wife of a poor fellow-actor, to an old woman trudging along the road while he passed in a post-chaise, or to the benevolent fund of a theatre a hundred and twenty miles away. There is a trivial entry in his journal for 25 November 1806 that is very revealing.

> I sauntered to the theatre, and then took a circuitous walk to Storey's-gate to dinner. My mind was not at all set on dining there, but at my last two breakfasts, I had not given the waiter a fee, and he being a very civil young fellow, I went there more on his account than my own.[1]

And there are many other records of his concern for others less well-off than himself. In his Dublin journal of 1798 he recorded a brief incident with one of the servants of the theatre, and then became introspective.

> Chancing to look out of the window, Joe, the caller at the theatre, was passing; I desired him to come up, without having any business with him. Joe, who is quite a male gossip, had I shown the least inclination, would have entertained me with stories until midnight, but after a short time, perceiving me indifferent and inattentive, took his leave. I could not help thinking there was something strange and capricious in my manner, not to say absurd and saucy. – Calling a man up, merely to ask a few insignificant questions, and then appearing to be tired of his conversation! Had any person of a superior station of life to myself served me so, how should I have felt? It would very likely have soured my temper, and sent me home dissatisfied for the evening. Would we sometimes

place ourselves in the situation of our inferiors, they would not so often
have justice on their side, when they complain of our conduct towards
them. I have several times, particularly in this kingdom, been shocked
and disgusted at the behaviour of many whom I have had the occasion of
observing, for their arrogant and even cruel behaviour to servants; and
often for no other reason (if I may upon such an occasion use the word)
but because they *were* servants. Is not the yoke of servitude sufficient,
without adding insult to the weight of it?[2]

This is far different from the insensitive boor of so many of the popular
anecdotes. Poverty, cruelty, injustice, were evils that moved him deeply;
though he confessed that while he believed they could be abolished, he did
not know precisely how.[3] Sober, he could be an excellent companion, and
his sense of humour could both entertain others, and enjoy a joke against
himself. Mrs. Mathews, who knew him well, recorded:

After we came to London, when Cooke was at the height of his celebrity,
he often visited us, and a more cautiously abstemious person could not
be found. Indeed, it was difficult to imagine that he could be ever
otherwise than the grave, dignified gentleman he then appeared.[4]

And yet Dibdin, who also knew him well, has an account of an evening they
spent together at about the same time, in which all the irrationality of the
other side of Cooke emerges. The session lasted all night.

After many nods and winks from my better half, who did not dare leave
the supper table and me at the mercy of the Manchester Roscius, at seven
o'clock in a cold November morning, there being no coach to be obtained, I accompanied my friend George on foot from Goodge-street to
Martlett-court, Bow-street. As we crossed Oxford-street from Rathbone-
place, Cooke gave me some papers, begging me to take care of them, as
being of the greatest consequence in respect to a suit then pending
between his wife (once my wife's bridesmaid, and now Mrs. Windsor of
Bath) and himself in the court of Consistory . . . I, of course, promised to
take great care of these papers, when Cooke turned short round on me,
and asked, "What for? give me them back: I shall have them used
against me else." I conceived I was answerable to Mr. Harris for Mr.
Cooke being properly disposed of after having dined and supped with
me, and therefore took not the slightest notice of anything he said, which
might appear offensive; and finding he every moment halted to tell a
long story, I observed, I had heard that when in the army, he had always
been accounted a bad one at a march, from not being able to step in

time. On his looking terrifically indignant, I expressed my disbelief of the calumny; and to give him an opportunity of disproving it, I proposed to whistle a quick march, and observe whether or not he did not keep just time: he chuckled, with a sort of contempt, at the proposal; and we went, at a tolerable steady quick step, as far as the middle of Greek-street, when Cooke, who had passed his hand along all the palisades and shutters as he marched, came in contact with the recently painted new front of a coachmaker's shop, from which he obtained a complete handful of wet colour. Without any explanation to me as to the cause of his anger, he rushed suddenly into the middle of the street, and raised a stone which, in respect to its magnitude, Polypheme might not have rejected in his desire to crush the shepherd Acis. This fragment Cooke was going to hurl against the unoffending windows; but I was in time to save them from destruction, and him from the watch-house. On my asking the cause of his hostility to the premises of a man who could not have offended him, he replied with a hiccup, "What! not offend? a d—d ignorant coachmaker, to leave his house out, new-painted, at this time of night!" I agreed it was infamous conduct, and advised him to let me lay a complaint at Bow-street next day, which quite satisfied poor George; and after whistling him the rest of the way to Martlett-court, I returned home, planning a line of conduct to be observed respecting him in future. All London was at this time on the *qui vive* respecting Cooke's recent impression on the public; and I have often thought what curiosity would have been excited to see him marching home in merry quick time, with the author of "Mother Goose" as his fife-major, – and what a subject the duo would have furnished to Rowlandson or Cruikshanks.

I forgot to say that he stopped in the middle of Soho-square, and with thundering emphasis uttered the interjection "Hah!" in a tone about ten degrees beyond the strongest aspiration of our stoutest street-paviors. "There!" said Cooke, "tell Harris what my voice effected, after a hard drinking-bout, at seven in the morning, in Soho-square." "I will, my good friend!" said I. "Will you indeed," replied Cooke, "be such an enemy to your old friend? 'What business,' Harris will say, 'had Cooke in Soho-square at seven in the morning?' and thus, through your forward friendship, I shall lose my situation!" He uttered much more nonsense; compared the bright moon to Mr. Harris, and a dark cloud to Mr. Kemble, with whom, he said, he would play any part by way of wager for – for – yes, for a god."[5]

Dibdin knew his man of old, and knew how to minimise the damage that might otherwise have been done. To those who did not, at such times the slightest provocation, intended or unintended, might lead to one of Cooke's fits of near-madness. In such moods he could insult or attack friends or complete strangers, individuals or even massed audiences, like that at Liverpool. An affront, real or imagined, could then turn him arrogant and insulting, sometimes violent. And once he had taken up an attitude in such circumstances his obstinacy was such that usually no argument of reason or moderation could move him, no matter how much he was damaging himself in the process.

There were other symptoms of irrationality. Examples have already been given of how in these moods he would suddenly decide not to perform. Sometimes he could be persuaded to change his mind: at others, nothing would move him – or he would disappear, perhaps for several days. Then, when he disappointed an audience in this way, either by not appearing as billed, or by being drunk and unable to play properly, an apology might be made and accepted; but if the playgoers did not adequately support his later performances – for reasons perfectly natural and understandable – he would feel himself unfairly treated, once more seek consolation in a bottle, as a result of which he would behave badly again, and so the vicious circle was perpetuated. This happened in London, for example, over his later benefit performances, and again in New York. Managers suffered most, perhaps, from his unreliability, but so too did his friends and colleagues. After defaulting at one of Munden's Benefit performances Cooke apologised and entreated to be allowed to make up for it on a future occasion; so in the end Munden

> put him in the bill for his benefit in a new character, and took the pains to call upon him and ascertain that he was studying the character previous to the rehearsal. In order that there might be no allurement this time, Munden invited him to dinner, saw that he took only a moderate quantity of wine, and walked arm and arm with him to the theatre. At the door, Cooke shook his friend by the hand, and said, "I wish you a bumper, Joe! I am going up to dress." When the time arrived for the prologue to be spoken, Munden inquired, in all directions, "Where is Cooke?" "Mr. Cooke, Sir," said the door-keeper; "Why he left the house the moment he parted from you."[6]

Wise in the ways of Cooke, Munden had taken the precaution of having a good understudy; and it is significant both of their characters and their relationship that Munden's son could comment – "To quarrel with such a man would have been absurd." To survive such incidents, Cooke's friendships must have been based on a recognition of something in his character that transcended such maltreatment.

S. W. Ryley, another of Cooke's colleagues who had worked with him in Manchester and elsewhere, summed up the dual nature of Cooke in his book *The Itinerant*. He wrote:

In some characters he is as much superior to any actor of the present day as Garrick was to those of his time; but they are limited to such parts as suit his figure, which wants grace and proportion; when these can be dispensed with, he has no competitor. As a man in private life, he is the gentleman, the scholar, the friend, the life of every party, an enemy to scandal and detraction, and benevolent even to imprudence. Such is George Cooke in his sober hours; but when stimulated by the juice of the grape, he acts in diametrical opposition to all this. No two men, however different they may be, can be more at variance than George Cooke sober and George Cooke in a state of ebriety. At these times his interesting suavity of manners changes to brutal invective; the feelings of his nearest and dearest friends are sacrificed; his best benefactor wounded, either in his own person, or that of his tenderest connection, and the ears of delicacy assaulted by abuse of the grossest nature. Such are the unfortunate propensities of this singular man; unfortunate, I say; because he seems incapable of avoiding them, although they have a tendency to ruin his health, injure his property, and destroy his social connections. No one can more regret these failings than he does in his hours of sanity, or make more handsome apologies, and if at night he creates enemies, his conciliatory manners in the morning are sure to raise double the number of friends.[7]

Why should it have been so? It was not that Cooke was unaware of the problem, and the various unfinished confessional journals show that from time to time he did try to gain control of himself. Dublin in 1798 was one of these, and he reflected on the advice given him by a friend more than two decades before,

to take a quarter of an hour's consideration every morning, to regulate the affairs, and arrange, as far as I could, the transactions intended or expected, for the day. I am sorry to say, I have very seldom availed myself of this advice; if I had, I am fully persuaded, I should have avoided many disagreeable and dangerous circumstances, which have perplexed and embittered a great part of my life. So small a space of time as a quarter of an hour, may be taken from the most urgent calls . . .[8]

During that same tour he played cards a good deal with some of his

colleagues, to pass the time – though without gambling; but then Cooke
brooded over the waste of precious time.

It will very little assist me in defending myself to say, that I have
frequently wasted my time in much worse manner; when a man reconciles himself to himself by making degrees of sin, he is in the utmost
danger of advancing to, instead of receding from, the utmost depth of
iniquity ... It is a doubt with me whether a Gamester (here I take the
word in its utmost latitude) or a drunkard, be the most vicious character,
or the most dangerous to society. The former, without deranging his
faculties, exerts them all for the avowed purpose of plundering everyone
he plays with, his dearest friends not excepted, (if such a wretch can have
a friend) and when by superior villainy, or some unforeseen chance or
change of fortune he in his turn is stripped and beggared, his mind,
having lost all the fine feelings of nature, is easily wrought on to embrace
the most abandoned and wicked project that human nature, depraved,
can possibly suggest. He starts not at murder! & his flagitious career
often ends in self-destruction. Let no one imagine this picture is too
highly coloured; there have been too many dreadful examples to prove
the truth of the painting.(9)

"When a man reconciles himself to himself by making degrees of sin
..." There is a clear-sighted intelligence at work here; if he could see so
clearly what he was doing, why on earth could he not stop? For such
periods rarely lasted for very long. A temporary reversal of fortune or the
blandishments of an old friend or acquaintance, and the good resolutions
vanished. The "easiness of his temper" Ward had called it. Cooke could
rarely say "no", and if he did it was probably on the wrong occasion and
for the wrong reason.

It is, of course, the crucial, and ultimately unanswerable question. Certainly there was a failure of the will. But it would be an oversimplification
to use that as the sole explanation. Adequately motivated to himself, as we
have seen, Cooke could be obstinate to a fault. Why was his motivation so
perverse?

We can, of course, do no more than speculate. But after reading and re-
reading the journals, one becomes more and more aware of two factors – Cooke's extreme sensitivity, and at the same time his failure ever fully
to face the facts about himself. The journals may be intended as a piece of
self-analysis, but they rarely dig deep enough. In Appleby, for instance, he
never refers openly to why he is there or what are the negotiations he is
carrying out; references are always guarded and oblique – even in a journal
written for himself alone. In Buxton he looks at himself – but again

211

obliquely, only through the reflecting mirror of the drunken clergyman. He exhorts himself to "remember Sunday 20th of April 1806 at Bath"; but does not specify why.[10] It is as though he could not bear to admit, even to himself, the difference between his image of what he would like to be, and the reality of what he was. Without first accepting that, amendment could not begin.

And so he ran away from the truth, or from a difficult problem when it arose, either by attempting to ignore it, or by using alcohol to take it out of his mind. But to the sensitive mind escape of this kind can have a cumulative, boomerang effect – problems that, if faced, can be solved comparatively easily, once left, or ignored, or run away from, can grow great out of all proportion; and so they become progressively more difficult and more impossible of solution – a kind of geometric progression of intractability is at work. Ultimately the only way out becomes some kind of a breakdown, after which it is possible to start again, for a while, until the next build-up develops. Cooke's life, as we have seen, had its regular sequence of crises of this kind.

Perhaps he came closest to looking clearly at himself in the Irish journals of 1798–1800. In them he noted, though he did not understand, a malaise in himself; for instance, at certain times he found himself quite unable to write.

> I am at times possessed with a certain restlessness of disposition, and an indecisive turn of mind, that prevents me from adhering to any one object, unless for a very short time. When these fits are on me I feel, and seem perplexed, and nothing but a change of scene will banish them. I cannot exactly account for their intrusion, but observe, I am chiefly visited by them, when affairs or business are a little embarrassed and unsettled.[11]

Across the Irish Sea, on the coast of North Somerset, or among the mountains of Cumberland, Samuel Taylor Coleridge would have understood.

It was in such moods that Cooke clouded his intellect with alcohol so that he no longer needed or was able to think. But when the alcohol released his rational control over himself then so often he became, as we have seen, arrogant, self-assertive, domineering. Was this, perhaps, the cover for a deep-seated sense of insecurity?

If it were so, again we can do no more than speculate as to the cause. Was it related to his obscure birth and lack of contact with his parents? Did the frustration of his early years contribute to it, when, conscious of his ability, he was for so long unable to make a way in his chosen profession? His need for, and lack of, a durable relationship with the opposite sex may also have been relevant. In his last years especially, overwork and overstrain may well have been contributing factors, too; not just the strain of the rivalry with Kemble, but the overwork of those touring summers when, night after night, with the minimum of rehearsal and after arduous and weary journeys, he was expected to give star performances backed by mediocre companies.

Yet other men have survived strains as great or greater. George Cooke could not. Physically he must have been immensely tough to have survived as long as he did the enormous strain he put upon his body. But mentally, emotionally, he was not strong enough. Perhaps subconsciously that was why he chose the actor's profession. There he could counterfeit the power and the drive and the will that inwardly he did not possess. The assumption of the mask could cover the face he was too vulnerable to reveal.

We have already recorded how in 1794, reflecting on the drunken clergyman he saw at Fairfield, he wrote –

From the general temper of the world it is too probable, with respect to the gentleman I am writing of, that a long and faithful discharge of the duties of his office will be almost forgotten, while the hours of his frailty, or to speak stronger, the periods of his vice and folly, will be clearly remembered and distinctly related.[12]

This, as perhaps Cooke divined intuitively at the time, is precisely what has happened to his own reputation. Both in his lifetime and since, the popular anecdotes have been those of his vice and folly, and they have overshadowed the compensating virtues of the man, and the long and faithful discharge, for much of the time, of his duties in the theatre.

In the beginning it was one aim of this biographical study to see if it were possible to redress the imbalance of such a view. But as the work proceeded that purpose became subsumed in a growing fascination with, and sympathy for, the paradoxes of the man himself. No human being is a single amalgam of qualities, but few are as overtly complex as George Cooke. In many ways he was a tragic figure – his great potential never fully realised because of his inability to marshal his powers and keep them under control. But something of his quality emerged from that very indiscipline itself, and might not have been revealed without it. In the final analysis it is presumptuous to attempt the precise categorisation of an accountant's balance sheet. Like the Richard he made to live again so vividly up and down the crowded playhouses of the United Kingdom, he was a unique phenomenon, he was himself alone.

George Frederick Cooke. *Requiescat.*

Appendix I

Bibliography

The extent of my debt to individual sources is indicated in the preceding notes. Here they are listed alphabetically by categories.

1. Manuscripts

George Frederick Cooke: Memorandum Book No 2. (Harvard Theatre Collection)

George Frederick Cooke: Ms. Diary – fragments from 1794–1807 (Harvard Theatre Collection M.S. Thr. 20.1)

J. P. Kemble's Memoranda Books 1788–1815. (British Museum Add. Mss. 31, 972–5)

Johnson: Liverpool Theatrical Material 1772–1945 (Picton Library, Liverpool)

The Stretton Mss. (Nottingham Reference Library. Pub. 1910)

2. Newspapers and Journals

Bath Chronicle
Bath Journal
(Aris') Birmingham Gazette
Bristol Gazette
(Felix Farley's) Bristol Journal
New Cork Evening Post
Cork Advertiser
Chester Chronicle
(Drewry's) Derby Mercury
Dublin – The Hibernian Journal
The Public Register, or Freeman's Journal

Edinburgh Evening Courant
Glasgow Courier
Glasgow Herald
Kentish Gazette
Limerick Chronicle
(Gore's) Liverpool Advertiser
Liverpool Chronicle
London – Bell's Weekly Messenger
          Commercial Chronicle
          Morning Chronicle
          Monthly Mirror
          Morning Post
          The Porcupine
          The Sun
          The Times
(Harrop's) Manchester Mercury
Manchester Newspaper Cuttings Book (Central Reference Library)
Newcastle Chronicle
Newcastle Courant
Norfolk Chronicle
Norwich Mercury
(Cresswell and Burbage's) Nottingham Journal
Salisbury Journal
Sheffield Advertiser
Sheffield Register
York Chronicle
Yorkshire Magazine

3. Playbills

British Library – Burney Collection
British Library – Covent Garden Playbills
British Library – Provincial Playbills
Victoria & Albert Museum – Enthoven Collection
Bath Playbills – City Reference Library
Birmingham Theatre Royal Playbills – Birmingham Reference Library
Bristol – Richard Smith Collection – Bristol Central Reference Library
Dublin – Trinity College
Lincoln – Central Library
Manchester Theatre Royal Playbills – Central Reference Library
York – Hailstone Collection – Minster Library

4. Public Records

Berwick-on-Tweed – Registers of Trinity Church (copies in Newcastle Central Reference Library)

Berwick-on-Tweed – Roll of Freemen (Northumberland County Record Office)

Dublin – Volumes of the Parish Register Society (The Castle)

Dublin – Watson's Almanack – Lists of General and Field Officers of Regiments in Ireland, Barrack Officers, Barrack Masters, etc. (The Castle)

Edinburgh – Register of Proclamations and Marriages, 1808 (New Register House)

London – Proceedings of the Consistory Court of London at Doctor's Commons, 1801 (Greater London Record Office)

5. Prompt Copies

Macklin:	The Man of the World	Enthoven Collection, Victoria and Albert Museum
Shakespeare:	Cymbeline	Harvard Theatre Collection
Shakespeare:	Cymbeline	Folger Library
Shakespeare:	Hamlet	Library of the Literary and Philosophical Society, Newcastle-upon-Tyne
Shakespeare:	Henry VIII	Birmingham Reference Library
Shakespeare:	Henry VIII	Harvard Theatre Collection
Shakespeare:	Henry VIII	The Players, New York
Shakespeare:	King Lear	Harvard Theatre Collection
Shakespeare:	King Lear	University of Michigan
Shakespeare:	Macbeth	New York Public Library
Shakespeare:	Merchant of Venice	Folger Library
Shakespeare:	The Merry Wives of Windsor	Folger Library
Shakespeare:	Othello	Harvard Theatre Collection
Shakespeare:	Richard III	Harvard Theatre Collection
Shakespeare:	Richard III	Folger Library

6. Memoirs, etc.

(Unless otherwise specified, place of publication is London)

Anon: Thoughts on the late Disturbance at the Theatre Royal Newcastle (Newcastle 1789)

Anon: The Secret History of the Green Room (1795)

Anon: Remarks on the Character of Richard III as played by Cooke and Kemble (2nd ed. 1801)

Anon: The Queen Street Ghost, or Theatrical Spectre (Glasgow 1806)

Bernard, J.: Retrospections of America 1797–1811 (1887)

Censor, C.: The Thespian Mirror (Manchester 1793)

Boaden, J.: Memoirs of the Life of John Philip Kemble (1825)

Cobbett, W.: The Autobiography of William Cobbett (ed. Reitzel 1947)

Dibdin, T.: Reminiscences (1827)

Dunlap, W.: The Life of George Frederick Cooke (2nd ed. revised 1815)

Everard, E. C.: Memoirs of an Unfortunate Son of Thespis (Edinburgh 1818)

Fuller, J.: A History of Berwick-on-Tweed (1799)

Garrick, D.: Letters (ed. D. Little and G. Kahrl 1963)

Genest, J.: Some Account of the English Stage (Bath 1832)

Hunt, L.: Critical Essays on the Performers of the London Theatres (1807)

Hutton: History of Derby (1791)

Inchbald, Mrs. E.: Memoirs (ed. Boaden 1833)

Kelly, M.: Reminiscences (1826)

Kemble, F.: Record of a Girlhood (1878)

Kirkman, J. T.: Memoirs of the Life of Charles Macklin (1799)

Lamb, C.: Essays of Elia (1835)

Lennox, Lord W. P.: Celebrities I Have Known (1876)

Lewes, C. L.: Memoirs (1805)

Lockhart, J. G.: Memoirs of Sir Walter Scott (1837)

Macready, W. C.: Reminiscences (ed. Pollock 1875)

Mathews, C.: Memoirs (ed. Mrs. A. Mathews 1838–9)

Mathews, Mrs. A.: Anecdotes of Actors (1844)

Moritz, C. P.: Journeys of a German in England in 1782 (ed. Nettel 1965)

Munden, J. S.: Memoirs (1846)

Roach, J.: Authentic Memoirs of the Green Room (1796)

Ryley, S. W.: The Itinerant (1808)

A Veteran Stager (? G. Grant): An Essay on the Science of Acting (1828)

Wilkinson, T.: The Wandering Patentee (York, 1795)

Winston, J.: The Theatric Tourist (1805)

7. Secondary Sources

Appleton, W. W.: Charles Macklin (Cambridge, Mass, 1960)

Armstrong, N.: The Edinburgh Stage 1715–1820 (3 vols. Typescript – Edinburgh Public Library) ·

Baker, H. B.: Our Old Actors (1878)

Baynham, W.: The Glasgow Stage (1892)

Broadbent, J. B.: Annals of the Liverpool Stage (1908)

Broadbent, J. B.: Annals of the Manchester Theatre 1735–1845 (3 vols. typescript 1913. Manchester Central Library)

Byrne, M.: "The Earliest *Hamlet* Prompt Book in an English Library" *Theatre Notebook* Vol. XV, No. 1. pp. 21–31

Clark, W. S.: The Irish Stage in the County Towns (1965)

Hare, A.: The Georgian Theatre in Wessex (1958)

Hare, A.: (ed.): Theatre Royal Bath – the Orchard Street Calendar 1750–1805 (Bath 1977)

Hare, A.: "George Frederick Cooke's Early Years in the Theatre" *Theatre Notebook* Vol. XXXI, No. 1 pp. 12–21

Hodgkinson, J. and Pogson, R.: The Early Manchester Theatre (1960)

Macmillan, D.: Drury Lane Calendar (1938)

Manvell, R.: Sarah Siddons (1970)

Oswald, H.: The Theatres Royal in Newcastle-upon-Tyne (Newcastle 1936)

Price, C.: The English Theatre in Wales (1948)

Price, C.: "Joseph Austin and His Associates 1766–89" *Theatre Notebook* Vol. 4 pp. 89–94

Price, C.: "An 18th Century Theatrical Agreement" *Theatre Notebook* Vol. 2 pp. 31–4

Richards, J.: "Thomas Shafto Robertson and The Theatric Tourist" *Theatre Notebook* Vol. XXIX No. 1 pp. 4–9

Rosenfeld, S.: The York Theatre (1948 Typescript York Public Library)

Rosenfeld, S.: "St George's Hall, King's Lynn" *Theatre Notebook* Vol. 3 pp. 24–7

Scholes, P.: The Great Dr. Burney (1948)

Shattuck, C. H.: The Shakespeare Prompt Books (Illinois 1965)

Sheldon: The History of Berwick-on-Tweed (1849)

Stone, G. W. (ed.): The London Stage 1747–76 (Illinois 1962)

Hogan, C. B. (ed.): The London Stage 1776–1800 (Illinois 1967)

Wilmeth, D. B.: "The Posthumous Career of George Frederick Cooke" *Theatre Notebook* Vol. XXIV, No. 2 pp. 68–74

Wilmeth, D. B.: "Cooke Among the Yankee Doodles" *Theatre Survey* Vol. XIV, No. 2 1973

Appendix II

Cooke's Repertory 1774–1812

Notes

1. Date of publication of all post-Restoration plays is given to show whether Cooke's performance is of a new play or a revival. *Allardyce Nicoll: A History of English Drama 1660–1900 Vol. VI – Alphabetical Catalogue of Plays (1965)* has been used as the standard for titles and dates.

2. The years of Cooke's first and last known performances are given as an approximate indication of the length of time the part remained within his repertory.

Character	Play	Date	Author	Period Played
Lord Abbeville	The Fashionable Lover	1772	Cumberland	1778
Abbot	Henry II	1773	Hull	1784
Aboan	Oroonoko	1695	Southern	1788
Capt. Absolute	The Rivals	1775	Sheridan	1785–1796
Sir Anthony Absolute	The Rivals	1775	Sheridan	1795
Adam	As You Like It	—	Shakespeare	1785–1792
Aimwell	The Beaux Stratagem	1707	Farquhar	1784–1791
Lord Aimworth	The Maid of the Mill	1765	Bickerstaffe	1774–1792
Sir George Airy	The Busybody	1709	Mrs. Centlivre	1781–1797
Albert	The Sorrows of Werter	1785	Reynolds	1787
Alberto	The Child of Nature	1788	Mrs. Inchbald	1801
Alexander	The Rival Queens	1677	Lee	1774–1797
Alfonso	Alfonso, King of Castile	1801	Lewis	1803
Marquis Almanza	The Child of Nature	1788	Mrs. Inchbald	1796–1798
Count Almaviva	The Follies of a Day	1784	Holcroft	1792
Alonzo	The Revenge	1721	Young	1784–1785
Alonzo	Columbus	1792	Morton	1793
Prince of Altenburg	Adrian and Orrila	1806	Dimond	1806–1808
Alwin	The Countess of Salisbury	1765	Hartson	1784–1791
Angelo	Measure for Measure	—	Shakespeare	1803
Antonio	The Merchant of Venice	—	Shakespeare	1784–1790
Apollo	Midas	1762	O'Hara	1775
Archer	The Beaux Stratagem	1707	Farquhar	1788
King Arthur	King Arthur	1691	Dryden	1775
Aubrey	The Fashionable Lover	1772	Cumberland	1787–1790
Austin	The Count of Narbonne	1781	Jephson	1799–1800
Lord Avondale	The School of Reform	1805	Morton	1805–1806
Bajazet	Tamerlane the Great	1701	Rowe	1802–1805
Count Baldwin	Isabella	1694	Southern	1786
Banquo	Macbeth	—	Shakespeare	1792

Character	Play	Date	Author	Period Played
Barbarossa	Barbarossa	1754	Brown	1784
George Barnwell	The London Merchant	1731	Lillo	1792–1793
Bastard	King Lear	—	Shakespeare	1800
Mr. Beauchamp	Which is the Man?	1782	Mrs. Cowley	1787
Beau Mizen	The Fair Quaker of Deal	1710	Shadwell	1774–1775
Bedamar	Venice Preserv'd	1682	Otway	1778
Bellair	More Ways than One	1783	Mrs. Cowley	1784
Young Belmont	The Foundling	1784	Moore	1779–1787
Belvile	The School for Wives	1773	Kelly	1774–1775
Belvile	Which is the Man?	1782	Mrs. Cowley	1786–1789
Benedick	Much Ado about Nothing	—	Shakespeare	1784–1799
Bertodo	The Maid of Honour	1785	Massinger/J. P. Kemble	1785
Capt. Bertram	The Birthday	1799	T. J. Dibdin	1799–1802
Sir Stephen Bertram	The Jew	1794	Cumberland	1800
Beverley	The Gamester	1753	Moore	1792
Beverley	All In The Wrong	1761	Murphy	1775
Beverley	The Man of Business	1774	Colman sen.	1775
George Bevil	Cross Purposes	1772	O'Brien	1778
Young Bevil	The Conscious Lovers	1722	Steele	1789–1790
Biron	Isabella	1694	Southern	1793–1799
Sir Phillip Blandford	Speed the Plough	1800	Morton	1800–1803
Lord Burleigh	The Unhappy Favourite	1681	Banks	1784
Dick Buskin	Wild Oats	1791	O'Keeffe	1791–1793
Sir Callaghan O'Brallaghan	Love à la Mode	1759	Macklin	1794
Dr. Cantwell	The Hypocrite	1768	Bickerstaffe	1792
Young Cape	The Author	1757	Foote	1782
Don Carlos	A Bold Stroke for a Husband	1783	Mrs. Cowley	1787–1804
Don Carlos	Love Makes a Man	1700	Cibber	1784–1792
Don Carlos	Lovers' Quarrels	1790	King	1792
Carlton	More Ways Than One	1783	Mrs. Cowley	1785

Character	Play	Date	Author	Period Played
Castalio	The Orphan	1680	Otway	1778
Catarach	Bonduca	1778	Beaumont and Fletcher/Colman sen.	1808
Cato	Cato	1713	Addison	1789–1810
Chamont	The Orphan	1680	Otway	1789
Charles	The Busybody	1709	Mrs. Centlivre	1778
Clairville	Notoriety	1791	Reynolds	1792
Sir John Classick	The Married Man	1789	Mrs. Inchbald	1792
Claudio	Much Ado about Nothing	—	Shakespeare	1784–1791
Claudius	Hamlet	—	Shakespeare	1784–1785
Clerimont	The Old Maid	1761	Murphy	1788–1791
Clytus	The Rival Queens	1677	Lee	1782–1811
John Cockle	The King and the Miller of Mansfield	1737	Dodsley	1787–1809
Cohenburg	The Siege of Belgrade	1791	Cobb	1804–1805
Columbus	Columbus	1792	Morton	1794
Comus	Comus	1772	Milton/Colman sen.	1786–1803
Conjurer	The Devil to Pay	1731	Coffey and Mottley	1778
Cromwell	King Charles I	1737	Havard	1791–1792
Captain Constant	The Ghost	1767	(Unknown)	1778
Sir Christopher Curry	Inkle and Yarico	1787	Colman jun.	1790–1808
Damaetas	Midas	1762	O'Hara	1774
Dashwood	Know your own Mind	1777	Murphy	1786
Lord Davenant	The Mysterious Husband	1783	Cumberland	1790–1806
Delaval	He's Much to Blame	1798	Holcroft	1798
Dick	The Confederacy	1705	Vanbrugh	1790
Dionysius	The Grecian Daughter	1772	Murphy	1792
Doricourt	The Belle's Stratagem	1780	Mrs. Cowley	1786
Sir William Dorrillon	Wives as They Were, and Maids as They Are	1797	Mrs. Inchbald	1797–1800

Character	Play	Date	Author	Period Played
Sir John Dormer	A Word to the Wise	1770	Kelly	1790
Harry Dornton	The Road to Ruin	1792	Holcroft	1792–1794
Derington	The Man of Ten Thousand	1795	Holcroft	1796
Douglas	Douglas	1756	Home	1784
Sir William Douglas	The English Merchant	1767	Colman sen.	1790–1791
Earl Douglas	Percy	1777	Mrs. More	1787–1798
Colonel Downright	I'll Tell You What	1785	Mrs. Inchbald	1787
Young Dudley	The West Indian	1771	Cumberland	1776–1788
Lord Guilford Dudley	Lady Jane Grey	1715	Rowe	1790
Duke	Measure for Measure	—	Shakespeare	789
Lord Duke	High Life Below Stairs	1759	Townley/Garrick	1774
Dumont	Jane Shore	1714	Rowe	1776–1806
Mr. Dupely	The Maid of the Oaks	1774	Burgoyne	1775–1791
Durand	Venice Preserv'd	1682	Otway	1786
Eastern Magician	Harlequin Sorcerer	—	(Unknown)	1781–1782
Edgar	King Lear	—	Shakespeare	1778–1789
King Edward	The Earl of Warwick	1766	Francklin	1786
Edward	Edward the Black Prince	1749	Shirley	1793
Epicene	The Macaroni	1773	Hitchcock	1774
Essex	The Earl of Essex	1751	Jones	1790
Eustace de St Pierre	The Surrender of Calais	1791	Colman jun.	1794
Anthony Euston				1794
Evander	The Grecian Daughter	1772	Murphy	1781–1799
Exeter, Earl of	Henry V	—	Shakespeare	1790
Fairfax	King Charles I	1737	Havard	1784
Fairfield	The Maid of the Mill	1765	Bickerstaffe	1799
Falconbridge	King John	—	Shakespeare	1791
Falstaff	Henry IV	—	Shakespeare	1788–1812
Falstaff	Merry Wives of Windsor	—	Shakespeare	1790–1811
Faulkland	The Rivals	1775	Sheridan	1794

223

Character	Play	Date	Author	Period Played
Capt. Faulkner	How to Get Married	1795	(Unknown)	1796–1802
Colonel Feignwell	A Bold Stroke for a Wife	1718	Mrs. Centlivre	1789
Don Felix	The Wonder	1714	Mrs. Centlivre	1774–1808
Ferdinand	The Tempest	—	Shakespeare	1774–1775
Filch	The Beggar's Opera	1728	Gay	1774
Mr. Fitzherbert	Which is The Man?	1782	Mrs. Cowley	1784–1791
Sir Clement Flint	The Heiress	1786	Burgoyne	1787–1793
Floriville	The Dramatist	1789	Reynolds	1792
Sir John Flowerdale	Lionel and Clarissa	1768	Bickerstaffe	1798
Frederick	The Miser	1733	Fielding	1778–1782
Frederick	The Wonder	1714	Mrs. Centlivre	1778
Farmer Freehold	The Farmhouse	1789	J. P. Kemble	1789
Freeman	A Bold Stroke for a Wife	1718	Mrs. Centlivre	1778
Freeport	The English Merchant	1767	Colman sen.	1788–1794
Fuzee	The Modish Wife	1761	Gentleman	1774–1775
Frankly	The Suspicious Husband	1747	Hoadley	1782–1794
Gambler	The Indian Chief	—	Williams	1784
Gayless	The Lying Valet	1741	Garrick	1778
Sir George	The Rage	1794	Reynolds	1795
Gibby	The Wonder	1714	Mrs. Centlivre	1809
Ghost	Hamlet	—	Shakespeare	1792–1804
Glanville	Cleone	1758	Dodsley	1784
Glenalvon	Douglas	1756	Home	1778–1811
Gloster	Jane Shore	1714	Rowe	1786–1807
Gondibert	The Battle of Hexham	1789	Colman jun.	1790
Granville	Clementina	1771	Kelly	1774
Grey	The Chapter of Accidents	1780	Lee	1788–1800
The Guardian	The Guardian	1759	Garrick	1790–1800
Hamlet	Hamlet	—	Shakespeare	1774–1802
Mr. Hammond	Modern Breakfast	1790	Siddons	1791

Character	Play	Date	Author	Period Played
Lord Hardy	The Funeral	1701	Steele	1774
Mr. Harlow	The Old Maid	1761	Murphy	1778
Harmony	Everyone Has His Fault	1792	Mrs. Inchbald	1793-1801
Harry	The Mock Doctor	1732	Fielding	1778
Lord Hastings	Jane Shore	1714	Rowe	1774-1805
Sir George Hastings	A Word to the Wise	1770	Kelly	1774
Haswell	Such Things Are	1787	Mrs. Inchbald	1788-1806
Mr. Heartly	The Guardian	1759	Garrick	1791-1803
Heartwell	The Guardian	1759	Garrick	1790
Henry	The Deserter	1773	C. Dibdin	1774-1775
Henry II	Henry II	1773	Hull	1774-1785
Henry V	Henry V	—	Shakespeare	1790-1805
King Henry	Richard III	—	Shakespeare	1784-1800
Henry VIII	Henry VIII	—	Shakespeare	1810-1811
Lord Hildebrand	The Carmelite	1784	Cumberland	1790
Colonel Holberg	The Disbanded Officer	1786	Johnstone	1787
Robin Hood	Robin Hood and Little John	1730	(Unknown)	1790
Horatio	The Fair Penitent	1703	Rowe	1795-1811
Horatius	The Roman Father	1750	Whitehead	1792-1810
Hortensio	Catherine and Petruchio	1756	Garrick	1778
Hotspur	Henry IV	—	Shakespeare	1775-1794
Hubert	King John	—	Shakespeare	1804
Iachimo	Cymbeline	—	Shakespeare	1789-1807
Iago	Othello	—	Shakespeare	1792-1812
Inkle	Inkle and Yarico	1787	Colman jun.	1788-1792
Capt. Ironsides	The Brothers	1769	Cumberland	1799-1807
Jaffier	Venice Preserv'd	1682	Otway	1774-1793
Jaques	As You Like It	—	Shakespeare	1789-1808
King John	King John	—	Shakespeare	1796-1811
Don Juan	The Castle of Andalusia	1782	O'Keeffe	1784

225

Character	Play	Date	Author	Period Played
Don Juan	The Duke of Braganza	1775	Jephson	1794
Don Julio	A Bold Stroke for a Husband	1783	Mrs. Cowley	1784–1785
Kent	King Lear	—	Shakespeare	1808
King	The King and the Miller of Mansfield	1737	Dodsley	1793–1809
King	The Mourning Bride	1697	Congreve	1786
King	The King in the Country	1789	Waldron	1793
Kiteley	Everyman in his Humour	—	Jonson	1793–1811
Sir John Lambert	The Hypocrite	1768	Bickerstaffe	1784
Friar Lawrence	Romeo and Juliet	—	Shakespeare	1794–1799
Las Casas	Pizarro	1799	Sheridan	1800
Lavensforth	To Marry or Not to Marry	1805	Mrs. Inchbald	1805
Lear	King Lear	—	Shakespeare	1774–1812
Leon	Rule a Wife and Have a Wife	—	Beaumont and Fletcher	1801
Lennox	Sprigs of Laurel	1793	O'Keeffe	1805
Leontes	The Winter's Tale	—	Shakespeare	1789
Leonidas	The Fate of Sparta	1788	Mrs. Cowley	1788–1790
Lionel	Lionel and Clarissa	1768	Bickerstaffe	1774–1775
Loveless	A Trip to Scarborough	1777	Sheridan	1786–1800
Loveless	Reparation	1784	Andrews	1789
Mr. Lovemore	The Way to Keep Him	1760	Murphy	1774–1789
Lovewell	The Clandestine Marriage	1766	Colman sen. and Garrick	1778–1791
Lusignan	Zara	1736	Hill	1790
Mahomet	Mahomet	1744	Miller	1790
Malville	Know you own Mind	1777	Murphy	1784–1789
Charles Marlowe	The Choleric Man	1774	Cumberland	1775
Young Manley	The Fugitive	1792	Richardson	1792–1793
Don Manuel	The Regent	1788	Greathead	1788–1792
Mark Antony	Julius Caesar	—	Shakespeare	1793–1796
Young Marlow	She Stoops to Conquer	1773	Goldsmith	1774–1794

226

Character	Play	Date	Author	Period Played
Marplot	The Busybody	1709	Mrs. Centlivre	1775
Master of the Shop	The Toyshop	1735	Dodsley	1797
Young Meadows	Love in a Village	1762	Bickerstaffe	1774-1775
Jack Meggot	The Suspicious Husband	1747	Hoadley	1774
Sir John Melville	The Clandestine Marriage	1766	Colman sen. and Garrick	1785-1792
Mentevole	Julia	1787	Jephson	1788
Mercutio	Romeo and Juliet	—	Shakespeare	1801
Midas	Midas	1762	O'Hara	1798
Moddy	The Country Lasses	1715	Johnson	1778-1790
Monoses	Tamerlane	1710	Rowe	1784-1787
Moody	The Country Girl	1766	Garrick	1789-1800
Morcar	Matilda	1775	Francklin	1775
Sir Edward Mortimer	The Iron Chest	1796	Colman jun.	1796-1802
Mortmer	Laugh when you Can	1798	Reynolds	1805
Myrtle	The Conscious Lovers	1722	Steele	1788
Macbeth	Macbeth	—	Shakespeare	1774-1812
Macduff	Macbeth	—	Shakespeare	1791-1804
Donald MacIntosh	The Register Office	1761	Reed	1805
Colin Macleod	The Fashionable Lover	1772	Cumberland	1808-1810
McLaughlan	Bantry Bay	1797	Reynolds	1797
Ensign Maclaymore	The Reprisal	1757	Smollett	1784-1793
Sir Archy MacSarcasm	Love a la Mode	1759	Macklin	1796-1812
Sir Pertinax MacSycophant	The Man of the World	1781	Macklin	1792-1812
The Natural Son	The Natural Son	1784	Cumberland	1787
Nevile	The Dramatist	1789	Reynolds	1790-1791
Old Norval	Douglas	1756	Home	1793-1799
Mr. Oakley	The Jealous Wife	1761	Colman sen.	1787-1808
Major Oakley	The Jealous Wife	1761	Colman sen.	1789-1810
Octavian	The Mountaineers	1793	Colman jun.	1794-1802

Character	Play	Date	Author	Period Played
Major O'Flaherty	The West Indian	1771	Cumberland	1791
Lord Ogleby	The Clandestine Marriage	1766	Colman sen. and Garrick	1775
Mr. Ordeal	Fashionable Levities	1785	Macnally	1787–1788
Orestes	The Distressed Mother	1712	Phillips	1784
Orloff, the Russian Slave	A Day in Turkey	1791	Mrs. Cowley	1792–1793
Oroonoko	Oroonoko	1695	Southern	1775–1792
Orsino	Alfonso, King of Castile	1801	Lewis	1802–1805
Earl Osmond	The Castle Spectre	1797	Lewis	1799–1804
Osmyn	The Morning Bride	1697	Congreve	1797
Othello	Othello	—	Shakespeare	1786–1801
Sir Giles Overreach	A New Way to Pay Old Debts	—	Massinger	1796–1812
Paris	The Judgment of Paris	1730	Langford	1774
Paris	The Golden Pippin	1772	O'Hara	1775
Earl of Pembroke	Lady Jane Grey	1715	Rowe	1782
Penruddock	The Wheel of Fortune	1795	Cumberland	1797–1812
Peregrine	John Bull	1803	Colman jun.	1803–1809
Petruchio	Catherine and Petruchio	1756	Garrick	1786–1807
Philotas	The Grecian Daughter	1772	Murphy	1784–1787
Pierre	Venice Preserv'd	1682	Otway	1801–1812
Pizarro	Pizarro	1799	Sheridan	1800–1806
Sir Charles Pleasant	The Fair Quaker	1773	Thompson	1784
Captain Plume	The Recruiting Officer	1706	Farquhar	1789–1792
Posthumous	Cymbeline	—	Shakespeare	1774–1791
Prattle	The Deuce is in him	1763	Colman sen.	1775
Prospero	The Tempest	—	Shakespeare	1789–1807
Earl Raby	Percy	1777	Mrs. More	1784–1786
Sir Robert Ramble	Everyone has his Fault	1792	Mrs. Inchbald	1794
Ramilie	The Miser			1774
Ranger	The Suspicious Husband	1747	Hoadly	1784–1792
Raymond	The Countess of Salisbury	1765	Hartson	1784–1785

228

Character	Play	Date	Author	Period Played
Raymond	The Count of Narbonne	1781	Jephson	1786–1787
Reginald	The Castle Spectre	1797	Lewis	1799
Sir John Restless	All in the Wrong	1761	Murphy	1786–1788
Revel	The Note of Hand	1774	Cumberland	1774–1775
Count Ribemont	The Surrender of Calais	1791	Colman jun.	1792–1793
Count Ribemont	The Black Prince	1667	Boyle	1792
Richard III	Richard III	—	Shakespeare	1774–1812
Richard	Richard Coeur de Lion	1786	Burgoyne	1792
Riches	Harlequin Fortunatus	1753	Woodward	1774–1775
Rolla	Rolla	1799	Lewis	1704–1805
Romeo	Romeo and Juliet	—	Shakespeare	1775–1791
Rosse	Macbeth	—	Shakespeare	1786
Rover	Wild Oats	1791	O'Keefe	1791–1794
Earl of Salisbury	Countess of Salisbury	1765	Hartson	1799
Salmandore, the genius of the Peak	Rape of Proserpine	1727	Theobald	1782
Saville	The Belle's Stratagem	1780	Mrs. Cowley	1781–1785
Sciolto	The Fair Penitent	1703	Rowe	1784–1805
Sealard	The Conscious Lovers	1722	Steele	1793
Sir Harry's Servant	High Life Below Stairs	1759	Townley/Garrick	1778
Shylock	A Merchant of Venice	—	Shakespeare	1786–1812
Siffrid	Tancred and Sigismunda	1745	Thomson	1784
Southampton	The Earl of Essex	1751	James	1778–1792
Spatter	The English Merchant	1767	Colman sen.	1774–1784
Spatterdash	The Young Quaker	1783	O'Keeffe	1785
Dr. Specific	The Jew and the Doctor	1798	T. J. Dibdin	1799
Sir George Splenderville	Next Door Neighbours	1791	Mrs. Inchbald	1791–1792
Colonel Standard	The Constant Couple	1699	Farquhar	1789–1790
Sir Hubert Stanley	A Cure for the Heartache	1796	Morton	1797
Stedfast	The Heir-at-Law	1797	Colman jun.	1798–1799

229

Character	Play	Date	Author	Period Played
Stockwell	The West Indian	1771	Cumberland	1775–1800
The Stranger	The Stranger	1798	Thomson	1799–1808
Mr. Strictland	The Suspicious Husband	1747	Hoadly	1790–1807
Stukeley	The Gamester	1753	Moore	1785–1811
Sultan	Such Things Are	1787	Mrs. Inchbald	1787
Joseph Surface	The School for Scandal	1777	Sheridan	1782–1810
Sir Oliver Surface	School for Scandal	1777	Sheridan	1795
Colonel Talbot	He wou'd be a Soldier	1786	Pilon	1787–1798
Colonel Tamper	The Deuce is in him	1763	Colman sen.	1791
Tamerlane	Tamerlane the Great	1701	Rowe	1775–1782
Tancred	Tancred and Sigismunda	1745	Thomson	1791
Sir Peter Teazle	School for Scandal	1777	Sheridan	1784–1788
Tobine	The Suicide	1778	Colman sen.	1794
Tom	The Conscious Lovers	1722	Steele	1775
Sir George Touchwood	The Belles' Stratagem	1780	Mrs. Cowley	1787–1798
Lord Townly	The Provok'd Husband	1728	Vanbrugh and Cibber	1782–1808
Luke Traffic	Riches	1810	Burges	1810
Tressel	Richard III	—	Shakespeare	1778
Lord Trinket	The Jealous Wife	1761	Colman sen.	1774
Trueman	The London Merchant	1731	Lillo	1778
Friar Tuck/ Baron Fitzherbert	Robin Hood	—	(Unknown)	1784–1785
Tybalt	Romeo and Juliet	—	Shakespeare	1778
Valentine	Love for Love	1695	Congreve	1790
Valerius	The Roman Father	1750	Whitehead	1784
Mr. Vandercrab	New Peerage	1787	Lee	1787
Varanes	Theodosius	1680	Lee	1788
Ventidius	All for Love	1677	Dryden	1806
Count Connoly Villars	The School for Arrogance	1791	Holcroft	1792
Villeroy	Isabella	1694	Southern	1784–1786

Character	Play	Date	Author	Period Played
Colonel Vortex	Match Making	1808	Mrs. C. Kemble	1808
Warford	How to Grow Rich	1793	Reynolds	1793
The Earl of Warwick	The Earl of Warwick	1766	Francklin	1790–1791
Whitle	The Irish Widow	1772	Garrick	1774
Baron Wildenheim	Lover's Vows	1798	Mrs. Inchbald	1799–1809
Wilding	The Gamesters	1757	Garrick	1774
Young Wilding	The Citizen	1761	Murphy	1778–1794
Sir Thomas Wildmay	The Outcasts	1796	Cherry	1797
Mr. Wingrove	The Fugitive	1790	O'Keeffe	1792
Wolsey	Henry VII	—	Shakespeare	1784–1793
Zamor	Alzira	1736	Hill	1790–1791
Zanga	The Revenge	1721	Young	1774–1812

231

Appendix III

Cooke's First Appearances in London 1800–1810

(Newspaper reviews containing material of critical significance are indicated.

Key: MC – Morning Chronicle; MP – Morning Post; P – The Porcupine; T – The Times; BWM – Bell's Weekly Messenger; MM – The Monthly Mirror)

1800

Oct 31   Richard III   (MC, MP, T 1/11/00; BWM 2/11/00;
                                    P 7/11/00; MP 8/1/01; MM 11/00;
                                    MP 14/9/01; MC, MP,
                                    20/10/01; MP 4/1/02)

Nov 10   Shylock   (P 13/11/00; MM 11/00;
                                    MP 5/2/01)

       13   Sir Archy   (MM 11/00)

       28   Iago   (P. 1/12/00; MC 4/12/00;
                                    MP 24/1/01)

Dec 5   Macbeth   (MC, MP, P 6/12/00; BWM 7/12/00;
                                    P 15/12/00; MP 15/1/01)

       17   Kitely   (MC, MP, T 18/12/00; MP 13/1/01)

1801

Jan 27   The Stranger   (MC 28/1/01; MP 30/1/01;
                                    BWM 1/2/01)

Mar 28   Sir Giles
               Overreach
Nov 27   Stukeley   (MC 28/11/01)

1802

Jan   2   Jaques   (MC 4/1/02)

Jan	4	Zanga	(MC, MP, 5/1/02)
	8	Lear	(MC, MP 9/1/02)
	15	Orsino	(MC, MP 16/1/02)
		(in *Alfonso*)	
Feb	24	Falstaff (H 1V)	(MC 25/2/02)
Apr	10	Sir Pertinax	(MC 12/4/02)
	28	Falstaff (MWW)	
May	7	Sir Edward Mortimer	
	24	? in *Ward of Honour*	
	29	Pierre	(MC 24/12/08)
Jun	3	Bajazet	
	9	Sir Philip Blandford	
Sep	27	Hamlet	(MC, MP 28/9/02; MP 5/10/02)
Dec	23	Cato	(MC, MP 24/12/02)

1803

Mar	5	Peregrine	(MP 7/3/03)
Apr	20	Comus	
May	20	King John	(MC 21/5/03)
Oct	6	Glenalvon	(MP 7/10/03)
	17	Pizarro	(MC 18/10/03; MC 21/10/03)
Nov	5	Sciolto	(MC, MP 7/11/03)
	21	Angelo	(MC 22/11/03)
	28	Macduff	

1804

Jan	17	Falstaff	(MC 18/1/04)
		(H IV 2)	
	23	? in *Love gives the Alarm*	
Apr	26	Haswell	
May	30	Osmund	
Oct	18	Strictland	(MC 19/10/04)
	22	Ghost (*Hamlet*)	

1805

Jan	15	Lord Avondale	
Feb	16	Lavensforth	(MC 18/2/05)
Apr	1	**Cohenburg**	
	6	Mortimer	

1806

Jan	1	Dumont	
	4	Lord Davenant	
	18	Iachimo	(MP 20/1/06)
Nov	15	Prince of Altenburg	

1807

Feb	16	Major Oakley
May	4	Prospero

1808

May	3	Catarach
	18	Kent
Jun	2	Sir Christopher Curry
	3	Don Felix

1809

May	1	John Cockle
	9	Gibby
	10	Baron Wildenheim
Nov	27	Horatius

1810

May	5	Henry VIII
	30	Joseph Surface

Notes

Chapter I (pp. 1–5)

1 W. Dunlap, *The Life of George Fred. Cooke*, 2nd ed. (London, 1815), II, pp. 178–81.
2 Ibid., II, p. 176.
3 Ibid., II, pp. 180–1.
4 Ibid., II, pp. 229–38.
5 Ibid., II, pp. 279–81. "Sarah" was, of course, Mrs. Siddons.
6 Ibid., II, pp. 283–5.

Chapter II (pp. 6–17)

1 Dunlap, I, p. 2.
2 Ibid., II, p. 372.
3 Ibid., II, p. 271.
4 *Thespian Dictionary* (1802) q. in J. B. Broadbent, *Annals of the Manchester Theatre* (Typescript, Manchester, 1913). It is not possible to confirm this in Dublin. The relevant records disappeared with the destruction of the Four Courts in 1922. No officer called Cooke appears in the army lists in Watson's Almanack in Dublin for the relevant years.
5 A Veteran Stager, *An Essay on the Science of Acting* (London, 1828), pp. 106–7.
6 Dunlap, I, pp. 2 and 5.
7 *Monthly Mirror*, X, Dec. 1800.
8 *Albion*, 8 Dec. 1800. Manchester Scrapbook (collection of newspaper cuttings relating to theatrical matters, Manchester Central Library).
9 A Veteran Stager, p. 106.
10 Registers of Trinity Church, Berwick-on-Tweed. Copies in the Newcastle-upon-Tyne Reference Library, Vol. D.
11 Registers, Vol. C.
12 A Veteran Stager, p. 106.
13 Dunlap, I, pp. 17–18.
14 Walter Baynham, *The Glasgow Stage* (Glasgow, 1892), p. 67.
15 Dunlap, I, p. 428.
16 V. Sheldon, *The History of Berwick-on-Tweed* (London, 1849).
17 Dunlap, I, p. 3, quoting Cooke's Ms. Chronicle.
18 *The London Stage 1660–1800*, 4/3, p. 1289.
19 *The Secret History of the Green Room* (London, 1795), I, pp. 209–13.
20 Dunlap, I, p. 5.
21 Ibid., I, pp. 6–7.
22 Ibid., I, pp. 7 8.
23 Ibid., I, pp. 8–9.
24 Ibid., I, p. 10.

25 Ibid., pp. 11–13.

26 This has been reproduced more than once of recent years. Sybil Rosenfeld, *Strolling Players and Drama in the Provinces* (Cambridge, 1939) and Bernard Miles, *The British Theatre* (London, 1948) both contain it.

27 Dunlap, I, p. 13. John Taylor is listed on the Roll of Freemen of Berwick from 1761 onwards, as are several members of the Cook family. In January 1767 Edward Cook is recorded as being apprenticed to John Horguson, a Burgess of the Borough. But no record linking George Cooke and John Taylor survives. (Documents in Northumberland County Record Office.)

28 John Fuller, *The History of Berwick-upon-Tweed* (London, 1799).

29 Dunlap, I, pp. 13–16.

30 Ibid., I, p. 14.

31 Ibid., I, p. 17.

32 Ibid., I, pp. 17–20. He gives the casts as: Oroonoko – Savigny; Aboan – Bensley; Blandford – Hull; Capt. Driver – Dunstall; Daniel – Quick; Imoinda – Miss Miller; Charlotte – Mrs. Baker; Widow – Mrs. Pitt. And in *Midas*: Midas – Shuter; Apollo – Mattocks; Pan – Dunstall; Silenus – Baker; Daphne – Mrs. Baker; Nysa – Mrs. Mattocks. The only occasion this could have been was Wednesday 2 October 1771. *V. The London Stage*, 4/4, p. 1573.

33 Cooke's Appleby Memorandum Book No. 2, entry for 16 Nov. 1807.

34 *Monthly Mirror*, X, p. 347; Dunlap, I, p. 18.

35 Dunlap, I, p. 20.

36 A Veteran Stager, p. 108.

37 Arthur Murphy in his farce *The Apprentice* satirises such clubs affectionately; *v.* also J. A. Thieme, "Spouting, Spouting Clubs and Spouting Companions," *Theatre Notebook*, XXIX, 1, pp. 9–16.

38 Dunlap, I, pp. 29–30. E. C. Everard, *Memoirs of an Unfortunate Son of Thespis* (Edinburgh, 1818), p. 78, says he had heard Cooke at Spouting Clubs, in the plural.

39 A Veteran Stager, pp. 108–9.

40 Ibid., p. 135.

Chapter III (pp. 18–36)

1 A Veteran Stager, pp. 110–11.

2 The detailed evidence is assembled in A. Hare, "George Frederick Cooke's Early Years in the Theatre," *Theatre Notebook*, XXXI, 1, pp. 12-21. *V.* also J. L. Hodgkinson and R. Pogson, *The Early Manchester Theatre* (London, 1960), p. 52. Mr. Lou Warwick, the historian of the Northampton Theatre, informs me that Whitley was never in any real sense the "Northampton manager". But that Henry Lee, a fellow-manager and contemporary, could make the mistake indicates how easy such confusion was. *V.* H. Lee, *Memoirs of a Manager* (Taunton, 1830).

3 *Lincoln, Rutland and Stanford Mercury*, 24 April 1829. Enquiries in Boston have failed to produce any surviving contemporary confirmatory evidence.

4 J. Winston, *The Theatric Tourist* (1805); J. Richards, "Thomas Shafto Robertson and the Theatric Tourist," *Theatre Notebook*, XXIX, 1, pp. 4–9.

5 *V.* Whitlock's advertisements in the *Chester Chronicle*.

6 *V.* pp. 33–4 *supra*.

7 Dunlap, I, p. 30, and, e.g., H. B. Baker, *Our Old Actors* (London, 1878); J. Knight, "George Frederick Cooke," *Dictionary of National Biography*.

8 *V.* P. Scholes, *The Great Dr. Burney* (Oxford, 1848), I, pp. 69–71.

9 *V.* R. Southern, "Concerning a Georgian Proscenium Ceiling," *Theatre Notebook*, 3, 1, pp. 6–12, and S. Rosenfeld, "St. George's Hall, King's Lynn," ibid., 3, 2, pp. 24–27.

10 C. L. Lewes, *Memoirs* (London, 1805), pp. 70–4. Lewes has a number of anecdotes of Herbert and Whitley.

11 Hodgkinson and Pogson, pp. 44–59.

12 A Veteran Stager, pp. 113–14; Everard, p. 101.

13 Lewes, p. 76.

14 Ibid., p. 46.

15 Playbills in Burney Collection, British Library. Cooke's complete repertoire, so far as it is known, is recorded in Appendix II.

16 A Veteran Stager, p. 111.

17 Ibid.

18 J. T. Kirkman, *Memoirs of the Life of Charles Macklin, Esq.* (London, 1799), I, pp. 59–60.

19 A Veteran Stager, p. 110.

20 Everard, p. 95.

21 Henry Thornton was later to go into management and build up a circuit which included Windsor, Newbury and Chelmsford. James Shafto Robertson subsequently became manager of the Lincolnshire company, as in turn did his son Thomas (probably the "Master Robertson"). Glassington was prompter at Bath and Bristol 1799–1801, a Miss Glassington was at China Hall 1776–78.

22 It may have been Mary Ann Canning, who joined Drury Lane in November 1773 but did not act there between December 1773 and April 1774. I owe this reference to Miss Kathleen Barker.

23 This was Roger Wright's description of him at the Spouting Club (A Veteran Stager, p. 110).

24 Dunlap (presumably relying on the Chronicle) refers to this as the opening of the season. In fact the season opened on 19 September with *All's Well that Ends Well* (*London Stage*, 4/3, pp. 1833 and 1845).

25 Dunlap, I, p. 22.

26 *London Stage*, 4/3, pp. 1851 and 1894.

27 Playbills in Burney Collection, British Library.

28 Dunlap, I, p. 22. For a detailed account of this episode *v.* W. Appleton, *Charles Macklin* (Cambridge, Mass., 1960), Chapter X.

29 *London Stage*, 4/4, p. 1894.

30 Dunlap, I, p. 27.

31 Ibid., p. 28; Everard, p. 78.

32 Playbills for 6, 15, 18, 20, 22 September, 2 October 1775, Lincoln Central Library. *V.* also Hare, *Theatre Notebook*, XXXI, 1.

33 Dunlap, I, p. 30.

34 Everard, p. 97.

35 Dunlap, I, pp. 31–2.

36 Everard, p. 97.

37 Dunlap, I, p. 33; *Morning Post*, 8 April 1778. *V.* also *The London Stage*, 5/1, p. 162.

38 Everard, pp. 74–7; *v.* also C. B. Hogan, "The China Hall Theatre, Rotherhithe," *Theatre Notebook*, 8, 4, pp. 76–80.

39 Dunlap, I, p. 35.

40 Everard, pp. 77–80. Fourteen performances involving Cooke are recorded in *The London Stage*, 5/1, pp. 176–83.

41 Dunlap, I, pp. 33–4; *London Stage*, 5/1, pp. 166–67, 235, 256.

42 Ibid., and Everard, pp. 91–93.

43 Ibid., p. 91.

44 In Dublin in 1794, for instance, when we know from his correspondence that the young Charles Mathews was playing small parts, his name rarely appears on the bills.

45 *Kentish Gazette*, 31 Jan. 1780 et seq.; (T. S. Munden) *Memoirs of Joseph Shepherd Munden, comedian* (London, 1844), p. 14.

46 *Norwich Mercury* and *Norfolk Chronicle, passim.*

47 *Kentish Gazette*, Jan.–May 1780. 17 lists only survive over a period of five months. Cooke could, by coincidence, not have been playing on each of those nights. But it is giving the arm of coincidence a rather long pull.

48 A Veteran Stager, p. 112. Swords is mentioned in the Canterbury cast lists.

49 *Kentish Gazette*, 4 Aug. 1781 et seq.

50 A Veteran Stager, p. 112.

51 *V. Kentish Gazette.*
52 The Stretton Mss. (Nottingham, 1910), pp. 162, 164.
53 Cresswell and Burbage's *Nottingham Journal*, 3 Jan. 1778, 25 Nov. 1780; Hodgkinson and Pogson, p. 58.
54 *Nottingham Journal*, 20 and 27 Oct. 1781. The bill announces the various places from which tickets could be bought, including "G. Burbage and Son".
55 *Nottingham Journal, passim*, particularly 19 Jan. 1782.
56 Hutton, *History of Derby* (London, 1791), contains an exterior engraving. Unlike its Nottingham counterpart the outer fabric of this building still recognisably survives at the time of writing, though now in use for office purposes.
57 Drewry's *Derby Mercury*, 7 Feb. 1782.
58 Ibid., 7 March 1782.
59 Ibid., *passim.*
60 *Stamford Mercury*, 6 June–11 July 1782.
61 Dunlap, I, p. 35.
62 Playbills for Theatre Royal, Bath, 8 March, 20 and 21 May, 28 June 1783; 21 Feb. and 9 March 1784. *V.* A. Hare (ed.), *Theatre Royal Bath: The Orchard Street Calendar* (Bath, 1977), 1782–83, 1783–84.
63 Dunlap, I, p. 36.

Chapter IV (pp. 37–46)

1 Dunlap, I, p. 36.
2 *V.* Hodgkinson and Pogson, pp. 75–129.
3 Dunlap, I, p. 36.
4 This and other quotations from Küttner are translated in Hodgkinson and Pogson, pp. 107–12.
5 Harrop's *Manchester Mercury*, 25 May 1784.
6 J. B. Broadbent, *Annals of the Liverpool Stage* (London, 1908), p. 72.
7 Dunlap, I, p. 38.
8 H. Brooke, *Liverpool during the Last Quarter of the Eighteenth Century*, quoted in Broadbent, p. 54.
9 Gore's Liverpool Advertiser, 13 Jan. 1785.
10 Ibid., 20 Jan. 1785.
11 Dunlap, I, p. 39.
12 British Library Playbills Vol. 307; *Chester Chronicle*, 1785, *passim.*
13 The Cooke Promptbook is in the Library of the Literary and Philosophical Society of Newcastle-upon-Tyne. *V.* M. St. Clare Byrne, "The earliest *Hamlet* prompt book in an English Library," *Theatre Notebook*, XV, 1, pp. 21–31 and plates 5–8; *Chester Chronicle* 4 Nov. 1785. Platt played the Ghost, Kemble Horatio, Whitlock Laertes, Mrs. Kemble Ophelia, Mrs. Taplin the Queen, and Munden Polonius.
14 The bills (B.L. Vol. 307) refer merely to "The Theatre in Roper Street"–but the Whitehaven theatre was in Roper Street, and was on the Austin-Whitlock circuit. On 28 January 1786 Mrs. Cooke made her first appearance in Newcastle as Miss Neville in *She Stoops to Conquer (Newcastle Courant).*
15 *Yorkshire Magazine*, July 1786, p. 198 *et seq.*
16 Ibid., p. 255.
17 S. Rosenfeld, *The York Theatre* (Typescript, 1948, in York Public Library), has a fuller account of this episode.
18 Playbills in the Hailstone Collection, Minster Library, York.
19 Dunlap, I, p. 43.
20 Ibid., I, 39–40.
21 *Chester Chronicle*, Sept.–Nov. 1786, *passim.*
22 Mrs. Cooke reappears on 30 December 1786 as Miss Neville in *She Stoops to Conquer* (B. L. Playbills, Vol. 307).
23 York Playbills, Hailstone Collection; *York Chronicle*, Dec. 1786– May 1787.

24 *York Chronicle* 3 April 1787. S. Rosenfeld, *York Theatre*, Chap IV, records the incident more fully.

25 Hare (ed.), *Theatre Royal, Bath*, p. 111.

Chapter V (pp. 47–64)

1 D. Macmillan, *Drury Lane Calendar* (Oxford, 1938). There are two letters from Garrick to Austin in D. M. Little and G. M. Kahrl (eds.), *The Letters of David Garrick* (London, 1963), I, pp. 329–31. *V.* also Cecil Price, "Joseph Austin and his Associates 1766–1789," *Theatre Notebook*, 4, 4, pp. 89–94.

2 V. H. Oswald, *The Theatres Royal in Newcastle-upon-Tyne* (Newcastle, 1936).

3 J. Winston, *The Theatric Tourist* (London, 1805), p. 44.

4 B. L. Provincial Playbills, Vol. 307. *V.* also Cecil Price, "An 18th Century Theatrical Agreement," *Theatre Notebook*, 2, 1, pp. 31–4.

5 S. W. Ryley, *The Itinerant* (London, 1808), Chapter XI; Munden, p. 18; B. L. Playbills, Vol. 307.

6 Belfill, Bellfill, Bellfield, Belville – there are so many variant spellings of her name that I have used whichever was current in the source I quote. But the lady was the same.

7 Ryley, pp. 122–23.

8 Munden, p. 18.

9 Charles Lamb, *Essays of Elia*, "On the Acting of Munden."

10 Munden, p. 17.

11 Quoted in R. Manvell, *Sarah Siddons* (London, 1970), p. 117.

12 Fanny Kemble, *Record of a Girlhood* (London, 1878), I, pp. 66–67.

13 Price, "Joseph Austin," p. 92. See also *Sheffield Register*, 10 Dec. 1790.

14 Munden, p. 119.

15 Tate Wilkinson, *The Wandering Patentee* (York, 1795), III, p. 23.

16 Ryley, p. 119.

17 *Newcastle Chronicle*, 15 March 1788.

18 *Chester Chronicle*, 6 Nov. 1789.

19 Dunlap, I, p. 40.

20 A Veteran Stager, pp. 114–15.

21 Ibid., pp. 115–18.

22 Both bills are reproduced in facsimile in Oswald.

23 A Veteran Stager, pp. 118–20.

24 15–30 September 1789 – *v.* Chester Chronicle and B.L. Provincial Playbills, Vol. 275.

25 Evidence of the *Newcastle Chronicle* and *Courant*.

26 *Chester Chronicle*, 28 Nov. 1788.

27 *Thoughts on the Late Disturbance at the Theatre Royal* (Newcastle, 1789), p. 16.

28 Ibid., p. 9.

29 Ibid., p. 12.

30 Ibid., p. 14.

31 *Newcastle Chronicle*, 28 March 1789.

32 *Thoughts* etc., pp. 18–9.

33 Ibid., p. 19.

34 Munden, p. 20.

35 A Veteran Stager, p. 121.

36 Hare (ed.), *Theatre Royal, Bath*, 1789–92.

37 Munden, p. 23. In Bristol she became ill; Munden sent her money, in due course paid for her burial, and saw that the children were sent to join their sisters in Newcastle.

38 It should be borne in mind, therefore, that in the Austin-Whitlock bills "Mrs. Munden" up to April 1789 at Newcastle, and from November 1789 at Sheffield, are two different people.

39 *Chester Chronicle*, 6 Nov. 1789; *Newcastle Chronicle*, 13 March 1790.

40 *Chester Chronicle*, 24 Sept., 1 Oct. 1790.

41 Ibid., 22 Oct. 1790.

42 Ibid., 19 Nov. 1790.
43 Munden, p. 184.
44 *Sheffield Register*, 21 Jan. 1791.
45 *Sheffield Advertiser*, 17 Dec. 1790.
46 Ibid.
47 Dunlap, I, p. 57.
48 Oswald, p. 32.

Chapter VI (pp. 65–80)

1 Manchester Theatre Royal Playbills, Vol. III.
2 A Veteran Stager, p. 123 *et seq.* 1791 is the most likely year for this account. The Stager is, as usual, muddled and imprecise about dates, and it has not proved possible to confirm the Bolton date by independent evidence. But the two Buxton visits for 1791 and 1794 are confirmed by Cooke's Chronicle in Dunlap, and Grist was at Sheffield in Kemble's company in September 1791 – *v. Chester Chronicle*, 30 Sept. 1791.
3 A Veteran Stager, pp. 125–26.
4 Ibid., pp. 127–28.
5 Ibid., p. 124.
6 Ibid., pp. 123–24; Dunlap, I, p. 60.
7 *Chester Chronicle*, 2 Sept. 1791.
8 Ibid., 23 Sept. 1791.
9 Ibid.; Manchester Playbills; *Manchester Mercury.*
10 Hogkinson and Pogson, p. 141.
11 Ryley, III, p. 87.
12 C. Censor, *The Thespian Mirror or Poetical Strictures on the Professional characters of (members) of the Theatre Royal Manchester, Liverpool & Chester* (? Manchester, 1793).
13 T. Dibdin, *Reminiscences* (London, 1827).
14 *V.* Hare (ed.), *Theatre Royal, Bath,* 1787–91; Tate Wilkinson, IV, pp. 55–6. For Mrs. Simpson's later history, *v.* A. Hare, *The Georgian Theatre in Wessex* (London, 1958), p. 180.
15 *Chester Chronicle*, 7 Oct, 1791.
16 Ibid., Oct.–Nov. 1791.
17 Ibid., 19 Oct. 1792.
18 Ibid., 8, 15 Nov. 1793; Hodgkinson and Pogson, p. 139.
19 In Chester the soldiers' Benefit raised £78; but Mrs. Siddons had already produced £93 for herself. *V. Chester Chronicle.*
20 *Chester Chronicle*, 7 Dec. 1792.
21 Manchester Theatre Royal Playbills, Vol. IV.
22 Proceedings in the Consistory Court of London at Doctor's Commons 2 May 1801. T. Dibdin, II, p. 388.
23 C. Censor, pp. 25–26.
24 Dibdin, II, pp. 388–89.
25 *Chester Chronicle*, 23 Nov. 1792.
26 Manchester Theatre Royal Playbills, Vol. III.
27 *Chester Chronicle*, 13 Dec. 1793.
28 *B.L. Provincial Playbills*, Vol. 226.
29 G.F.C. Ms. Journal Harvard Theatre Collection, MS Thr 20. Dunlap, I, pp. 65–80. Dunlap (p. 65) has him again in Liverpool for the summer of 1793, but there is no trace of this in the bills for that year (B.L. Vol. 227).
30 Manchester Theatre Royal Playbills, Vol. III.
31 Dibdin, I, pp. 120–21.
32 C. Censor, pp. 3–5.
33 Ryley, III, pp. 75–79.
34 Dunlap, I, p. 49. He adds that Cooke read the story in his presence in Philadelphia in 1811, and did not deny it.

35 Ibid., I, pp. 68–9.
36 Ibid., I, p. 70.
37 Cooke's Ms. Journal, 6 Sept. 1794.
38 Dunlap, I, pp. 77–9.

Chapter VII (pp. 81–97)

1 Cooke's Memoir; Dunlap, I, p. 81.
2 Mrs. A. Mathews, *Memoirs of Charles Mathews Comedian* (London, 1838–9), I, p. 130.
3 Ibid., I, p. 90.
4 *The Public Register, or, Freeman's Journal*, 6 Nov. 1794
5 Mathews, I, p. 93.
6 Dunlap, I, p. 84.
7 The list has been compiled from *The Public Register* and the *Hibernian Journal*. The comments are from Charles Mathews. The "lady" was in fact male – *v.* W. S. Clark, *The Irish Stage in the County Towns* (Oxford, 1965), pp. 136–37.
8 *Public Register*, 20 Nov. 1794.
9 Mathews, I, p. 128.
10 *Public Register*, 22 Nov. 1794; Mathews, I, p. 128.
11 *Public Register*, 9 Dec. 1794; 1 Jan. 1795.
12 Mathews, I, p. 129.
13 Dunlap, I, pp. 84–5.
14 Ibid., pp. 85–91.
15 Mathews, I, pp. 131–38.
16 Ibid., I, pp. 129–30, 141.
17 Ibid., I, p. 131.
18 Ibid., I, p. 147.
19 Ibid., I, p. 131.
20 Ibid., I, p. 148.
21 Ibid., I, p. 153.
22 A Veteran Stager, p. 129.
23 Mathews, I, pp. 150–51.
24 Kemble's Memoranda Books, 1788–1815 (B.L. Add. Mss. 31, 972).
25 Mrs. Mathews quotes one in Cooke's handwriting from her husband's autograph collection. "When a sober, moderate, and silent man drinks wine in a quantity more liberal than ordinary, it has the effect of cherishing and rousing his spirits and genius, and rendering him more communicative. If taken still more freely, he becomes talkative, eloquent, and confident of his abilities. If taken in still larger quantities, it renders him bold and daring, and desirous to exert himself in action. If he persist in a more plentiful dose, it makes him petulant and contumelious. The next step renders him mad and outrageous. Should he proceed still farther, he becomes stupid and senseless." Mathews, I, p. 140.
26 W. Reitzel (ed.), *The Autobiography of William Cobbett* (London, 1947), pp. 25–6.
27 Dunlap, I, p. 91; A Veteran Stager, p. 129. It is typical of the Stager's unreliability as to detail, that he has the regiment bound for the Quiberon Bay Expedition, which took place in 1759, when Cooke was about three years old!
28 Dunlap refers to him as Maxwell and calls him the manager of the Portsmouth Theatre. Maxfield was to become this eventually, but only after Collins' death in 1807. At this time he was a leading actor in the company. V. Hare, *Georgian Theatre*, Chap. VIII.
29 Dunlap, I, pp. 92–3.
30 *Monthly Mirror*, April 1796, I, p. 373; A Veteran Stager, p. 130; Dunlap, I, p. 96.
31 Records of the Consistory Court of London, case heard before Sir John Nicholl, Ll.D.–surrogate of Sir William Scott, at Doctor's Commons, 2 May 1801. Greater London Record Office.
32 *Monthly Mirror*, March 1797, III, pp. 180–82.
33 *Manchester Mercury*, 4 Jan., 14 Feb. 1797.
34 Ibid., 26, 30 May 1797.

35 Dunlap, I, pp. 97, 107. They were at Preston on 28 July, as was Cherry. B.L. Playbills (Burney Collection).

Chapter VIII (pp. 98–112)

1 Clark, p. 141.
2 *Public Register*, 14 Nov. 1797.
3 G.F.C. Ms. Journal 2 Feb. 1800; Appleby Memorandum Book No. 2, 20 Nov. 1807. Much – though not all – of the journal of this period survives in the original Ms. Dunlap quotes from it, but his transcripts are frequently inaccurate, and in some cases he seems to have re-written beyond the bounds of editorial licence. I have therefore quoted the original wherever possible.
4 Ms. Journal 29 and 31 Jan. 1800; Appleby Memorandum Book No. 2, 21 Nov. 1807.
5 Clark, p. 140.
6 *Public Register*, 27 Jan. 1798.
7 *Public Register,* 27 Jan. 1798, and *Hibernian Journal*, 29 Jan. 1798.
8 Ibid.
9 G.F.C. Ms. Journal, 31 Jan. 1800.
10 Dunlap, I, pp. 118–19.
11 Hare (ed.), *Theatre Royal, Bath*, 1798–99 *et seq.* Mrs. Cooke remained with the Bath company, becoming in due course Mrs. Windsor, after her re-marriage to a local musician. She eventually died after collapsing dramatically on stage during a performance at the new theatre in Beauford Square, on 28 April 1826 (*v. Bristol Journal* and *Bristol Mirror*, 6 May 1826).
12 *New Cork Evening Post*, 13 Sept., 22 Nov. 1798.
13 G.F.C. Ms. Journal, 17 Sept. 1798.
14 *Cork Evening Post*, 17, 24, 27 Sept. 1798.
15 *V.* Chapter XIV.
16 G.F.C. Ms. Journal, 27 Sept. 1798.
17 Dunlap, I, pp. 125–28.
18 *Limerick Chronicle*, 6 Oct. 1798.
19 *Public Register*, 18 Dec. 1798 and later December issues.
20 G.F.C. Ms. Journal, 21 Jan. 1800.
21 *Public Register*, 11 and 14 May 1799.
22 *Cork Advertiser*, 24 Aug. 1799.
23 *Public Register and Hibernian Chronicle.* The former on 25 January 1800 reported that *The Stranger* was drawing as much money this year as *The Castle Spectre* did last.
24 G.F.C. Ms. Journal, 31 Dec. 1799, 3 and 26 Jan., 26 Feb. 1800.
25 Ibid., 19–20 Jan. 1800.
26 Ibid., 31 Jan. 1800.
27 E.g., ibid., 16 Jan., 1 and 3 Feb. 1800.
28 Ibid., 29 Jan. 1800.
29 Ibid., 28 Feb. 1800.
30 Dunlap, I, p. 111. *Freeman's Journal*, 7 June 1800.
31 *Cork Advertiser*, 30 Sept. 1800.
32 Clark, p. 143.
33 Dunlap, I, p. 143.

Chapter IX (pp. 113–34)

1 Dunlap, I, p. 143. C. G. Playbills, B.L.
2 *Monthly Mirror*, X, Nov. 1800.
3 *Morning Post*, 1 Nov. 1800.
4 *Morning Chronicle*, 1 Nov. 1800.
5 *Times*, 1 Nov. 1800.
6 *Sun*, 1 Nov. 1800. Newspaper Cuttings Book, Manchester Public Library.

7 Ibid., 6 Nov. 1800.
8 *Monthly Mirror*, X, Nov. 1800.
9 *Morning Post* and *Times*, 1 Nov. 1800.
10 Dunlap, I, p. 145.
11 Munden, p. 88.
12 Munden, pp. 81–4 contains an account of the dispute. There is much relating to it in the newspapers of the time.
13 L. Hunt, *Dramatic Essays* (ed. Archer; London, 1894), p. 44.
14 *The Porcupine*, 13 Nov. 1800.
15 *Morning Chronicle*, 4 Dec. 1800; *Porcupine*, 1 Dec. 1800.
16 *Morning Post*, 1 Dec. 1800, 24 Jan. 1801.
17 Ibid., 6 Dec. 1800.
18 *Porcupine*, 6 Dec. 1800.
19 *Morning Post*, 18 Dec. 1800, 13 Jan. 1801; *Morning Chronicle* and *Times*, 18 Dec. 1800.
20 *Morning Post*, 28 Jan. 1801.
21 *Bath Chronicle*, 15 Oct. 1801.
22 Dunlap, I, pp. 180–81; Covent Garden Playbills, B.L. *Bell's Weekly Messenger*, 1 Feb. 1801; *Morning Post*, 30 Jan. 1801; and *Morning Chronicle*, 28 Jan. 1801 also have long reviews of *The Stranger*.
23 Dunlap, I, pp. 169–70.
24 B.L. Playbills, Vol. 184; Birmingham Theatre Royal Playbills 1801–5 (Birmingham Reference Library); Aris' *Birmingham Gazette*, 22, 29 June 1801; Dunlap, I, p. 190.
25 Norma Armstrong, *The Edinburgh Stage 1715–1820* (3 vols. typescript in Edinburgh Public Library) contains a valuable Calendar of this theatre, abstracted from newspaper and playbill sources. *Monthly Mirror*, XII, Aug. and Sept. 1801.
26 Dunlap, I, p. 192.
27 *Monthly Mirror*, loc. cit.
28 *Glasgow Courier*, 21 July–4 Aug. 1801.
29 *Newcastle Chronicle*, 19 Sept. 1801.
30 B.L. Provincial Playbills, Vol. 228. Johnson's Ms. is in the Picton Library, Liverpool.
31 B.L. Provincial Playbills, Vol. 228.
32 *Liverpool Advertiser*, 10 Aug. 1801.
33 *Monthly Mirror*, XII, Sept. 1801.
34 *Manchester Mercury* of appropriate dates: *Monthly Mirror*, loc. cit.
35 Dunlap, I, p. 195.
36 *Morning Post*, 15 Sept. 1801.
37 Dunlap, I, pp. 195–97; *Morning Post*, loc. cit.; *Commercial Chronicle*, 10 Sept. 1801.
38 Ms note on the file copy of the playbill in B.L. collection.
39 *Morning Post*, 15 Sept. 1801.
40 Ibid.
41 *Newcastle Chronicle*, 19 Sept. 1801.
42 *Bell's Weekly Messenger*, 20 Sept. 1801.
43 Dunlap, I, pp. 200–01.
44 *Morning Post*, 20 Oct. 1801; v. also *Morning Chronicle* of same date, and Dunlap, I, pp. 202–03.

Chapter X (pp. 135–48)

1 *Morning Chronicle*, 28 Nov. 1801.
2 *Morning Post, Morning Chronicle*, 4 Jan. 1802.
3 Ibid., 5 Jan. 1802.
4 Dunlap, I, pp. 111–12.
5 *Morning Chronicle, Morning Post*, 9 Jan. 1802.
6 Covent Garden Playbills, B.L. According to the *Commercial Chronicle*, 19 Sept. 1801.

(Manchester Cuttings Book), Storace was to receive £1500 and Braham £1000 for the season.

7 *Bath Journal*, 7 and 14 June 1802. Evidence of the Covent Garden playbills.
8 *Felix Farley's Bristol Journal*, 19 and 26 Dec. 1801; *Bath Chronicle*, 17 and 24 December 1801. Playbill of Theatre Royal Bristol, 18 Dec. 1801, in Richard Smith Collection, Bristol. The *Bath Chronicle's* account of his illness was that after his exertions as Iago he "imprudently drank a quantity of cold water" which shortly afterwards gave him violent stomach cramps and confined him to bed. This is, of course, perfectly possible. There is no need to suppose it a cynically humorous covering up by the management of an indiscretion involving stronger liquids – though that too might be possible. Alicia (Daniels again, after the: marriage annulment of the previous summer) was now a leading singer with the Bath–Bristol company, but she does not appear in any of the bills of his visits; presumably it was arranged that they kept out of each other's way.
9 Playbill, 5 April 1802, Richard Smith Collection; *Bath Journal*, 5 April 1802 and *Felix Farley's Bristol Journal*, 10 April 1802. Cooke returned on this occasion by way of Portsmouth, where he gave two performances of Richard (Dunlap, I, p. 242). As he had last been there in 1795 on his escape from the army, the change of circumstances must have given him pleasure.
10 This summary is compiled from the relevant playbill collections and newspapers already noted, and Dunlap, I, Chapter 12.
11 Dunlap, I, pp. 250–82.
12 Ibid., pp. 254–55.
13 Ibid., p. 259.
14 Ibid., pp. 265–67.
15 Ibid., pp. 269–71; Covent Garden playbill.
16 Ibid., p. 251.
17 *Morning Post*, 16 Sept. 1802.
18 *Morning Chronicle*, 28 Sept. 1802.
19 *Morning Post*, 28 Sept. 1802.
20 Dunlap, I, p. 286.
21 *Morning Post*, 5 Oct. 1802. That the critic should do so is indication of his desire to be fair.
22 Dunlap, I, p. 287.
23 *Morning Post*, 15 Oct. 1802.
24 Covent Garden playbills, B.L.
25 Dunlap, I, pp. 375–76 has Cooke's comments on it in 1806.
26 Covent Garden playbills, B.L.; *Monthly Mirror*, XV, May 1803. It was on the occasion of the Johnstons' Benefit in the previous year that he had been drunk as Orsino.
27 *Morning Chronicle*, 21 May 1803. Covent Garden playbill 20 May 1803 (B.L.).
28 Dunlap, I, pp. 298–322.
29 Manchester Theatre Royal Playbills Vol. IX; *Chester Chronicle*, B.L. Provincial Playbills Vol. 275.
30 Dunlap, I, pp. 322–23; B.L. Provincial Playbills Vol. 248; *Monthly Mirror*, XVI, Aug. 1803.
31 *Derby Mercury*, 26 Aug. 1803; *Nottingham Journal*, 3 Sept. 1803.

Chapter XI (pp. 149–63)

1 J. Boaden, *Memoirs of the Life of John Philip Kemble* (London, 1825), pp. 374–76.
2 Ibid., pp. 381–82.
3 Munden, p. 108.
4 Dunlap, II, p. 49; *Monthly Mirror*, N.S. 111, March 1808, p. 271.
5 Boaden, p. 108.
6 Ms. note on playbill of 22 Oct. 1804, B.L. Cooke and Kemble had played these parts together in Dublin in 1800 – *v.* playbill 30 May 1800, Library of Trinity College Dublin.
7 Evidence of the playbills. Dunlap, II, p. 45.

NOTES

8 Dibdin, pp. 288–89.

9 (T. Hook, ed.) *Reminiscences of Michael Kelly* (London, 1826), pp. 213–15. After this incident Cooke started (on 23 November) another of his Journals, which he kept till the end of December.

10 Ibid., p. 216.

11 *Morning Post*, 12 Dec. 1806. *The Tempest* had its first night on 8 December.

12 Ms. inset in Covent Garden playbills, B.L. Vol. 89.

13 Evidence of the Covent Garden playbills, B.L.

14 The figures are based on an analysis of the Covent Garden playbills. There is, of course, always the possibility with Cooke that the occasional performance announced may not have been given or completed, without annotation on the bill. But with that reservation, they indicate roughly the scale of popularity of the major roles.

15 He played Macbeth and Prospero because Kemble was ill with rheumatism and asthma. *Monthly Mirror*, May 1807.

16 Covent Garden playbills, 1 April 1805, 3 June 1806, 26 Jan. 1807; *Monthly Mirror*, XIX, p. 347; new series, I, p. 143.

17 Dunlap, I, e.g. pp. 333–38, 367, 383, 394–401.

18 Playbills in the collections at Birmingham, Manchester, B.L.; *Manchester Mercury, Aris' Birmingham Gazette, Monthly Mirror*, XX; Dunlap, I, pp. 348, 364.

19 *Bristol Gazette, Bristol Mirror, Felix Farley's Bristol Journal, Bath Journal*; Dunlap, I, pp. 378–79, 423.

20 Harvard Theatre Collection, Ms. Thr. 20; Dunlap, I, pp. 384–87.

21 *Glasgow Herald*, 16 June 1806; *Glasgow Courier*, 24 June 1806, et seq.; Dunlap, I, pp. 387–89. Cooke played Zanga for his Benefit and took £170.

22 *Freeman's Journal*, 7 June 1806 et seq.; B.L. Provincial Playbills Vol. 230, Liverpool.

23 Mrs. Anne Mathews: *Anecdotes of Actors* (London, 1844), p. 99; *Liverpool Chronicle*, 3 Sept. 1806. Munden, pp. 182–83, has another account of this affair differing in detail but not in essentials.

24 *Salisbury Journal*, 16 Mar. 1807.

25 B.L. Provincial Playbills, Vol. 252; *Manchester Mercury*, 16 and 23 June 1807.

26 Dunlap, I, p. 429; *Glasgow Herald*, 29 June 1807 et seq.

27 Dunlap, I, p. 429.

28 B.L. Provincial Playbills, Vol. 230.

29 The earliest authority for this account is Broadbent's *Annals of the Manchester Stage 1735–1845* (3 Vols. Typescript in Central Library, Manchester). Unfortunately Broadbent does not give his source, and all attempts so far to locate contemporary evidence have failed. But it is so much in character and fits the known facts, that I have tentatively accepted it. It does not however, dispose of all problems. The earliest of Cooke's surviving Memorandum Books (No. 2) begins on 16 November, and he refers later to 4 December as "(5W)" and 18 December as "(7W)" – presumably meaning 5th or 7th week of the journal. This would give its commencement at c. 30 October or 6 November depending on whether one interprets 5W as the beginning or end of the 5th week. But he also says on 19 December (Dunlap, II, p. 33) that for the last 10 weeks he has been on a limited diet and has lived as if at sea. This may suggest the beginning of his confinement as early as 10 October. But if, as we know, he was expected in Liverpool at the end of August, what was he doing for about six weeks through September to the beginning of October? Perhaps it was another more extended alcoholic bout like that in Marlborough the previous year. *V.* also Hodgkinson and Pogson, pp. 173–75.

30 Dunlap, I, p. 432. The Memorandum Book belonged at one time to Sir Henry Irving, and passed through his grandson Laurence Irving to Sir Bernard Miles. It is now in the Harvard Theatre Collection. It is a small exercise book bound in a marbled paper cover.

31 All the foregoing extracts are from Memorandum Book No. 2.

32 Dunlap, II, pp. 12–15.

33 Ibid., p 33. The partridge had been sent to him by Captain Dent of the local militia (p. 28) – one of the local gentry whose company he had spurned?

34 Ibid., p. 38; *Glasgow Courier* confirms.

Chapter XII (pp. 164–78)

1 Dunlap, II, pp. 39–42; *Glasgow Courier* and *Herald; Edinburgh Evening Courant.*
2 Dunlap, II, p. 44.
3 Monthly Mirror, N.S. 111, March 1808, pp. 268, 270; *Morning Post*, 11 March 1808.
4 Munden, pp. 133–34.
5 Evidence of Covent Garden playbills, B.L. *V.* Chapter II *ante.*
6 *Newcastle Chronicle*, 25 July 1808 et seq.
7 B.L. Provincial Playbills, Vol. 327 (York), 11 and 16 August 1808; Vol. 230 (Liverpool), 12 Sept. 1808; *Edinburgh Evening Courant*, 27 Aug. 1808.
8 Entry in Register of Acclamations and Marriages, General Register Office, Edinburgh; Dunlap, II, p. 72. Another fragmentary journal reveals Cooke corresponding with several of his new relatives during the winter, e.g., pp. 75, 82, 86. He spells the name variously Lamb and Lambe.
9 The press carried full accounts. *V.*, e.g., *Monthly Mirror*, N.S. IV, Sept. 1808.
10 The best collection of Covent Garden bills for this season is in the Enthoven Collection at the Victoria and Albert Museum.
11 *Bath Journal, Bristol Gazette*, playbills in Richard Smith Collection, Bristol.
12 Dunlap, II, pp. 96–7. But as John Brandon was "a party in the business", it may have been a theatrical matter. Or was it to do with Cooke's debt to Harris?
13 Lord William Pitt Lennox: *Celebrities I have Known* (London, 1876), I, pp. 269–82. His account is reprinted as Appendix IV in Hare: *Georgian Theatre in Wessex*, pp. 210–217.
14 B.L. Provincial Playbills Vol. 230 (Liverpool), 1809; *Manchester Mercury*, 27 June 1809; Dunlap, II, p. 98.
15 *Edinburgh Evening Courant*, 3 July 1809 et seq.
16 Dunlap, II, pp. 99–101.
17 B.L. Covent Garden Playbills. *Monthly Mirror, Morning Post, Morning Chronicle, Porcupine* passim. Dunlap, II, pp. 101–19.
18 B.L. Provincial Playbills Vol. 155 (Birmingham); Dunlap, II, pp. 117–19. In Birmingham he was billed as "The Inimitable Cooke". The adjective is precise.
19 B.L. Covent Garden Playbill, 26 Dec. 1809; *Post* and *Chronicle*, 27 and 29 Dec. 1809.
20 Playbill, 8 Jan 1810. *Morning Chronicle*, 9 Jan. 1810.
21 E.g., Dunlap, II, p. 125.
22 *Monthly Mirror*, N.S. VII, Jan. 1810, pp. 56–7.
23 B.L. Provincial Playbills, Vol. 288 (Warwick), 31 March, 5, 6, 7 April 1810.
24 Cooke's marked copy of the play in the Shakespeare Memorial Library in Birmingham has much fuller markings for Wolsey than Henry VIII.
25 *Morning Post*, 31 Oct. 1809, reprints the prologue. *V.* playbill (B.L.) 22 June 1810. Dunlap gives Cooke's last performance in London as Falstaff on 5 June. In fact the annotated bill for that night makes it clear Cooke was unable to perform and the play was changed.
26 Munden, p. 179.
27 B.L. Provincial Playbills, Vol. 230 (Liverpool), Vols. 387, 298 (Preston).
28 Dunlap, II, Chapters 24 and 25.
29 Dunlap says Cheltenham, Hereford, and other places; but *Nottingham Journal* of 1 Sept. 1810 makes it clear that he was engaged for and expected at Nottingham and Derby. Unless otherwise indicated, the account of this incident is based on Dunlap.
30 *Monthly Mirror*, N.S. VIII, Oct. 1810, pp. 315–16; Dunlap, II, pp. 165–67.
31 Munden, p. 181.
32 Dunlap, II, p. 162.
33 Monthly Mirror, loc. cit.
34 Munden, p. 187.

Chapter XIII (pp. 179–89)

1 This short account of the American tour is based principally on Dunlap, who devotes over a quarter of his book to the last eighteen months of Cooke's life (II, Chapters 26–35).

Using the American sources, D. B. Wilmeth has published an account of this period, "Cooke Among the Yankee Doodles," *Theatre Survey*, XIV, 2. Here I draw attention only to the essential details.

2 *V.* Chapter I ante. Dunlap, II, p. 267.

3 *V.*, e.g., Dunlap, II, pp. 178, 257–64, 265–6, 372.

4 Ibid., pp. 187–78, 195–99.

5 Ibid., pp. 200. 204–05.

6 John Bernard, *Retrospections of America 1797–1811* (London, 1887), p. 369.

7 Dunlap, II, pp. 243, 284–85.

8 Ibid., p. 249.

9 Ibid., pp. 269, 277, 332–33.

10 Ibid., p. 333.

11 Ibid., pp. 308–09.

12 Ibid., pp. 372, 376–77, 317, 201.

13 Ibid., pp. 392–94.

14 Ibid., pp. 293–95, 346. Mrs. Mathews has a variant account of this incident.

15 Dunlap, II, pp. 348–50.

16 Ibid., pp. 292, 319, 322–26.

17 Ibid., pp. 281–85. *V.* also Chapter I ante.

18 Ibid., pp. 314–16.

19 Ibid., pp. 245, 303–04, 330, 306.

20 Ibid., p. 338.

21 Ibid., pp. 247, 353, *V.* also D. B. Wilmeth, "The Posthumous Career of George Frederick Cooke," *Theatre Notebook*, XXIV, 2. The marriage took place on the evening of 20 June, the day after his return to New York.

22 Ibid., p. 356.

23 Ibid., pp. 353–60.

24 Ibid., pp. 363–69.

25 Ibid., p. 370.

26 Ibid., p. 369.

27 Munden, pp. 186–87; Dunlap, II, p. 379.

28 Correspondence of Thomas Harris, British Theatre Museum.

29 Dunlap, II, pp. 377–78.

30 Ibid., pp. 383–93, which includes a long letter from Dr. Hosack outlining Cooke's medical history.

31 *V.* Wilmeth, "Posthumous Career".

32 *V.*, e.g., *Monthly Mirror*, N.S. IX, Jan. 1811, p. 63.

Chapter XIV (pp. 190–205)

1 The extant promptbooks are listed in the Bibliography, Appendix I. *Remarks on the Character of Richard III as played by Cooke and Kemble* (London, 2nd edn. revised and corrected, 1801).

2 *Othello* Promptbook, Harvard Theatre Collection, T.S. 2493, 50.

3 *Monthly Mirror*, X, Nov. 1800.

4 *Richard III* Promptbook, Harvard Theatre Collection, T.S. 2587, 64.

5 *Remarks*, pp. 18–19.

6 Ibid., p. 23.

7 Ibid., p. 25.

8 Ibid., pp. 41–42.

9 *Morning Post*, 4 Jan. 1802.

10 *Porcupine*, 1 Dec. 1800; *Morning Chronicle*, 4 Dec. 1800.

11 *Monthly Mirror*, X, Nov. 1800.

12 *Morning Post*, 24 Jan. 1801. *V.* Chapter 9 ante.

13 *Morning Post*, 5 Feb. 1801.

14 Ibid. *V.* also *Morning Chronicle*, 9 Jan. 1802.

15 *Morning Post*, 7 Feb. 1801.
16 *Morning Chronicle*, 25 Feb. 1802.
17 *Bristol Gazette*, 24 Feb. 1814. I owe this reference to Miss Kathleen Barker.
18 Hunt, pp. 102–7.
19 *The Man of the World* Promptbook, Enthoven Collection, Victoria & Albert Museum.
20 Ibid., Act IV, p. 47.
21 Ibid., Act III, pp. 29–31.
22 *Bristol Gazette*, 10 April 1806. Again I am indebted to Miss Barker for drawing my attention to this account.
23 Hunt, pp. 106–07.
24 J. G. Lockhart, *Memoirs of Sir Walter Scott* (Edinburgh, 1837–8), II, pp. 262–63.
25 *Morning Chronicle* and *Morning Post*, 9 Jan. 1802.
26 *Morning Post*, 28 Sept. 1802.
27 *Morning Chronicle*, 28 Sept. 1802.
28 *Morning Post*, 5 Oct. 1802. L. Hunt, *Critical Essays on the Performers of the London Theatres* (London, 1807), p. 217.
29 Byrne, op. cit.
30 V. A. C. Sprague, *Shakespeare and the Actors* (New York, 1963), p. 155 et seq.
31 *Hamlet* Promptbook, Newcastle Lit. & Phil. Soc. Library, pp. 46–47.
32 T. Sadler (ed.), *Diary, Reminiscences and Correspondence of H. C. Robinson* (London, 1869), I, pp. 82–83.

Chapter XV (pp. 206–13)

1 Dunlap, I, p. 393.
2 G.F.C. Ms. Journal 16 Sept. 1798, Harvard Theatre Collection Mss. Thr. 20.
3 Dunlap, II, pp. 92, 95–96.
4 Mathews, p. 139.
5 Dibdin, pp. 282–85.
6 Munden, pp. 92–93.
7 Ryley, pp. 140–41.
8 Dunlap, I, p. 116.
9 G.F.C. Ms. Journal 27 Sept. 1798.
10 V. Chapters VI and X ante.
11 G.F.C. Ms. Journal 20 Sept. 1798.
12 Dunlap, I, pp. 77–78.

Index

INDEX

Hammerton, Jacob 96, 98, 106–7, 110
Hargrave, Mr. 82
Harlequin Fortunatus 25
Harper's Daughter, The 146
Harris, Thomas 111, 113, 117, 122, 129,
    131–3, 137, 142–3, 145, 147, 149,
    151–2, 156, 165–8, 173, 175, 177, 183,
    185, 188, 205, 208
Hart, Miss Polly (later Mrs. Reddish) 48
Hastings 29
Hayes, Mrs. 34
Heatton, Michael 47
Heir-at-Law, The 100
Heiress, The 46
Helvetsloeys 14
Henderson, John 35, 116–17
Henry IV 195
Henry V 73
Herbert, Dennis 18, 20, 24, 34
Herbert, Mr. 107
He's Much to Blame 103
He Wou'd be a Soldier 84
Highland Reel, The 50
High Life Below Stairs 19, 22
Hitchcock, Thomas 81, 88
Hitchcock, Mrs. 82, 106
Hodgkinson, John 49, 55, 59–60
Holcroft, Thomas 155
Holland (Manager) 15
Holland, Mr. 82
Hollingsworth, Mr. 40
Holman, Joseph 75, 118, 157, 189
Hotel, The 105
Huddart, Mr. 107
Huddersfield 97
Hudson, Mr. 34–5
Hudson, Mrs. 34
Hull, Mr. 44–5, 168
Hunn, Mr. & Mrs. 49
Hunt, Leigh 118–19, 197–9
Huntley, Mrs. 34
Hurst (Manager) 32
Hurst, Mr. 60, 82–3

Inchbald, Mrs. Elizabeth 46
Incledon, Charles 108, 112, 118, 154
Inkle and Yarico 52, 106
Irish Theatrical Fund 107–8
Irish Widow, The 19, 22
Iron Chest, The 137

Jackson, John 125, 156, 159
Jane Shore 22, 28, 42, 44, 82, 155
Jew and the Doctor, The 107
John Bull 145, 182–3
Johnston, Henry 119, 138, 146, 150
Johnston, Mrs. 119, 138, 146

Jones, Frederick Edward 97–100, 112, 157,
    161
Jordan, Mrs. Dorothy 44, 54–5, 64
Judgment of Paris, The 22

Kean, Edmund 189
Kearney's Inn 7, 109
Kell, Mrs. 34
Kelly, Michael 152–3
Kelly, Mrs. 82
Kemble, Charles 153–4, 166, 168, 171–2,
    183, 189
Kemble, Miss Fanny 49, 51
Kemble, John Philip 39, 40, 42, 44, 52, 62,
    64, 66, 84, 90, 111–12, 115–17, 122,
    127, 135–7, 139, 143–4, 148–55, 165–6,
    170–1, 173, 179, 183, 189, 192–3,
    199–201, 204–5, 208, 213
Kemble, Stephen 40, 42, 44, 49, 51, 62–4,
    67, 125, 128–30, 167, 196
Kemble, Mrs. Elizabeth 42, 49, 72
Kennedy, Mr. & Mrs. 49, 82
Keymer, Mr. 34
Kilkenny 82
King, Mr. 11, 48, 69, 82, 95, 98, 100
King, Mrs. 11, 48, 104
King and the Miller of Mansfield, The 75, 168
King Arthur 26
King Charles I 75
King John 146
King Lear 22, 45, 84, 136–8, 168, 199–200
Kings Lynn 18–27, 45
Knight, Thomas 46, 48, 118, 121, 169
Knight, Mrs. Margaret (formerly Miss
    Farren) 46
Kniveton, Mrs. 40
Know Your Own Mind 54
Kuttner, C. G. 38

Lady Jane Grey 34
Lamash, Philip 99–100, 110, 161
Lamb, Charles 194
Lambe, Miss Sarah Harvey (later Mrs.
    Cooke) 165, 167–8, 187
Lancaster 40–1, 47–8, 60, 97
Langrish, Mr. & Mrs. 40
Lassells, Mr. 99
Laurent, Mr. 99
Lee, Henry 18
Lee, Mr. 100, 103–4
Lee, Mrs. 103
Leeds 44
Leicester 170
Leister, Mrs. 49, 72
Lennox, Lord William Pitt 169
Leserve, Miss 119